31376   PR
                         6019
Wilson   09Z96

Re Joyce

Date Due

DEC 6 '68			
NOV 4 '68			
JE 2 '69			
MR 18 '70			
AG 13 '71			
MR 3 '72			
NOV 26 '74			
JUN 20 '22			
DEC 13 '78			
OCT 1 9 1992			

CHABOT
COLLEGE
LIBRARY

RE JOYCE

By Anthony Burgess

NOVELS

The Right to an Answer
Devil of a State
A Clockwork Orange
The Wanting Seed
Honey for the Bears
Nothing Like the Sun
The Long Day Wanes
A Vision of Battlements

NONFICTION

Re Joyce

Anthony Burgess

RE JOYCE

 W · W · NORTON & COMPANY · INC ·

New York

TO
CHRISTOPHER BURSTALL

Contents

FOREWORD   *page* 11

PART ONE: THE STONES

1 SOLEMNISATIONS   17
2 INHERITANCES   27
3 A PARALYSED CITY   35
4 MARTYR AND MAZE-MAKER   48
5 FREE FLIGHT   58
6 'YOU POOR POET, YOU!'   70

PART TWO: THE LABYRINTH

1 WAYS INTO THE LABYRINTH   83
2 TAKING OVER HOMER   88
3 TELEMACHUS   94
4 BEGINNING OF THE JOURNEY   106
5 HELL, WIND, CANNIBALS   114
6 HE PROVES BY ALGEBRA   126
7 LABYRINTH AND FUGUE   133
8 FIREWORKS   142
9 BULLOCKBEFRIENDERS   151
10 MEN INTO SWINE   157
11 HOME IS THE SAILOR   165
12 THE BEDSIDE LABYRINTH   177

PART THREE: THE MAN-MADE MOUNTAIN

1 BIG NIGHT MUSIC   185

Contents

2 BYGMESTER FINNEGAN   194

3 HERE COMES EVERYBODY   203

4 ALP AND HER LETTER   209

5 BROTHERLY HATE   219

6 MACTATION OF THE HOST   220

7 SHAUN TO JAUN TO YAWN   239

8 BED AND RICORSO   253

9 IN THE END IS THE WORD   264

   INDEX   273

Foreword

ANOTHER book about James Joyce? Yes, and very far from being the last or anywhere near the last. Indeed (What, will the line stretch out till the crack of Bloom?) it must be regarded as coming very early in the series. Innumerable Ph.D. candidates yet unborn have their thesis subjects waiting for them — an Old Norse word-count of *Finnegans Wake*, II. iii.; the identity of Magrath; the prosodic system of *Ulysses;* Joyce as Marxian allegorist; the misuse of stretto in the 'Sirens' episode; HCE and the schizophrenic syndrome — Joyce might as well, in has last great dense book, have left us twenty pages of possible titles (perhaps he did; I must look again). Twin heavens for the scholars, *Ulysses* and *Finnegans Wake* are, because of the amount of research that already fences them around, being more and more regarded as mystical codices and less and less as masterly novels intended to entertain.

My book does not pretend to scholarship, only to a desire to help the average reader who wants to know Joyce's work but has been scared off by the professors. The appearance of difficulty is part of Joyce's big joke; the profundities are always expressed in good round Dublin terms; Joyce's heroes are humble men. If ever there was a writer for the people, Joyce was that writer. The time is coming for both *Ulysses* and *Finnegans Wake* to be made available to the paperback audience that already knows the earlier, more orthodox, fiction. This audience needs the guidance of a sort of pilot-commentary, and that is what my book tries to be.

Naturally, I could not have written it without help from the scholars. I would like to acknowledge my debt to them now. I have been reading Joyce for the last thirty-odd years, and I have been reading books about him for the same length of time, so I cannot hope to mention all. But no Joyce student can do without *James Joyce's Ulysses — a study by Stuart Gilbert* (available in Vintage

9

paperback), since this learned commentary was sponsored by Joyce himself. *A Skeleton Key to Finnegans Wake*, by Joseph Campbell and Henry Morton Robinson (available in a Viking paperback) lacks the authority of Gilbert's book, but it is a remarkable attempt — both painstaking and imaginative — to uncover the narrative line that underlies Joyce's word-jungle. Adaline Glasheen's *A Census of Finnegans Wake* (Northwestern University) is unique in that it systematically — but also humbly and humorously — tames much of the thematic material of the book into a miniature encyclopaedia. I have always received help from it when help was wanted. The nearest approach to a Joyce's-voice guide to the great myth of death and resurrection is *Our Exagmination round his Factification for Incamination of Work in Progress* (New Directions; revised edition 1962), twelve essays by twelve men, behind all of whom the prodding master seems to stand.

The best Joyce criticism is still, I think, to be found in Edmund Wilson's *Axel's Castle* (Scribner, 1931) and *The Wound and the Bow* (Oxford University Press, 1947). Harry Levin's *James Joyce* (New Directions, revised edition 1960) is brilliant, but — as Henry Reed says in his useful essay, *Joyce's Progress*, in *Orion* in 1946 'he seems on the whole only to deepen the mystery'. There are many admirable essays on aspects of Joyce's work, but, as yet, few really important full-length critical studies. Needless to say, my own book is not presented as one of them. It is commentary rather than criticism.

Joyce was an autobiographical writer, and my reading of books about Joyce the man, husband and father has always helped to elucidate difficulties in his novels. Richard Ellmann's definitive biography *James Joyce* (Oxford University Press, 1959) is a large book that to some extent swallows up Herbert Gorman's earlier life (*James Joyce* — Bodley Head, 1941), Frank Budgen's *James Joyce and the Making of Ulysses* (Indiana, paper, 1960) and Stanislaus Joyce's unfinished memoir *My Brother's Keeper* (Faber and Faber, 1958), but these three maintain their own flavour and still ought to be ready. In *Letters of James Joyce*, edited by Stuart Gilbert (Viking, 1957), the enigmatic master sometimes says what he is trying to do in his enigmatic works.

The title of the British edition of *Re Joyce* is *Here Comes Everybody*. It comes from *Finnegans Wake*, whose hero Humphrey

Foreword

Chimpden Earwicker very frequently has his initials filled out to some appropriate phrase or slogan, like Howth Castle and Environs or Haveth Childers Everywhere. I do not mean to imply that Earwicker is Joyce's wry portrait of himself; rather, I want to stress the universality of Joyce's creations, the fact that they are as demotic as a 'come-all-ye'. Also I enfold there the hope that it will not be long before everybody comes to Joyce, seeing in him not tortuous puzzles, dirt, and jesuitry gone mad, but great comedy, large humanity, and that affirmation of man's worth that more popular writers stamp on in order to make money.

Chiswick   A.B.
August 1965

RE JOYCE

PART ONE

THE STONES

꒐

1: Solemnisations

I START THIS BOOK ON JANUARY 13TH, 1964 – THE TWENTY-THIRD
anniversary of the death of James Joyce. I can think of no other
writer who would bewitch me into making the beginning of a spell
of hard work into a kind of joyful ritual, but the solemnisation of
dates came naturally to Joyce and it infects his admirers. Indeed,
this deadest time of the year (the Christmas decorations burnt a
week ago, the children back at school, the snow come too late to be
festive) is brightened by being a sort of Joyce season. It is a season
beginning in Advent and ending at Candlemas. January 6th is the
Feast of the Epiphany, and the discovery of epiphanies – 'showings
forth' – of beauty and truth in the squalid and commonplace was
Joyce's vocation. February 1st is St Bridget's Day. February 2nd is
Joyce's birthday, and two massive birthday presents were the first
printed copies of *Ulysses* and *Finnegans Wake*; it is also Candlemas
Day and Groundhog Day. One is being very Joycean if one tempers
the solemnity by remembering the groundhogs. Overlooked by
Christmas shoppers, Saint Lucy, Santa Lucia, celebrated her feast on
December 13th. To Joyce, who struggled most of his life against eye-
disease, she had a special meaning, being the patron saint of sight,
and his daughter Lucia was named for her. The theme of the whole
season is light-out-of-darkness, and it is proper to rejoice (Joyce was
well aware of the etymology of his name) in the victory of the light.
We are to rejoice even in the death of the first Christian martyr on
Boxing Day, and we remember why Joyce appears under the name
of Stephen in his autobiographical novels. He too was a martyr,
though to literature; a witness for the light, self-condemned to exile,
poverty, suffering, vilification and (perhaps worst of all) coterie
canonisation in life, that the doctrine of the Word might be spread.
He was a humorous martyr, though, full of drink and irony. Out of
the stones that life threw at him he made a labyrinth, so that Stephen
earned the surname Dedalus. The labyrinth is no home for a

17

monster, however; it is a house of life, its corridors ringing with song and laughter.

In January, 1941, when the news of Joyce's death filtered through from Zürich, the world was distracted by other preoccupations, other deaths. Few of his admirers could take time off for a wake. I myself, a private soldier in snow-bound Northumberland, learned the news when I was polishing the windows of the Sergeants' Mess with a week-old copy of the *Daily Mail*. There it was, on the front page, rightly dwarfed by the bombing of Plymouth.

'Good God, James Joyce is dead.'

'Who the hell's he?' asked a sergeant.

'A writer. Irish. The author of *Ulysses*.'

'Aaaaah, a *dirty* book that is. Get on with the job.' So Joyce's quizzical photograph polished away, looking out at the snow ('faintly falling, like the descent of their last end, upon all the living and the dead'. A great writer modifies everything).

Ulysses, then, was generally known of among the so-called non-intellectuals, even though the name Joyce meant only an English traitor, broadcaster of Nazi propaganda. *Ulysses* (heavily accented on the first syllable) was one of the great dirty books, too dirty to be easily accessible, one of the trilogy of literary dirt completed by *Lady Chatterley's Lover* and *The Well of Loneliness*. Most of us are prurient and will buy the latest piece of literary erotica to be released by a court judgement; we will not join the queue, but we will watch for the queue to die down. I have never felt inclined to condemn people who look for dirt in literature: looking for dirt, they may find something else. I do not think that those of my fellow-soldiers who read paperback pornography for masturbatory thrills saw that sort of stuff as of the same order as *The Decameron* or Joyce's dirty book. In literature (recognisable as such through bulk, hard words, long stretches of boredom) they wanted confirmation that sexual desire, sexual exercise, and sexual obscenity were valid aspects of life. A solid book in hard covers solemnised the day of the groundhog and showed that holy candles were still phallic. Often it was enough for them just to find the word 'sex' in an evidently serious book. For a whole month, in my unit, there was talk of a dirty book in the guard-room—a book that was never, unsportingly, removed but left there to beguile the tedium of guard-duty. It turned out to be my lost copy of Lawrence's *Fantasia of the Unconscious*, a work of jaw-locking dullness.

The author of *Ulysses*, at the time of his death, was not, then,

18

regarded as a pornographic writer even on the lowest level: he was rather the creator of a big book in which, like ore in dull rock, dirt nestled. Twenty-three years after, thanks to the popularising media, his name is generally known and his other work is at least known of. Paperback copies of his earlier fiction, and even Harry Levin's *The Essential James Joyce*, may be bought on railway bookstalls; *Stephen D*–a dramatisation of *Stephen Hero* and *A Portrait of the Artist as a Young Man*–has been seen at peak-viewing hours on BBC television.[1] The glamour of smut has worn off *Ulysses* since Henry Miller and the didactic pornography of the East have appeared on the open market. Joyce is available as Ian Fleming is available, and at no higher price. But he remains, to the majority of library-borrowers and paperback-buyers, suspect. He is obscure, crafty, not straight-forward. The low priest of dirt, unfrocked, is the high priest of difficulty.

No one who has wrestled with *Finnegans Wake* will deny the difficulty there; after ton-loads of exegesis, parts of *Ulysses* still have to be puzzled out. But is the early work, the latest of it fifty years old, really difficult? In a way, though not an obvious way, yes. The stories in *Dubliners* are different from the stories of O. Henry, Guy de Maupassant, and W. Somerset Maugham: nothing seems to happen in them, there are no plots, they are not really stories at all. Anyone who has ever read a *Dubliners* story aloud to a class of adolescents or even adults will know the embarrassment of, at the end of the reading, meeting a wave of incredulity, disappointment, even anger: is it really all over?–why, there is no dénouement, no resolution, no twist. Joyce isn't playing fair; he's a confidence trickster; he pretends to be in the tradition but he's really walked out of it. As for *A Portrait of the Artist as a Young Man*, the very opening breaks the rules; this is not how an adult story ought to begin:

> Once upon a time and a very good time it was there was a moocow coming down along the road and this moocow that was coming down along the road met a nicens little boy named baby tuckoo . . .

But even the surface of his writing offends. After *Dubliners*, he decides to reject both inverted commas and hyphens. His lines of dialogue begin with a dash, in the Continental manner:

> – Hello, Stephanos!
> – Here comes The Dedalus!
> – Ao! . . . Eh, give it over, Dwyer, I'm telling you or I'll give you a stuff in the kisser for yourself . . . Ao!

[1] So has *Bloomsday*–Allan McClelland's dramatisation of *Ulysses* (June 10th, 1964).

– Good man, Towser! Duck him!
– Come along, Dedalus! Bous Stephanoumenos! Bous Stephaneforos!
– Duck him! Guzzle him now, Towser!
– Help! Help! . . . Ao!

His compound words have a German look about them: 'softhued', 'slateblue', 'darkplumaged', 'earsplitting'. Later, in *Ulysses*, he is to pervert conventional word-order as Milton did: 'Perfume of embraces all him assailed. With hungered flesh obscurely, he mutely craved to adore.' He is to pack and tighten his sentences as the Elizabethans used to: 'Ben Dollard's loose blue cutaway and square hat above large slops crossed the quay in full gait from the metal bridge.' Or, better, 'She dances in a foul gloom where gum burns with garlic. A sailorman, rustbearded, sips from a beaker rum and eyes her. A long and seafed silent rut.' He hates pure fill-in words, aquacities; he presses every drop of water out of his cooked cabbage.

His prose thus often looks odd when its intelligibility is not in doubt. It is a special kind of oddness which he shares with a poet– Gerard Manley Hopkins. These two, the renegade Catholic and the Catholic convert, the Jesuit-taught and the Jesuit teacher, have more in common than critics have been prepared to notice. Hopkins taught Greek at University College, Dublin, but long before Joyce was a student there: Joyce was only seven when Hopkins died. Hopkins's verse was not published till 1918, when Joyce's mature style was already formed. They were, independently and one ahead of the other, on the same track. 'Her fond yellow hornlight wound to the west, her wild hollow hoarlight hung to the height waste'–that is Hopkins, but it could be Joyce. 'Isobel, she is so pretty, truth to tell, wildwood's eyes and primarose hair, quietly, all the woods so wild, in mauves of moss and daphnedews, how all so still she lay, neath of the whitehorn, child of tree, like some losthappy leaf, like blowing flower stilled': here Joyce seems almost to parody Hopkins. 'Forwardlike, but however, and like favourable heaven heard these' is the Joycean last line of Hopkins's 'The Bugler's First Communion', written in 1879. Joyce's 'whitemaned seahorses, champing, bright-windbridled' would have delighted Hopkins.

There is more to it than a love of packed sentences and a dislike of hyphens. Joyce and Hopkins were led to a common view of art because of a common belief in the power of ordinary life to burst forth –suddenly and miraculously–with a revelation of truth. Joyce talked of 'epiphanies', Hopkins of 'inscape'; Joyce adopted Aquinas as his philosopher, Hopkins took to Duns Scotus; the one rejected the

Church (or thought he did), the other gave up all for it (or tried to: literature got in the way); both were so acutely aware of the numinous in the commonplace that they found it necessary to manipulate the commonplaces of language into a new medium that should shock the reader into a new awareness. The language of both of them – priest-poet and free-thinking fabulist – is fitted for naked confrontation with a world that seems newly created. It is the lack, not merely of the cliché, but of the rhythm that suggests a cliché, that makes both writers seem odd. Yet this oddness springs from nature: English is never abused, never given exotic flavouring; the compressions, re-orderings of the sentence, compound coinages, alliterations are native to the language. 'Our heart's charity's hearth's fire, our thoughts' chivalry's throng's Lord': so Hopkins addresses Christ, and we are listening to English rhythms that were old-fangled before the coming of the Reformation. 'Dead breaths I living breathe,' writes Joyce, 'tread dead dust, devour a urinous offal from all dead', and the Norman Conquest is not long behind us. Both writers build, not on the accumulations of the centuries, but on the freshly uncovered roots of English. This, then, makes them look odd.

Oddness is more easily excused in a poet than in a novelist. The poet's trade is with words, an odd trade anyway, and he has to arrange them oddly to draw attention to the mystery of language (a mystery which is a distraction in the market-place). But the novelist's trade is less with words than with people and places and actions. Most novel-readers want to get at the content of a novel without the intermediacy of a kind of writing that seems to obtrude, rivalling the plot in its claim to be looked at. In the works of the late Nevil Shute there is no such distraction:

He called the front basement room his clean workshop, and this was his machine shop. Here he had a six-inch Herbert lathe for heavy work, a three-and-a-half-inch Myford, and a Boley watchmaker's lathe. He had a Senior milling machine and a Boxford shaper, a large and a small drill press, and a vast array of tools ready to hand. A long bench ran across the window, a tubular light system ran across the ceiling, and a small camera and flashgun stood ready for use in a cupboard, for it was his habit to take photographs of interesting processes to illustrate his articles.

That is from *Trustee from the Toolroom*, a novel so readable that it slips down like an oyster. Consider also a passage from the late Ian Fleming's *Moonraker*:

The amenities of Blades, apart from the gambling, are so desirable that the Committee has had to rule that every member is required to win or lose £500 a year on the club premises, or pay an annual fine of £250. The food and wine are the best in London and no bills are presented, the cost of all meals being deducted at the end of each week *pro rata* from the profits of the winners. Seeing that about £5,000 changes hands each week at the tables the impost is not too painful and the losers have the satisfaction of saving something from the wreck; and the custom explains the fairness of the levy on infrequent gamblers.

The solidity of such prose is more apparent than real: it derives from the content, the hard inventories of fact; otherwise it is pedestrian enough. But the average novel-reader can only take descriptive prose of a static nature (that is, prose that is not dialogue and prose that does not present physical action) if it evokes the market-place. If a novel attempts static analysis of a scene, a situation, or an emotion, the average novel-reader becomes uneasy: if you cannot give us action, then give us an inventory. If the covers of a novel could contain a film rather than a book, such readers would be pleased. The film, the comic-strip adaptation, the *Reader's Digest* summary – these are, in order of easiness, the easiest ways of getting at the heart of a novel. They agree in finding many novels too wordy; words, a necessary evil in the days of primitive art, are rendered supererogatory by the new, mostly visual, media. This is the general view: it is *wrong* for the novel to be literature. The popular novel never has been literature, and that is why it is popular: the language is transparent, a window on to generalised situations and generalised characters. Joyce's novels are all too literary, his language horribly opaque.

All this means is that Joyce is a sort of prose-poet, and to be that is to be a cheat – the dry bread of a good yarn seems to be offered, but it turns out to be the stone (precious but still inedible) of words or symbol. The thing to do is to forget that the field of the novel is as limited as the cult of the contemporary best-seller is making it, and to consider that Joyce may be within his rights in turning language into one of the *characters* of *Ulysses* (perhaps in *Finnegans Wake* the only character). In *Ulysses*, the poeticising and the pastiche and parody serve, as we shall see later, a dramatic enough purpose; they also deepen the human characters by adding to their ordinary human dimensions the dimension, first, of history, then of myth. Here is the hero of *Ulysses* seen in his primary, Nevil Shute, aspect, though the language of this inventory has, in sheer sound, in sheer organisation of consonants and vowels, a distinction few popular novelists could reach:

Mr Leopold Bloom ate with relish the inner organs of beasts and fowls. He liked thick giblet soup, nutty gizzards, a stuffed roast heart, liver slices fried with crustcrumbs, fried hencod's roes. Most of all he liked grilled mutton kidneys which gave to his palate a fine tang of faintly scented urine.

Here he is seen in relation to one phase of past history:

Some man that wayfaring was stood by housedoor at night's oncoming. Of Israel's folk was that man that on earth wandering far had fared. Stark ruth of man his errand that him lone led till that house.

And here he is in one of his comic-mythic aspects:

And there came a voice out of heaven, calling: *Elijah! Elijah!* And he answered with a main cry: *Abba! Adonai!* And they beheld Him even Him, ben Bloom Elijah, amid clouds of angels ascend to the glory of the brightness at an angle of fortyfive degrees over Donohue's in Little Green Street like a shot off a shovel.

'Comic' is the key-word, for *Ulysses* is a great comic novel–though comic in a tradition that has been obscured by 'popular' conceptions of comedy–P. G. Wodehouse, Richard Gordon and the rest. The comedy of Joyce is an aspect of the heroic: it shows man in relation to the whole cosmos, and the whole cosmos appears in his work symbolised in the whole of language.

One idea that should now be emerging is that Joyce is a very traditional writer: he belongs to a period in which the warring notions of fine art and pop-art had no place; he antecedes, certainly, the popular novel in the sense in which we are using that term. He is very close to novelists like Cervantes, Fielding and Sterne, masters of the mock-epic. There is a great deal of Rabelais in him and not a little Dickens. He belongs, in fact, to the comic-heroic tradition of Western Europe–a tradition based on a kind of qualified humanism. Man is interesting and important enough to be examined in great detail and at great length, but he is not by any means the Lord of the Universe. The universe can be a mystery or an antagonist: against it the comic-epic hero opposes all he has, and it is not much–merely free will and a capacity for love. His defeats are inevitable but always contain the seed of a victory that the universe, a vast mass of organised ironmongery, is not equipped to understand. It is the victory of the stoic who, though the gods themselves crush him with superior weight, knows that his values are right and theirs are wrong. The heroes of the great mock-epics are, by an ironical twist, always more admirable, because more human, than the demi-gods of true epic whom they parody. Odysseus and Æneas are all for imposing their weight, little Mediterranean kings; they try to imitate the cosmos, and the cosmos is flattered into supporting them with occasional miracles. Don Quixote and Leopold Bloom merely want to improve society with decent acts. But the cosmos sees human society as a model of itself and does not want it disturbed, hence its resentment – expressed in thunder, practical jokes, gross coincidences.

It is evident that the mock-epic novel is not just spinning a yarn and cannot be content with the language appropriate to a plain tale. The difficulties of *Ulysses* and, very much more, of *Finnegans Wake* are not so many tricks and puzzles and deliberate obscurities to be hacked at like jungle lianas: they represent those elements which surround the immediate simplicities of human society; they stand for history, myth, and the cosmos. Thus we have not merely to accept them but to regard them as integral, just as the stars overhead are integral to the life of the man who, micturating in the open air, happens to look up at them. What is difficult in *Ulysses* and *Tristram Shandy* is meant to be difficult: the author is not coyly withholding a key.

James Joyce, starting on his literary career, said that one of his artistic weapons was to be that of the labyrinth-maker – not brute cunning but human cunning. The average reader, coming to Joyce for the first time, resents the cunning. Perhaps even more he resents another of the author's declared weapons – silence. No writer was more autobiographical than Joyce, but no writer ever revealed, in the telling of his story, less of himself. He keeps silent, he never judges, he never comments. I am convinced that many novel-readers go to a book not merely for the story but for the companionship of the teller of the story – they want a friend with a somewhat greater knowledge of the world than themselves, one who knows the clubs, a good cigar, Tangier and Singapore, who has perhaps dallied with strange women and read odd books, but remains friendly, smiling, tolerant but indignant when the reader would be indignant, always approachable and always without side. Read Nevil Shute and you will meet the no-damned-nonsense engineer who has no arty pretensions; read Ian Fleming and you will meet the globe-trotting clubman who is one of the lads; read Somerset Maugham and you will meet the sceptical *raisonneur* with a well-hidden heart of gold. These images are sometimes an unforced expression of nature, sometimes (as with Maugham) a very cleverly made *persona*. In the works of Dickens George Orwell saw a face:

It is the face of a man about forty, with a small beard and a high colour. He is laughing, with a touch of anger in his laughter, but no triumph, no malignity. It is the face of a man who is always fighting against something, but who fights in the open and is not frightened, the face of a man who is *generously angry*–in other words, of a nineteenth-century liberal, a free intelligence, a type hated with equal hatred by all the smelly little orthodoxies which are now contending for our souls.

No face shines through the novels of James Joyce, and this is disturbing. He is cut off from his own creation, as he is cut off from God's, and he has no comment to make about either. He cannot be enlisted in the cause of Irish nationalism, Fascism or Communism, though–like Shakespeare, a man legitimately faceless because he wrote plays and not novels–he has been invoked in the name of every ideology. Perhaps, among novelists, only Flaubert approaches him for self-effacement.

But, to the novel-reader brought up in a cosier tradition, such self-effacement looks like *hauteur*, the nose in the air, the swollen head, the snob. It ought not to look like that. Joyce's aim was the ennoblement of the common man, and this could best be achieved by letting the common man speak for himself. To watch over one's hero, coddle him, discuss him with the reader, offer him praise or pity– is not this perhaps the real posture of superiority, the imitation of God? We are given Leopold Bloom and Humphrey Chimpden Earwicker without apology and without the intermediacy of attitudes imposed on the reader. We have to make up our own minds as to whether we like them or approve of their actions (Bloom's masturbation, for instance, or Earwicker's incestuous fantasies); ultimately, liking and approbation do not apply–we become concerned with the harder discipline of love. The priest is the agent of solemn ceremonies, and we are never drawn to look at his face or consider what thoughts and feelings move behind it. Joyce, without blasphemy, saw his function as priestlike–the solemnisation of drab days and the sanctification of the ordinary.

It is this preoccupation, even obsession, with the ordinary that should endear him to ordinary readers. Nobody in his books is rich or has high connections. There is no dropping of titled names, as there is in the novels of Evelyn Waugh, and we enter no place more exalted than a pub or a public library. Ordinary people, living in an ordinary city, are invested in the riches of the ages, and these riches are enshrined in language, which is available to everybody. Given time, Joyce will flow through the arteries of our ordinary, non-reading, life, for a great writer influences the world whether the world

25

likes it or not, and the blessing of the ordinary must eventually trans-
figure it. We see Gerard Manley Hopkins in cornflake advertise-
ments ('gold-toasted, sugar-tossed, lighter-than-air, O crisp, they
crunch and crackle') and we hear Joyce's interior monologues in the
'think-tape' of television plays and documentaries, even hear something of his word-play in radio shows. But '*Introibo ad altare Dei*' is
the first spoken statement in *Ulysses*, and we are wisest if we get up
early and deliberately go to the great comic Mass, rather than merely
let its deformed and thinned echoes trickle through to us. It is not
a Black Mass, even though Guinness is drunk and bawdy songs
punctuate the golden liturgy; it is a solemnisation without solemnity.

2: Inheritances

BESIDES SILENCE AND CUNNING, JAMES JOYCE NEEDED ANOTHER condition for expressing himself in art–exile. It was, on the face of it, a more thorough exile than, say, Ovid or Dante had known; it looked like an almost sacramental disowning of family, city, race, and religion. But such gestures are usually less drastic and dramatic and self-denying than they sound, nor could this one be wholly fulfilled: Joyce ended his days as a son and a brother, a walking guide to Dublin past and present, an expatriate Irishman, a Mass-missing Catholic who knew as much as the priests. Exile was the artist's stepping back to see more clearly and so draw more accurately; it was the only means of objectifying an obsessive subject-matter. Joyce wanted to 'forge the uncreated conscience' of his own people, and exile was the smithy.

The heroes of Joyce's two greatest books are both family men. Family was important to Joyce, and he expressed its importance by cutting himself away from his father's decaying house and starting a family of his own. As for the umbilical cord, it does not seem to have exerted a very strong pull. *Amor matris* is a big theme in *Ulysses*, but only in one of its meanings. Stephen Dedalus remembers his mother with pity, but, when she rises from the dead in the late-night brothel scene, she is the enemy, making her son cry: 'The corpse-chewer! Raw head and bloody bones!' and smash the chandelier with his ashplant. She seems to provoke the same feelings as those two greater mothers, Ireland and the Church–a mixture of guilt, anger, terror and disdain. That earlier, remembered, incident where Stephen refuses to pray at his dying mother's behest, is not an exact representation of what happened in Joyce's own life, but it stands for the *non serviam* he wanted to shout at all his mothers. Joyce, unlike D. H. Lawrence, was no mother's boy. But the father-son relationship is a different matter; it was one that Joyce was able to enter into in both capacities and it had for him a 'mystical' significance: Bloom and Stephen come together despite the lack of a biological tie or even a cultural or racial affinity.

Of all the numerous family he begot, John Joyce seems to have been liked only by his eldest son James. Perhaps 'liked' is too strong or too weak a word: tolerance in youth gave place to a sort of guilty love in middle age. If Joyce's mother represented the *yin* side of the Irish psyche, all pregnancies and forbearance and superstition, Joyce's father was very much the *yang*–charm, virility, dissipation, improvidence, bibulous shiftlessness, the relics of old dacency, talent let run to seed. In *A Portrait* Stephen enumerates 'glibly his father's attributes':

–A medical student, an oarsman, a tenor, an amateur actor, a shouting politician, a small landlord, a small investor, a drinker, a good fellow, a storyteller, somebody's secretary, something in a distillery, a taxgatherer, a bankrupt and at present a praiser of his own past.

The variousness which the son put into his art the father put into his life, though to no profit. And yet he ends up, the eternal father-figure, in Earwicker in *Finnegans Wake*. More than that, only such a father could have begotten such a son, for James Joyce is his father with genius added, the peculiar chaos of his father organised into a cosmos. Stephen Dedalus says that Socrates learned dialectic from his shrewish wife Xantippe, and from his midwife mother 'how to bring thoughts into the world'. He does not say what he learned from his father. What Joyce learned, or inherited, from his own father was a voice, the gift of song and the gift of rhetoric.

John Joyce was not just a tenor but a fine tenor, and his eldest son was almost a great tenor. The importance of song in his books cannot be exaggerated. *Ulysses* sings all the way or, when it does not sing, it declaims or intones. It has been turned into a stage-play–*Bloomsday*; it could also be turned into an opera. The 'Sirens' episode is composed in the form of a fugue, but the symphonic nature of the whole work only appears when we come to the 'Circe' chapter–here we have a free fantasia or development section which gathers all the whirling fragments of the long day together and, in the sphere of the special logic of the imagination, relates one to the other. As for *Finnegans Wake*, parts of it are essentially bardic: they require the voice and the harp. But Joyce's father could do more than sing; he could speak as well. He had the gift of eloquence, especially in abuse, and this was heard at its best when he was denouncing his wife's family ('O weeping God, the things I married into'). The denunciatory rhetoric of the 'Cyclops' episode in *Ulysses* is pure John Joyce, while the highly idiosyncratic tropes of Simon Dedalus ('Shite and onions', 'Melancholy God', 'Jesus wept, and no wonder, by Christ') are no more than transcriptions of actuality.

The ear and the voice of Joyce's father produced, in his son, a prodigious appetite for language. Joyce wrung the English language nearly dry in *Ulysses* and, in *Finnegans Wake*, had to devise a new medium–a composite tongue, a kind of pan-European, in which the vocabulary was drawn from all the languages Joyce knew–a very considerable number. Joyce's urge to learn foreign languages began with a desire to communicate with the great Europe 'out there': he had no interest in learning Erse, a very insular tongue. While still an undergraduate, he wrote a letter of admiration to Ibsen in Dano-Norwegian. Italian was becoming his second language (later it was to be his first, and that of his wife and children). He could be creative in French. He learned German in order to translate Hauptmann. Even before he began to write his characteristic works, his world was becoming a world of sounds–meaningful or otherwise, though, as Leopold Bloom points out, everything speaks in its own way. Whether the primacy of the ear and the tongue in Joyce is, building on a natural endowment, fate's way of compensating him for weak sight and, later, near-blindness–this is a matter which it is not profitable to debate. Blind Homer is a strongly visual poet, blind Milton is not. The weak-sighted cherish what little they can see; the near-sighted turn themselves into microscopes. I am myself a novelist classified as 'partially sighted', but the visible world exists for me, especially in the close print of cigarette-ends in a dirty ashtray, segs on potato-peeling fingers, the grain of wood, the bubbles in tonic water, a painter's brushwork. There are plenty of visual minutiae in Joyce's novels but (contrast him here with another poor-sighted author, Aldous Huxley) there is not much interest in the visual arts– not because of poor vision but because of poor provision on the part of the world that reared him. The dim fairy water-colours of George Russell (AE) represent the approach of *fin de siècle* Dublin to the painter's art. Joyce as a young man knew pornographs and hagiographs–dirty pictures hidden up his bedroom chimney, the Sacred Heart and the BVM above the mantelpiece; what works of art he possessed in later life were dear to him because of their literary or verbal associations–weaving Penelope; a view of Cork framed in cork. The Dublin of his youth nourished his auditory gift. It was very much his father's city, keen on rhetoric and Italian opera; it found its colours and shapes in sounds.

29

Joyce left his father's house in order to convert his father into myth, but he encouraged one member of the family to follow him into exile and stay in exile – his brother Stanislaus. If James Joyce brought his father's voice and ear to his art, he took his father's capacity for disorder and improvidence into his private life, Trieste (his first place of exile) apparently encouraging him to promote the vices of shiftlessness and squalor on a spectacular, Continental, scale. Stanislaus, 'brother John', had been inoculated against all this: he was solid, reliable, and had a great appetite for order and responsibility. Against incredible odds he helped to keep the new Joyce ménage afloat, and his book about James was well-titled – *My Brother's Keeper*. But his importance to those who want to read Joyce, not just read about him, is mythical. *Finnegans Wake* presents, as one of its themes, the eternal opposition of brothers: Shem is an autobiographical study (Shem = James), the hard core of Shaun (= John) is Stanislaus.

Despite his temperamental inability to be solid, reliable, an earner of good wages, James Joyce had it in him to be a good husband and father. Though he ran off with Nora Barnacle in 1904, they did not legally marry till 1931 (at a London registry office, 'for testamentary reasons'). They were glued together by affection, not form. If John Joyce rightly saw that a girl with a name like that would never leave his son, James's need for Nora was beyond all fancy. She was unliterary, had no patience with her husband's bizarre projects (why couldn't he write an ordinary story that people could understand?), but she is firmly planted in both *Ulysses* and *Finnegans Wake* – not biographically but mythically. Joyce saw in her the essential virtues of woman. She was down-to-earth, anti-romantic, common-sensical, loyal, forgiving. If Stanislaus was his foil, she was his complement. As for Joyce's paternal gifts, these were as powerfully developed as we should expect from the creator of Bloom and Earwicker. One of the most affecting relationships in the whole of modern biography is that between himself and his daughter Lucia, the poor girl who inherited her father's genius in the form of dementia.

Joyce's unwillingness to 'regularise' his ménage had less to do with an antipathy to the forms of marriage than a total rejection of the Church. Marriage was a sacrament, therefore not for him. The alternative of a purely legal wedding would not do. Leaving the Catholic Church did not mean becoming a Protestant, for that would be merely the exchange of a logical absurdity for an illogical one; similarly, one did not spurn religion in order to fly into the arms of the State. '*Non serviam*' meant what it said. Joyce, who admired William Blake, had a lot of Blake in him: all laws were bad; damn braces, bless relaxes. And yet Joyce's rejection of Catholicism was far from absolute. The Jesuit's boast about conditioning a child's soul for ever is not an empty one, and Joyce was brought up by the Jesuits. He might refuse to take the sacraments, matrimony along with the Eucharist, but the disciplines and, in a tortured renegade form, the very fundamentals of Catholic Christianity stayed with him all his life.

There is a sense in which the novels of Evelyn Waugh and Graham Greene, both Catholic converts, are less Catholic than the works of the great Jesuit apostate. Waugh looks for an unbroken tradition of English Catholic aristocracy with a terrible hunger for certitude, but it is less an eschatological certitude than a social one; he wants a code of behaviour and a code of taste that are sponsored by the oldest possible tradition. Greene is a Jansenist, and Jansenism, with its emphasis on man's impotence to do good or obey the commandments, is too close to Calvinism to be good Catholicism, and, indeed, the Church has repeatedly condemned Jansenism as a heresy. But Joyce's residual Catholicism never really leaves the norm. As Buck Mulligan says of Stephen Dedalus, he has the Jesuit strain injected the wrong way. The blasphemies of *Ulysses* are a kind of affirmation (the following is a statement about discipline in the British Navy):

> They believe in rod, the scourger almighty, creator of hell upon earth, and in Jacky Tar, the son of a gun, who was conceived of unholy boast, born of the fighting navy, suffered under rump and dozen, was scarified, flayed and curried, yelled like bloody hell, the third day he arose again from the bed, steered into haven, sitteth on his beamend till further orders whence he shall come to drudge for a living and be paid.

That is meant to shock, just like 'The Ballad of Joking Jesus' and the story of Mary and Joseph and the pigeon. All through *Ulysses* and *Finnegans Wake* we catch echoes of the liturgy in parodic form ('Hail Mary, full of grease, the lard is with thee'), but we also meet learned chunks of theological speculation, as well as close Thomistic reasoning. It is typical of Joyce that, creating a religion of art to replace his Catholicism, he has to formulate his aesthetic in the terms of the schoolmen, and that his very premises come out of Aquinas. He cannot slough the Church off, he can never become completely emancipated. In *Ulysses* he is obsessed with the mystical identity of Father and Son; in *Finnegans Wake* his only real theme is that of the Resurrection.

31

The first words spoken in *Ulysses* are the opening words of the Mass. Buck Mulligan, robed, bearing a razor and a mirror crossed, ascends to the top of a tower to perpetrate the first blasphemy of the book: 'For this, O dearly beloved, is the genuine Christine: body and soul and blood and ouns.' But the blasphemy belongs to the character; the liturgical tone belongs to the book. Here, Joyce seems to say, a rite of solemn meaning, however comic the surface, is about to begin. And both of his major works *are* rituals: there is a hidden substance, a cunning planting of occult symbols, there is more than meets the eye. Every chapter of *Ulysses* performs several functions at one and the same time: it tells the story, signifies an art or science, stands for a part of the human body, has an appropriate symbol, is even dominated by an appropriate colour and (but this is not quite so esoteric, since the title of the book gives us a huge clue) has a parallel in Homer's *Odyssey* which is worked out in rich and secret detail. Behind the 'accidents' of a mock-epic lies a substance qualitatively different: in a sense, a sacrament is being administered. This very Catholic desire for the certitude of an organic system – and that seems to be one of the motives for writing *Ulysses* – is cognate with a priestly love of mysteries.

Joyce's attitude to Catholicism is the familiar love-hate one of most renegades. He has left the Church, but he cannot leave it alone: he attacks it to the priests but defends it from the protestants. Despite all the mockery and blaspheming, it is safe to put Joyce's works into the hands of the devout believer. The Church may be an absurdity, but its logic is not denied; nor is there any institution less absurd. The Church stands that it may be battered, but the fists that batter know their own impotence. And, even in small particulars, Joyce seems to add to the literature of the Church rather than the literature of the unbeliever:

The proud potent titles clanged over Stephen's memory the triumph of their brazen bells: *et unam sanctam catholicam et apostolicam ecclesiam*: the slow growth and change of rite and dogma like his own rare thoughts, a chemistry of stars. Symbol of the apostles in the mass for Pope Marcellus, the voices blended, singing alone loud in affirmation: and behind their chant the vigilant angel of the church militant disarmed and menaced her heresiarchs. A horde of heresies fleeing with mitres awry: Photius and the brood of mockers of whom Mulligan was one, and Arius, warring his life long upon the consubstantiality of the Son with the Father, and Valentine, spurning Christ's terrene body, and the subtle African heresiarch Sabellius who held that the Father was Himself His own Son. Words Mulligan had spoken a moment since in mockery to the stranger. Idle mockery. The

void awaits surely all them that weave the wind: a menace, a disarming
and a worsting from those embattled angels of the church, Michael's host,
who defend her in the hour of conflict with their lances and their shields.

Joyce's intellectual grasp of Catholicism was as beyond his
mother's simple faith as his refusal to make his Easter duty. But there
are shreds of peasant Catholicism left in him. His governess, Mrs
Conway ('Dante' in *A Portrait*), taught him to make the sign of the
cross when there was a flash of lightning and say, 'Jesus of Nazareth,
King of the Jews, from a sudden and unprovided for death deliver
us, O Lord.' In Joyce's books thunder is always the voice of a wrath-
ful God. In *Ulysses* it rumbles while the students in the maternity
hospital are mocking the forces of life. The language used for it is
full of primitive terror: 'Loud on left Thor thundered, in anger
awful the hammerhurler.' In *Finnegans Wake* thunder appears as one
of the characters, symbolised in a word of one hundred letters (like
'bababadalgharaghtakamminarronnkonnbronntonnerronntuonnthu-
nntrovarrhounawnskawntoohoohoordenenthurnuk!'), the power
which drives men to shelter but makes them start building civilisations. Joyce himself always trembled at the noise of thunder and, to
those who asked why, he said, 'You were not brought up in Catholic
Ireland.'

As for Joyce's Irishry, we need not make too much fuss about it,
for it is perhaps the least important element in his make-up. His
means of creating for Ireland the conscience it did not want was to
drag Ireland into Europe and, later, use Ireland as the nucleus of a
universal myth. He spent his nationalistic ardour very early in life,
though he retained throughout his exile a profound knowledge of the
history of Ireland's struggle for home rule. His work derives from
no Celtic originals (the part played by the *Book of Kells* in *Finnegans
Wake* is the least of the reader's worries); he had no role in the
literary movement which Yeats glorified; he did not even, like Synge,
eavesdrop on the flavoursome speech of the peasantry. His Irishry
was passive, merely innate, unpromoted; his aim was to be a European artist rather than the bard-senator of a backwater republic.
Dublin pub-crawlers claim him as their own, but official Ireland
rejects him. This is as it should be. Joyce's purpose in life was to
glorify the Dublin of pubs and poverty, not to further a shining
national image. He was a Dubliner as Bloom and Earwicker are
Dubliners, and both Bloom and Earwicker are foreigners.

Joyce's books are about Dublin, all of them. In the earlier sections
of *A Portrait* we visit other Irish places, but briefly. We home back

33

to Dublin with relief. But we are wrong if we think that Dublin *encloses* the work of Joyce, that a knowledge of the city is the key to understanding. The living Dubliner claims a superior appreciation of Joyce because he knows the distance from Sir John Rogerson's Quay to Mount Jerome Cemetery. This is a delusion. Dublin, in Joyce, is turned into an archetypal city, eventually into a dream city. Moreover, the Dublin of 1904 is, with romantic Ireland and O'Leary, dead and gone. Davy Byrne's is a smart bar now, not a boozer. The Martello Tower is a Joyce museum, an omphalos of petrifaction. It helps us to know something about Dublin, the real city of Joyce's memory, when we tackle the myths he has made out of it, but it is by no means essential. The real keys to an understanding of Joyce are given to the diligent reader, not to the purchaser of an Aer Lingus ticket. My own best claim to an appreciation of his work, apart from application to it, is a Lancashire Catholic upbringing, a superstitious grandmother called Finnegan, and a strong auditory bias. Dublin is a city I know far less intimately than Singapore or Leningrad.

But, plunging into Joyce's books, we plunge into a kind of Dublin. The Hill of Howth is man, and the river Liffey is woman, and the city ends as a metaphysical city, a place for the working out of the whole of human history. Before we reach that consummation we have to see it as a paradigm of all modern cities, a stage for the enactment of paralysis, the befouled nest of a poet.

3: A Paralysed City

JOYCE'S FIRST PIECE OF PUBLISHED JUVENILIA WAS A VERSE encomium on dead Parnell and an attack on Parnell's chief enemy. It was called *Et Tu, Healy* and it was written when he was nine. Here ends the bibliography of Joyce the committed or *engagé*. His student writings praised Ibsen and poured scorn on the Irish Literary Theatre ('The Day of the Rabblement'). Before leaving Ireland, almost for ever, he wrote a Swiftian—or Hudibrastic—poem called *The Holy Office*, in which the parochial poetlings of the Celtic Twilight have a few drops of acid thrown at them:

> So distantly I turn to view
> The shamblings of that motley crew,
> Those souls that hate the strength that mine has
> Steeled in the school of old Aquinas.
> Where they have crouched and crawled and prayed
> I stand, the self-doomed, unafraid,
> Unfellowed, friendless and alone,
> Indifferent as the herring-bone,
> Firm as the mountain-ridges where
> I flash my antlers on the air.

Bold words, and a bold manifesto:

> But all these men of whom I speak
> Make me the sewer of their clique.
> That they may dream their dreamy dreams
> I carry off their filthy streams
> For I can do those things for them
> Through which I lost my diadem,
> Those things for which Grandmother Church
> Left me severely in the lurch.
> Thus I relieve their timid arses,
> Perform my office of Katharsis.

Joyce, at twenty-two, had no doubt of his artistic function, nor of its importance. The office of purgation, of making art a kind of sewer for the draining-off of man's baser elements, was not what the Church

35

would call holy; still, Aristotle–who gave him the word *katharsis*–was sponsored by St Thomas Aquinas, and St Thomas Aquinas was not of the same world as the Christian Brothers and the Maynooth priests. Joyce has the image of a great traditional intellectual aristocracy, to which he himself belongs. Prettiness, fancy, devotionalism have no place in the austerity and self-dedication of its creed. It is demanding, and one must be prepared to be damned for it (Joyce sees himself in a sort of hell of artists, 'self-doomed, unafraid, unfellowed, friendless and alone'). And so the deliberate cutting-off, the exile.

The first big fruit of Joyce's exile was the volume of short stories, *Dubliners*. It seems a very mild purge to us now, chiefly because it is the first in a whole pharmacopoeia of cathartics to which we have developed a tolerance. To its eponyms it seemed strong enough; printers and publishers would not at first administer it; its little saga of rejections, bowdlerisations, burnings looks forward to the epic struggle of *Ulysses* (itself originally conceived as a story for *Dubliners*) to get itself first into print and then past the customs-houses. The book was mainly written in Trieste in 1905, worked up from notes Joyce had made while still in Dublin. Grant Richards, to whom it was first sent, would and would not publish it. In 1909, Joyce gave it to Maunsel and Co. in Dublin. In 1910, Maunsel and Co. grew frightened of it and postponed publication. In 1912, the type was broken up by the printer and Joyce, in a broadside called 'Gas from a Burner', made the printer say:

> . . . I draw the line at that bloody fellow
> That was over here dressed in Austrian yellow,
> Spouting Italian by the hour
> To O'Leary Curtis and John Wyse Power
> And writing of Dublin, dirty and dear,
> In a manner no blackamoor printer could bear.
> Shite and onions! Do you think I'll print
> The name of the Wellington Monument,
> Sydney Parade and Sandymount tram,
> Downes's cakeshop and Williams's jam?
> . . . Who was it said: Resist not evil?
> I'll burn that book, so help me devil.
> I'll sing a psalm as I watch it burn
> And the ashes I'll keep in a one-handled urn
> I'll penance do with farts and groans
> Kneeling upon my marrowbones.
> This very next lent I will unbare
> My penitent buttocks to the air

And sobbing beside my printing press
My awful sin I will confess.
My Irish foreman from Bannockburn
Shall dip his right hand in the urn
And sign crisscross with reverent thumb
Memento homo upon my bum.

But printing the name of the Wellington Monument and Downes's cakeshop was, after all, the thin end of the wedge. Admit the naturalism of a picture postcard and you must soon admit also *graffiti* on lavatory walls, the blaspheming of jarveys, and what goes on in the back bedrooms of Finn's Hotel. *Dubliners* was totally naturalistic, and no kind of truth is harmless; as Eliot says, mankind cannot bear very much reality.

And yet, first as last, Joyce did not want merely to record the current of ordinary life. There was this business of epiphanies, defined in *Stephen Hero* (the first draft of *A Portrait*):

By an epiphany he meant a sudden spiritual manifestation, whether in the vulgarity of speech or of gesture or in a memorable phase of the mind itself. He believed that it was for the man of letters to record these epiphanies with extreme care, seeing that they themselves are the most delicate and evanescent of moments.

Stephen Dedalus tells his friend Cranly (as, in *A Portrait*, he is to tell Lynch–more eloquently and at much greater length) that Aquinas's three prerequisites for beauty are integrity, symmetry and radiance. First the apprehending mind separates the object–'hypothetically beautiful'–from the rest of the universe and perceives that 'it is one integral thing'; it recognises its integrity or wholeness. Next, 'the mind considers the object in whole and in part, in relation to itself and to other objects, examines the balance of its parts, contemplates the form of the object, traverses every cranny of the structure'. As for the third stage–'radiance'–that is Stephen's translation of Aquinas's *claritas*–it is a sort of *quidditas* or whatness shining out of the object:

. . . finally, when the relation of the parts is exquisite, when the parts are adjusted to the special point, we recognise that it is *that* thing which it is. Its soul, its whatness, leaps to us from the vestment of its appearance. The soul of the commonest object, the structure of which is so adjusted, seems to us radiant. The object achieves its epiphany–

The term seems ironic when applied to the 'showings forth' of *Dubliners*, but, after all, the original Epiphany was ironic enough to the Magi–a child in a dirty stable.

37

The glory and mystery of art can lie in the tension between the appearance and the reality, or, rather, between the subject-matter and what is made out of it. The view that subject-matter should be in itself enlightening still persists, chiefly because a moral stock-response comes more easily to most people than a genuine aesthetic transport. When Grant Richards eventually got round to publishing *Dubliners*–as he did on June 15th, 1914: very nearly the tenth anniversary of the Bloomsday that had not yet happened–few people were ready for it: the taste was for the didacticism, the pedestrian moral lessons of a less naturalistic fiction. In *Dubliners* the reader was not told what to think about the characters and their actions, or rather inactions. There were no great sins, nor any performance of great good. Out of drab ordinariness a purely aesthetic *quidditas* leaps out.

All the stories in *Dubliners* are studies in paralysis or frustration, and the total epiphany is of the nature of modern city life–the submission to routines and the fear of breaking them; the emancipation that is sought, but not sought hard enough; the big noble attitudes that are punctured by the weakness of the flesh. The first story, 'The Sisters', presents the key-word in its very first paragraph:

Every night as I gazed up at the window I said softly to myself the word paralysis. It had always sounded strangely in my ears, like the word gnomon in the Euclid and the word simony in the Catechism. But now it sounded to me like the name of some maleficent and sinful being. It filled me with fear, and yet I longed to be nearer to it and to look upon its deadly work.

The narrator is a young boy. Behind the window Father Flynn lies dead. The boy, like Joyce himself, is drawn not only to the mystery of words but to the terrifying complexities of the rites that the priest has administered. As for the priest himself–old and retired and dying–the boy's feelings have been a mixture of awed fascination and repugnance. Father Flynn looks forward to the unpleasant priests of Graham Greene and the dramatic possibilities of the contrast between their function and their nature. He has been a messy snuff-taker. 'When he smiled he used to uncover his big discoloured teeth and let his tongue lie upon his lower lip.' But now he is dead, and the boy goes with his aunt to see the body in the house of the Misses Flynn, the sisters of the priest. He learns, over a glass of defunctive sherry, that Father Flynn's illness began with the breaking of a chalice, that this affected his mind: '. . . And what do you think but there he was,' says Eliza Flynn, 'sitting up by himself in the dark in his confession-box, wide-awake and laughing-like softly to himself?' Meanwhile, the dead priest is 'lying still in his coffin as we had seen him, solemn and truculent in death, an idle chalice on his breast'.

That is the whole story, and it is more an attempt at establishing a symbol than manufacturing a plot: a broken chalice, an idle chalice. The shameful discoveries about the adult world continue in the next

'An Encounter', in which the boy-narrator and his friend Mahony play truant from school for a day. Their heads full of *The Union Jack*, *Pluck*, and *The Halfpenny Marvel*, they meet adventure, but not in the form of the innocent violence of their little Wild West mythologies. A shabby man accosts them, full of perverse fantasies. Mahony runs away, but the narrator has to listen to the man's monologue about whipping boys who have sweethearts. 'He described to me how he would whip such a boy, as if he were unfolding some elaborate mystery. He would love that, he said, better than anything in this world; and his voice, as he led me monotonously through the mystery, grew almost affectionate and seemed to plead with me that I should understand him.' The narrator gets away from the demented babbling, calling Mahony. 'How my heart beat as he came running across the field to me! He ran as if to bring me aid. And I was penitent; for in my heart I had always despised him a little.'

'Araby' is the last of this opening trilogy of stories in which the world is seen from a child's-eye view. Here, though, the passionate frustration belongs to the boy himself. He is past the stage of encountering external mysteries – ritual and dementia – and is now learning about love's bitter mystery through pubescent experience. Here comes the eucharistic symbol: 'I imagined that I bore my chalice safely through a throng of foes. Her name sprang to my lips at moments in strange prayers and praises which I myself did not understand.' We are to meet this symbolism again, in the 'Villanelle of the Temptress' – named in *Stephen Hero*, presented in *A Portrait*. In 'Araby', though, the loved one is no temptress but a girl at a convent-school. She wants to go to the bazaar called Araby (this, like all the public events in Joyce, is historical: it was held in Dublin from May 14th to 19th, 1894, in aid of Jervis Street Hospital); unfortunately there is a retreat at the convent and she has to be disappointed. The boy promises to go instead and bring her back a present. It is the last night of Araby, he must get some money from his uncle, and his uncle comes home late and fuddled. When he arrives at the bazaar it is closing down; the lights are going out.

39

Gazing up into the darkness I saw myself as a creature driven and derided by vanity; and my eyes burned with anguish and anger.

The seeming triviality of the frustration and the violence of the language which expresses it are, as it were, reconciled by the aesthetic force of the epiphany: here, drawn from commonplace experience, is a symbol for the frustration of adolescence and, by extension, of maturity too.

The rest of the frustrations and cases of paralysis belong to the adult secular world. The heroine of 'Eveline' longs to escape from her drab Dublin life and she has her chance. But, on the very point of embarking for Buenos Aires with the man who loves her, 'all the seas of the world tumbled about her heart. He was drawing her into them: he would drown her.' Her heart says no; she sets 'her white face to him, passive, like a helpless animal. Her eyes gave him no sign of love or farewell or recognition.' Little Chandler, in 'A Little Cloud', re-meets the great Ignatius Gallaher, who has made good in London journalism (in *Ulysses* he has already become a Dublin newspaper-man's myth: he telegraphed details of the Phoenix Park murders to the *New York World*, using a code based on a *Freeman* advertisement. This was a memorable scoop). Little Chandler makes the inevitable comparison between the richness of Gallaher's life, all whiskey and advances from moneyed Jewesses, and his own – the mean job, the insipid wife, the bawling child. If only he could make his name with a little book of Celtic Twilight poems, go to London, escape ghastly provincial Dublin. But it is too late. The epiphany flowers in the rebukes of his wife for making the brat scream, while his cheeks are 'suffused with shame' and 'tears of remorse' start to his eyes. The cage is tight-shut.

One need not be a negative and timid character, like Eveline or Little Chandler, to exhibit the syndrome of soul-rot. Farrington, in 'Counterparts', is burly, red-faced, perpetually thirsty, and he fancies himself as a pub strong man. But he has the shiftlessness of all virile Dubliners, and even the job of copy-clerk in a solicitor's office is too much for him. The little heaven of release from actuality is always the 'hot reeking public-house', the tailor of malt, the dream of high-class women, but the money always runs out, the sponging cronies fade away, and heaven is thoroughly dissolved by the time he has reached the tram-stop on O'Connell Bridge. 'He cursed everything', waiting for the Sandymount tram. 'He had done for himself in the office, pawned his watch, spent all his money; and he had not even got drunk.' All that is left is to go home and beat his son Tom for letting the fire go out. Tom cries: 'I'll say a *Hail Mary* for you, pa, if you don't beat me . . . I'll say a *Hail Mary*. . . .' But a *Hail Mary* won't do for any of these Dubliners.

Nothing will really do. Lenehan, in 'Two Gallants' as in *Ulysses*, carries his seedy scraps of culture round ('That takes the solitary, unique, and, if I may so call it, *recherché* biscuit!') in the service of a sports paper and the office of jester to whoever–even a boor like Corley–has, or is able to get, a little bit of spending money. But even where there *is* money, and education, and a fair cultivated and cosmopolitan acquaintance, there is something missing. In 'After the Race' the city wears 'the mask of a capital' for Jimmy and his European friends, who have come 'scudding in towards Dublin, running evenly like pellets in the groove of the Naas Road' in their racing cars.

At the crest of the hill at Inchicore sightseers had gathered in clumps to watch the cars careering homeward, and through this channel of poverty and inaction the Continent had sped its wealth and industry. Now and again the clumps of people raised the cheer of the gratefully oppressed . . .

There are drinking and gambling and song on board the American's yacht in Kingstown Harbour, but Jimmy is fuddled and is one of the heaviest losers. 'They were devils of fellows, but he wished they would stop: it was getting late.' It is all folly, and he will regret it all in the morning. At the end of the story–Joyce's only incursion into the world of the moneyed–morning has come. 'Daybreak, gentlemen!'

High ideals are betrayed–not with renegade force but through submission to compromise, the slow silting away of conviction that, it seems, only the Irish fanatic can hold. Mr Henchy, in 'Ivy Day in the Committee Room', says:

'Parnell is dead. Now, here's the way I look at it. Here's this chap come to the throne after his old mother keeping him out of it till the man was grey. He's a man of the world, and he means well by us. He's a jolly decent fellow, if you ask me, and no damn nonsense about him. He just says to himself: "The old one never went to see these wild Irish. By Christ, I'll go myself and see what they're like." And are we going to insult the man when he comes over here on a friendly visit?'

It is Parnell's anniversary, and the corks pop round the fire in the committee room. The impending visit of Edward VII is folded into the warmth of convivial tolerance ('The King's coming here will mean an influx of money into this country'). Joe Hynes recites a poem called 'The Death of Parnell', in which the lost leader is presented as a betrayed Christ. There is applause, another cork pops, and Mr Crofton says that it is 'a very fine piece of writing'. Parnell has joined a harmless pantheon, no legitimate Jesus but an ikon. This is one of the stories that held back publication of the whole book. A libel on the Irish spirit, a too free bandying of the name of a living monarch, an intolerable deal of demotic speech: naturalism had gone too far altogether.

With 'Grace', the penultimate story, the heady wine of religious faith is decently watered for the children of this world, who–as the text of Father Purdon's sermon reminds us–are wiser in their generation than the children of light. The story begins with the fall of man:

Two gentlemen who were in the lavatory at the time tried to lift him up: but he was quite helpless. He lay curled up at the foot of the stairs down which he had fallen. They succeeded in turning him over. His hat had rolled a few yards away and his clothes were smeared with the filth and ooze of the floor on which he had lain, face downwards. His eyes were closed and he breathed with a grunting noise. A thin stream of blood trickled from the corner of his mouth.

This is Mr Kernan, 'a commercial traveller of the old school which believed in the dignity of its calling'. He is one of a group of small tradesmen, clerks, employees of the Royal Irish Constabulary, workers in the office of the Sub-Sheriff or the City Coroner–good bibulous men who are to be the backbone of *Ulysses*. Mr Power promises Mrs Kernan that he and his friends will make a new man of her husband: no more drunken fallings, regeneration with God's grace. And so, without solemnity and even with a few harmless Catholic jokes, we move towards a businessmen's retreat, a renewal of baptismal vows, and a sermon from Father Purdon. It is a manly, no-nonsense sermon, in which Jesus Christ is presented as a very understanding master, asking little, forgiving much.

We might have had, we all had from time to time, our temptations: we might have, we all had, our failings. But one thing only, he said, he would ask of his hearers. And that was: to be straight and manly with God. If their accounts tallied in every point to say:

'Well, I have verified my accounts. I find all well.'

But if, as might happen, there were some discrepancies, to admit the truth, to be frank and say like a man:

'Well, I have looked into my accounts. I find this wrong and this wrong. But, with God's grace, I will rectify this and this. I will set right my accounts.'

Thus this rather mean city is spread before us, its timidity and the hollowness of its gestures recorded with economy and a kind of muffled poetry, its bouncing cheques of the spirit endorsed with humour but with neither compassion nor censoriousness, for the author must be totally withdrawn from his creation. The book begins, in 'The Sisters', with the image of a paralysed priest and a broken chalice; it might have ended, in 'Grace', with the sacrament of provincial mock-piety and a blessing for small and dirty minds. But it does not end there. The longest and best story which concludes the book is an afterthought. Dublin may be an impotent city, but Ireland is more than Dublin. Life may seem to lie in exile, 'out in Europe', but it is really waiting coiled up in Ireland, ready to lunge from a wilder west than is known to the reading boys of 'An Encounter'. This story about life is called 'The Dead'.

Everything in Joyce's writing is an enhanced record of the author's own experience, but perhaps 'The Dead' is the most personal item in the long chronicle of Dublin which was his life's work. Gabriel Conroy is a sort of James Joyce–a literary man, college teacher, contributor of a literary column to the Dublin *Daily Express*, Europeanised, out of sympathy with Ireland's nationalistic aspirations, aware that his own culture is of a different, superior, order to that which surrounds him in provincial Dublin. He has married a girl of inferior education ('country cute' is what his own mother once called her), but he does not despise her: Gretta Conroy has the Galway firmness of character of her prototype, Nora Joyce; she is beautiful; Gabriel is a possessive husband. On New Year's Eve they go to the annual party given by Gabriel's aunts–Miss Kate and Miss Julia–and, as the house is some way out of Dublin, they have booked a hotel room for the night. It is a good convivial evening, full of piano solos, song, quadrilles, food. As Gabriel and Gretta go to their hotel room in the early hours, a wave of desire comes over him: the possessive wants to possess. But Gretta is distracted. At the end of the party the tenor Bartell D'Arcy sang a song called *The Lass of Aughrim*, and she is thinking about the song. A young boy she once knew in Galway used to sing it. His name was Michael Furey and he was 'in the gasworks'. He died young. Gabriel asks whether he died of consumption, and Gretta replies: 'I think he died for me.'

The complex of emotions which takes possession of Gabriel's soul on this disclosure and on Gretta's transport of re-lived grief needs something more than a naturalistic technique for its expression. We see the emergence of a new Joyce, the deployment of the

43

cunning of the author of *Ulysses*, and experience a visitation of terrible magic. As Gabriel analyses his tepid little soul we see that his name and that of his dead rival have taken on a strange significance – Gabriel the mild angel, Michael the passionate one; and that dead boy, possessed of an insupportable love, was rightly called Furey.

The air of the room chilled his shoulders. He stretched himself cautiously along under the sheets and lay down beside his wife. One by one, they were all becoming shades. Better pass boldly into that other world, in the full glory of some passion, than fade and wither dismally with age.

Gabriel becomes aware of the world of the dead, into which the living pass. That world goes on with its own life, and its purpose is to qualify, literally to haunt, the world of those not yet gone. The living and the dead coexist; they have strange traffic with each other. And there is a sense in which that dead Michael Furey is more alive, through the passion which killed him, than the living Gabriel Conroy with his bits of European culture and his intellectual superiority. Meanwhile, in the all too tangible world of Dublin, the snow is coming down, general all over Ireland. 'The time had come for him to set out on his journey westwards.' The west is where passion takes place and boys die for love: the graveyard where Michael Furey lies buried is, in a sense, a place of life. As for the snow, it unites the living and the dead and, by virtue of this supernatural function, it ceases to be the sublunary snow that drops on a winter city. Gabriel's soul swoons slowly as he hears 'the snow falling faintly through the universe and faintly falling, like the descent of their last end, upon all the living and the dead'. We have broken, with him, through the time-space veil; we are in the presence of a terrible ultimate truth.

Ellmann's biography of Joyce tells us, in detail, about the real-life materials which went to the making of 'The Dead'. Gabriel's revelation of the community of dead and living was also his creator's, derived from a similar jealousy of his wife's dead lover, a jealousy which had to yield to acquiescence and a sort of surrender. By extension, jealousy of a living rival becomes equally futile: it is best to accept philosophically, even gladly; we can even end by deliberately willing the cuckold's role. When, towards the end of *Ulysses*, Bloom reflects on his wife's adultery (multiple – the names of her fellow-sinners are fully listed), he considers the responses of 'envy, jealousy, abnegation, equanimity' and justifies the last of these with thoughts about 'the futility of triumph or protest or vindication; the inanity of extolled virtue; the lethargy of nescient matter; the apathy of the stars'. But, earlier, in the brothel scene, his imagination has called up the enactment of adultery between his wife and Blazes Boylan and he himself, in imagination, has urged it on:

BLOOM: (*His eyes wildly dilated, clasps himself*) Show! Hide! Show! Plough her! More! Shoot!

Similarly, Richard in the play *Exiles* has a shameful desire to give his wife to his friend Robert: '. . . In the very core of my ignoble heart I longed to be betrayed by you and her—in the dark, in the night—secretly, meanly, craftily. By you, my best friend, and by her. I longed for that passionately and ignobly, to be dishonoured for ever in love and in lust, to be . . .' This yielding urge, shared by three of Joyce's characters, and even given mythical status (it is imposed on Shakespeare, for instance) in *Ulysses*, is an aspect of the 'womanly' in the Joyce man, the *yin* that qualifies the *yang*. Bloom undergoes many metamorphoses in Mabbot Street, and perhaps the least spectacular of these is his change of sex.

As for the bigger, and more creative, theme of the one world of living and dead, this may be thought of as having its roots in Joyce's Catholicism: the striving living are militant and the beatified dead triumphant, but they are members of one Church. Dead and alive meet naturally in the phantasmagoria of the brothel scene; in the deeper dream of *Finnegans Wake* the unity of human history depends on the simultaneous existence of all its periods. But, in the interests of economy, one man and one woman must play many parts. The table called, Joyceanly, 'Who is Who When Everybody is Somebody Else' in Adaline Glasheen's *A Census of Finnegans Wake*, makes Earwicker play God the Father, Adam the sinner, Adam the father, Abraham, Isaac, Noah, Buddha, Mohammed, Finn MacCool, Tim Finnegan, King Leary and some twenty-odd other roles, and Earwicker's family is quick to find appropriate supporting parts. This is the Occam's Razor of the mature artist. At the close of 'The Dead' Gabriel feels his own identity fading out and his soul swooning as the solid world dissolves: it is dissolving, proleptically, into the huge empyrean of *Finnegans Wake*; the seeds are being sown.

The importance of *Dubliners* in the entire Joyce canon cannot be exaggerated. There may seem to be little remarkable in the technique nowadays, but this is because Joyce himself, through his followers as well as in the book, has habituated us to it: we take for granted the bareness of the prose, the fact that originality may well consist in taking away as much as in adding. Joyce's later work is, in fact, an art of adding, of building on to a simple enough structure incrustations of deeper and deeper richness: *Finnegans Wake* represents the possible limit of loading statements with layers of significance. In *Dubliners* his task was different. He had to deromanticise fictional prose, stripping off the coloured veneers that had passed for poetic brilliance in the heyday of the late Victorian novel. To write like Meredith or Hardy or Moore (or anybody else, for that matter) was not difficult for the author who was to create the 'Oxen of the Sun' episode in *Ulysses*. He naturally tended to richness, but richness was not wanted in this study of a drab modern city which should flash out its epiphanies from the commonplace. Where cliché occurs, cliché is intended, for most of the inhabitants of the city live in clichés. Where a stale bit of romanticism is used – as in 'Two Gallants': 'His harp, too, heedless that her coverings had fallen about her knees, seemed weary alike of the eyes of strangers and of her master's hands' – that also is in keeping, underlining the poverty of the Irish dream of the past. As for the management of humour, as in 'Grace' and 'Clay', this is as deadpan as anything in the contemporary American tradition and a world away from the whimsy and heavy-footed japing of what passed for comedy in Joyce's youth. But the miraculous ear for verbal nuance is seen best in the dialogue.

Joyce's books are about human society, and most social speech is 'phatic', to use Malinowski's useful term. It concerns itself less with conveying information, intention or need than with establishing or maintaining contact – mere comfortable noise in the dark. Irish town speech is the most phatic of the entire English-speaking world: it is all colour, rhythm and gesture. It is the very voice of charming apathy and shiftlessness, a deadly Siren trap for the author who is concerned with strong plot and dramatic action, for the creation of Irish characters within the structure of a plot must either lead to the destruction of the plot or the falsifying of those who must enact it. When we see *Juno and the Paycock* we feel somehow let down when action occurs: the play stands or falls on what the characters say, and what they say does not take us towards a final curtain. Joxer and the Paycock, like *Finnegans Wake* itself, are destined to go round and round in a circle, lamenting the 'chassis' of the world but never doing anything about it, asking 'What is the stars?' but never troubling to find out. And so with Joyce's Dubliners, whose totem is Johnny the horse in Gabriel Conroy's story:

'And everything went on beautifully until Johnny came in sight of King Billy's statue: and whether he fell in love with the horse King Billy sits on or whether he thought he was back again in the mill, anyhow he began to walk round the statue. Round and round he went . . .'

The exactly caught speech of these harnessed citizens is the true voice of paralysis. Realising how essential its tones are to Joyce's art, we begin to understand his need for finding action outside, for his garrulous pub-crawlers will not generate it. Action has to come from an exterior myth, like that of the Odyssey, or a circular theory of history which suggests, even if it does not fulfil, an image of purposive movement.

Finally, *Dubliners* is important because it provides *Ulysses* with a ready-made cast of extras. We shall meet them all again or, if they are dead, hear about them—Bartell D'Arcy, Mr Power, Martin Cunningham, Hynes, Mrs Sinico and the rest. If we have not yet met Mr Bloom, it is because, though he was intended for this gallery, he had to be lifted out to be groomed for greater things. And if we have not yet met Stephen Dedalus and his university cronies, it is because they had already been set down in a novel of their own, along with a roaring father and a sweet doomed mother.

4: Martyr and Maze-maker

JOYCE'S FIRST ATTEMPT AT FORGING A PIECE OF IMAGINATIVE prose out of his own artistic genesis belongs, apparently, to 1904, Bloomsyear, when the genesis was still going on. The Dublin intellectuals Eglinton and Ryan were bringing out a magazine called, after the Irish earth-goddess, *Dana*. Joyce wrote a story about himself–the renegade Catholic discovering his creative soul through sin, then striding forward to change the world–in which the technique of the Symbolists was charged with the spirit of Ibsen. Stanislaus Joyce suggested 'A Portrait of the Artist' as a title; under this name it was submitted to *Dana* and promptly rejected. Still, nothing was lost. Indeed, writers are sometimes quietly relieved about rejections: they will often have second thoughts as soon as the package has slid into the post-box, seeing in their subject-matter a bigger potential than was at first apparent: many a big book has started as something for a magazine. Joyce was quick to observe that his theme deserved to be developed on the scale of a full-length novel, and so he conceived a *Bildungsroman* of some three hundred thousand words. Thus *Stephen Hero* was born. The writing of it seems to have proceeded, first in Dublin, then in Trieste, *pari passu* with the sketches for *Dubliners*, but Joyce was never to publish *Stephen Hero*. Most of the completed manuscript was apparently burnt–perhaps in a mood of dejection–but nearly four hundred pages survived, to be published posthumously as *Stephen Hero: Part of the first draft of 'A Portrait of the Artist as a Young Man'*.

That is how we read this long fragment–as a groping towards a masterpiece. We can see why Joyce abandoned his original scheme: it had too little shape to it, there was too much concern with recording life warm, as it was lived. The vitality of *Stephen Hero* derives mainly from its passionate egoism, the need to set down–as in a journal–everything that happens as soon as it happens, for every grain of experience is food for the greedy growing soul of the artist.

48

Joyce always wants the whole of something. His inability to encompass, in *Stephen Hero*, the whole of a growing life, together with what that life feeds on, teaches him to be content with smaller wholes–the whole of a day in *Ulysses* and the whole of a night in *Finnegans Wake*. In every major artist there seems to be a conflict between the urge to swallow everything and the desire to select and shape. Joyce must have seen the dangers implicit in the writing of *Stephen Hero* more clearly because of his solution of the problem of *Dubliners*. It was not enough to gather a bunch of casual epiphanies and impose unity on them through the fact of mere common citizenship: Joyce arranged his stories cunningly, in a sort of genetic pattern, beginning with childhood, moving on to adolescence, adulthood, public life, and modulating to the Church through motherhood; finally, all the living and the dead, the young, the old, the frail forts they build against time and corruption, are wrapped together under the metaphysical snow. For his autobiographical novel he conceived a cognate design but was bolder in his drawing on the resources of symbolism.

The growth of the embryo and the growth of the soul mirrored each other in Joyce's personal symbolism. In the 'Oxen of the Sun' episode in *Ulysses*, a history of English literature–which is a good enough record of the spiritual history of a nation–is used to symbolise embryonic growth; in *A Portrait of the Artist as a Young Man*, embryonic growth is used to symbolise the spiritual history of a young poet. There was no element of the cold and considered choice of symbols here: Joyce, as a medical student, had become fascinated by embryology; the conception and birth of his daughter Lucia pointed the mystery; his idiosyncratic passion for Nora avoided the filial but often–in his letters to her–expressed itself in the foetal. The static and passive organism, which does not move of its own volition but on which growth is miraculously imposed, is a very Joycean concept.

As soon as we meet the name of Joyce's hero we recognise that symbolism is at work, but in *Stephen Hero* that particular symbolism sticks out like a sore thumb, especially in the implausible form 'Daedalus'. Joyce was quick to change this to 'Dedalus', which will just about stand in a naturalistic novel, but the name can only really radiate significance in a symbolic context. So the 'Stephen Dedalus' of *A Portrait*, which makes naturalism serve symbolism, can sound all its harmonics–the self-elected martyrdom of literature, the wren which, in the song, is the 'king of all birds' and is sacrificed on St

Stephen's Day, the stones which killed a saint and which built a labyrinth, the invention of flight–flight for exile and flight for poetic creation, the image of a bird which unites the pagan name and the Christian.

A Portrait of the Artist as a Young Man has many symbols, but the fundamental one is of a creature trying to escape from the bondage of the grosser elements, earth and water, and learning painfully how to fly. The first of the five big chapters into which the book is organised begins with a child's discrete impressions–the father's fairy tale (the father comes first), the stumbling of an infant's tongue that is not yet a poet's, so that 'O, the wild rose blossoms' becomes 'O, the green wothe botheth', the smells of bed and father and mother, water. The embryonic soul is surrounded by a sort of amniotic fluid – urine and the sea (Stephen dances a hornpipe); as for the land, it has two colours–red and green. These are also heraldic or political colours: 'Dante had two brushes in her press. The brush with the maroon velvet back was for Michael Davitt and the brush with the green velvet back was for Parnell.' But the embryo is better used to darkness, and so Stephen hides under the table. Dante (Mrs Riordan, his nurse) foretells his future.

> . . . His mother said:
> –O, Stephen will apologise.
> Dante said:
> –O, if not, the eagles will come and pull out his eyes–
> > Pull out his eyes,
> > Apologise,
> > Apologise,
> > Pull out his eyes.

The eagle, not the wren, is still the king of all birds, but he knows who is threatening to usurp his eyrie and he counter-threatens the poet with blindness.

This opening page is a swift miracle, the sort of achievement which, in its immediacy and astonishing economy, ought to make the conventional novelist ('My first memories are of my father, a monocled hirsute man who told me stories') ashamed. Prose and subject-matter have become one and inseparable; it is the first big technical breakthrough of twentieth-century prose-writing and, inevitably, it looks as if anybody could have thought of it. The roots of *Ulysses* are here – to every phase of the soul its own special language; *Finnegans Wake* must seem, not a wilful aberration from sense, but a logical conclusion from that premise. If we recognise the rightness of 'When you wet the bed first it is warm then it gets cold. His mother put on the oilsheet. That had the queer smell', we must accept the inevitability of 'Till thousendsthee. Lps. The keys to. Given! A way a lone a last a loved a long the.'

The section that follows takes Stephen to Clongowes Wood College. He is still a child, a creature of responses and not of thought, and he tries to hide from the boisterous world. The eye-pecking eagle has become a football: 'the greasy leather orb flew like a heavy bird through the grey light'. In the pale and chilly evening air he feels 'his body small and weak amid the throng of players'; his eyes are 'weak and watery'. He is surrounded by mud and cold but he is also ill: a boy called Wells (appropriate name) shouldered him into the slimy water of the square ditch because he would not swop his snuff-box for a hacking chestnut. The soul is kept pushed down to its primal water and earth. Stephen hears one boy call another a 'suck' and at once he hears and sees water going down a lavatory basin. The colours of earth assert themselves: '. . . he remembered the song about the wild rose blossoms on the little green place. But you could not have a green rose. But perhaps somewhere in the world you could.' A class-mate, Fleming, has coloured the earth and clouds on the first page of the geography book–the earth green and the clouds maroon. We are back to Dante's brushes and–gross forces which will try to hold the emergent soul to a particular spot of earth–Irish politics. Parnell is in Stephen's mind as he shivers in the study hall:

He wondered which was right, to be for the green or for the maroon, because Dante had ripped the green velvet back off the brush that was for Parnell one day with her scissors and had told him that Parnell was a bad man. He wondered if they were arguing at home about that. That was called politics. There were two sides in it: Dante was on one side and his father and Mr Casey were on the other side but his mother and Uncle Charles were on no side.

When he is taken off to the school infirmary and his soul almost resigns itself to the earth ('How beautiful the words were where they said *Bury me in the old churchyard!*') he has a watery vision, full of the noise of waves, with the cry 'Parnell! He is dead!' coming up from the crowd by the sea's edge. Dante, in maroon and green velvet, walks proudly and silently past.

The red of holly and the green of ivy usher in the Christmas dinner scene, with its terrible quarrel about politics and the Church and Mr Casey's heartbroken cry of 'Poor Parnell! My dead king!'

Stephen, old enough now to sit at table with his elders, raises a terror-stricken face to see his father's eyes full of tears. The soul is learning about the world–loyalty, treachery, the bitter divisions of faith. Other lessons come when he is back at school–the crimes of adolescence and just punishments for those crimes. But Stephen himself is punished for nothing: his glasses are broken and (the eagles are at work) he cannot see well enough to write. The prefect of studies comes into the classroom, calls Stephen a lazy little schemer and–in one of the most excruciatingly painful passages in all modern literature–beats him with a pandybat:

A hot burning stinging tingling blow like the loud crack of a broken stick made his trembling hand crumple together like a leaf in the fire: and at the sound and the pain scalding tears were driven into his eyes. His whole body was shaking with fright, his arm was shaking and his crumpled burning livid hand shook like a loose leaf in the air. A cry sprang to his lips, a prayer to be let off. But though the tears scalded his eyes and his limbs quivered with pain and fright he held back the hot tears and the cry that scalded his throat.

–Other hand! shouted the prefect of studies.

The peculiar objectivity of Joyce's method can be seen even in isolated words. In the paragraph that follows, Stephen draws back 'his shaking arm in terror' and bursts out 'into a whine of pain'. 'Whine' is not usually for heroes, but it is the exact word that is wanted here. Similarly, the Stephen of *Ulysses* is as capable of sneering as of picking his nose. Let traditionally unheroic connotations go hang.

And now the earthbound spirit, pandybatted to shameful lowliness, finds the courage to attempt the air. Nasty Roche tells Stephen to complain to the rector; a fellow in second of grammar says: 'The senate and the Roman people declared that Dedalus had been wrongly punished.' His name is a great name, like the names of great classical men in Richmal Magnall's Questions; the eagles are on his side. He complains to the rector, who gives him a kind hearing and says that it will not happen again, and walks away faster and faster towards the air. He tells his schoolfellows what he has done, and they fling their caps into the air, cheering. They hoist him up on their locked hands and carry him. He is airborne and the leitmotif is 'air'. But, when he is alone again, the smell of evening in the air reminds him of fields and the digging up of turnips. The sound of the cricket-balls being bumped in the distance is 'pick, pack, pock, puck: like drops of water in a fountain falling softly in the brimming bowl'. We are back to the amniotic fluid. The foetus has had a premonition of release, but there is still a long time to go before emancipation.

In the second chapter the prose becomes staider and more periodic, suggesting the tortuous groping towards the soul's expression through school essays and reading in nineteenth-century literature. Stephen, under the old trainer Mike Flynn, is learning to run if not to fly. But words are already suggesting to him that another element awaits his fledging:

Words which he did not understand he said over and over to himself till he had learnt them by heart; and through them he had glimpses of the real world about him. The hour when he too would take part in the life of that world seemed drawing near and in secret he began to make ready for the great part which he felt awaited him the nature of which he only dimly apprehended.

Dreams out of *The Count of Monte Cristo* nourish his pride. His first image of woman comes to him in the form of Mercedes, filling his blood with unrest. Meanwhile, the ruin of his family is under way, and he is not to go back to Clongowes. But, says his father, 'there's a crack of the whip left in me yet, Stephen, old chap. We're not dead yet, sonny. No, by the Lord Jesus (God forgive me) nor half dead.' And so the furniture-caravans move the Dedalus chattels to Dublin, and the subject-matter awaits the artist. The key-words are 'unrest', 'dissatisfaction', 'embittered silence', 'anger': the growing soul is dragged down more than ever before by its sense of circumambient squalor. We have the first vague glimpse of the 'temptress'–the young girl at the party, Emma Cleary, who appears only in her initials, a cipher at the head of the poem he writes for her, under A.M.D.G. and over L.D.S.

Stephen goes to Belvedere College, so that he is still receiving a Jesuit education. The steady thickening of the prose-style matches the 'scum of disgust' that coats his palate for life; an immense amount of detail is marked–as in the description of the Whitsuntide play in which Stephen performs–but there is no emergence of any single image. The sheer multiplicity of daily life bewilders the soul, and the tortures of pubescence additionally hold back flight. But one bird, his schoolfriend Heron, has achieved one kind of emancipation–the giggling world of bazaars and tennis-parties and cigarettes. Heron taunts Stephen with Emma's interest in him ('And what part does Stephen take, Mr Dedalus? And will Stephen not sing, Mr Dedalus?') and, threatening playfully to strike him with his cane, tries to make Stephen admit that he is a sly dog. This easy world of banter and flirtation is one the young poet cannot enter. Heron is superficial, philistine Ireland with little, though painful, claws. It was Heron, Stephen remembers, who, over a year ago, had tried to make him admit that Byron was no good – a bad man and an atheist, hence (in Irish logic) a poor poet. Then Stephen had not given in and he had been beaten with a cabbage stump as well as a cane; it was the beginning of his literary martyrdom. Now he glibly recites the *Confiteor* to the indulgent laughter of Heron and his friend Wallis. He cannot really hold anger or resentment for very long; like peel from a fruit, all strong emotion becomes swiftly and smoothly detached from him. He is preparing for the single commitment of art. Meanwhile, he has to act the part of an aged pedant in the school play. The curtain falls and, in a complex and intolerable seizure of emotions he cannot understand – pride (wounded), hope (fallen), desire (baffled) – he runs and runs, as once before down the corridor leading from the rector's study at Clongowes. But this time it is down a hill – 'at breakneck speed'. At the bottom of the hill the smell of horse-piss and rotted straw calms his heart. He must prepare for a greater descent into further squalor. He is still not ready for take-off.

Stephen goes with his father to Cork, Simon Dedalus's old city. Some vague business connected with saving the family itself from a too precipitous descent takes them there. Stephen's pubescent torments find images of shame. In the Queen's College, where Mr Dedalus was once a medical student, he meets the word *Foetus* cut several times on a desk. 'The sudden legend startled his blood.' Unbidden and derived from no known memory, a vision of the act of inscription springs up before him:

A broadshouldered student with a moustache was cutting in the letters with a jack knife, seriously. Other students stood or sat near him laughing at his handiwork. One jogged his elbow. The big student turned on him, frowning. He was dressed in loose grey clothes and had tan boots.

Stephen is to know other, seemingly pointless, epiphanies of this order. The present visionary shock frames a significant word. He is still held down in the womb of matter, longing for birth but compelled to remain an embryo driven by an enclosing will to take further, more grotesque, shapes before release into the air. He recognises his formlessness, the sleep of pre-birth which is represented to him as death. 'His childhood was dead or lost and with it his soul capable of simple joys and he was drifting amid life like the barren shell of the moon.'

The shell is a specious one. The outer life of Stephen is one of academic success, and he even wins thirty-three pounds as an exhibition and essay prize. With the money he tries 'to build a breakwater of order and elegance against the sordid tide of life without him and to dam up, by rules of conduct and active interests and new filial relations, the powerful recurrence of the tide within him'. But he fails, recognises that he must succumb to sin, and lets the tide break. In the brothel district of Dublin he finds what he must have.

Can the soul descend any lower? The world that Joyce now describes is one of dull light, through which the soul thuds and blunders, taking a kind of crass pleasure in its own degradation. Sin follows sin, fumblings with whores are matched by a gross appetite for greasy mutton stews. Matter has reasserted itself, but the clogged soul has no desire to be free. Yet one exalted image prevails, though hopelessly: Mercedes has appropriately changed to the Blessed Virgin, an allomorph of the *Ewig-weibliche*, the eternal woman.

If ever his soul, reentering her dwelling shyly after the frenzy of his body's lust had spent itself, was turned towards her whose emblem is the morning star, 'bright and musical, telling of heaven and infusing peace', it was when her names were murmured softly by lips whereon there still lingered foul and shameful words, the savour itself of a lewd kiss.

As for the lips of the embryo artist himself, they seem to have forfeited the right of golden utterance. At the beginning of the book they stuttered ('O, the green wothe botheth'); now they have yielded to a pressure 'darker than the swoon of sin'. They cannot receive the Eucharist, not yet.

The soul can, of course, descend lower, for it can descend to the Pit. Now follows the incredible and most unjesuitical retreat, in which Father Arnall's sermons on hell are presented unedited, the utter limit of naturalism. Here is the final victory of natural elements which have taken on divine intensity and duration. There is no air now, only stench and corruption and fire. Stephen's terror is so great that it breeds hallucinations: faces watch and voices murmur:

–We knew perfectly well of course that although it was bound to come to the light he would find considerable difficulty in endeavouring to try to induce himself to try to endeavour to ascertain the spiritual plenipotentiary and so we knew of course perfectly well–

The verbal technique moves closer to *Ulysses*. The image of personal hell is almost a stage direction out of the brothel scene:

A field of stiff weeds and thistles and tufted nettlebunches. Thick among the tufts of rank stiff growth lay battered canisters and clots and coils of solid excrement. A faint marsh light struggling upwards from all the ordure through the bristling greygreen weeds. An evil smell, faint and foul as the light, curled upwards sluggishly out of the canisters and from the stale crusted dung.

The field is full of grey satyrs. The horror of the vision is intensified by the trivial sordidness of some of the properties – the canisters, stale excrement, a torn flannel waistcoat round the ribs of one of the creatures. It is authentic hell. Stephen cries for air.

He is not the only one. I still find it difficult to read the hell-chapter without some of the sense of suffocation I felt when I first met it, at the age of fifteen, myself a Catholic looking for emancipation. I was hurled back into conformity by this very sermon and this very vision. As for Stephen, he runs blindly to confession and, in a white dream of holiness recaptured, receives the Eucharist. Everything is white – pudding, eggs, flowers, the altar cloth, the wafer, Stephen's soul. The lips that kissed a whore at the end of the preceding chapter now open for the reception of Christ. But, by a fine irony, the elevation that the soul has awaited belongs to a different order of reality from what religion represents. Stephen's long penance, with its curious mortifications of the flesh, seems to bear no real spiritual fruit. He finds himself in bondage to a quantitative concept of salvation which expresses itself in very materialistic terms:

He seemed to feel his soul in devotion pressing like fingers the keyboard of a great cash register and to see the amount of his purchase start forth immediately in heaven, not as a number but as a frail column of incense or as a slender flower.

He is still waiting for the real ciborium, and – the irony maintained – he senses its coming when his spiritual director asks him whether he has ever felt that he had a vocation. He nearly says yes, but he withholds the word. The priest means something very specific. 'The Reverend Stephen Dedalus, S.J.' Stephen is aware of temptation, but the vision of himself as a priest is at once confused with the images of the soul's repression we have already met in the Clongowes episodes. 'His lungs dilated and sank as if he were inhaling a warm moist unsustaining air, and he smelt again the moist warm air which hung in the bath in Clongowes above the sluggish turfcoloured water.'

Stephen at last knows that literature is his vocation, priestly enough since its function is the transmutation of lowly accidents to godly essence. Through art he can come to terms with the down-dragging stuff of material life:

The faint sour stink of rotted cabbages came towards him from the kitchen gardens on the rising ground above the river. He smiled to think that it was this disorder, the misrule and confusion of his father's house and the stagnation of vegetable life, which was to win the day in his soul.

He walks towards the sea and observes the raw white bodies of his old schoolfellows, foetuses that will never emerge to outer life, flopping about in the water. But they at least recognise, even in joke, the 'mild proud sovereignty' of the poet, and his name, which they call, 'seemed to him a prophecy' – 'Stephanos Dedalos! Bous Stephanoumenos! Bous Stephaneforos!' And now, for the first time, Stephen sees a winged form over the waves, slowly mounting the sky. It is Daedalus, the fabulous artificer. The soul at last takes wing:

His heart trembled in an ecstasy of fear and his soul was in flight. His soul was soaring in an air beyond the world and the body he knew was purified in a breath and delivered of incertitude and made radiant and commingled with the element of the spirit. An ecstasy of flight made radiant his eyes and wild his breath and tremulous and wild and radiant his windswept limbs.

He wants to cry out his sense of deliverance, in the voice of a hawk or eagle. Fire, which had been presented to him as a property of hell, is part of the air-world: his blood and body burn for adventure. All that is now needed to mediate between earth and heaven is some angelic vision of a woman who is neither a whore nor the Virgin Mary. Stephen sees a girl standing in a rivulet, 'alone and still, gazing out to sea'. No word passes between them, but her image enters his soul for ever. She embodies the call of life. He falls asleep in rapture on the earth, and the earth takes him to her breast. The grosser elements no longer drag him down: they have become sanctified by his newly found power of flight. The earth is for wandering and the sea for travel. He is master of the four elements. And then we remember the inscription on the fly-leaf of the young Stephen's geography, back in Clongowes:

> Stephen Dedalus
> Class of Elements
> Clongowes Wood College
> Sallins
> County Kildare
> Ireland
> Europe
> The World
> The Universe.

It is, we see, a manifesto of conquest, and now it is beginning to be fulfilled.

5: Free Flight

THE MATERIAL OF THE FEW SCORE PAGES WHICH MAKE UP THE final chapter of *A Portrait* is a distillation of hundreds of pages of *Stephen Hero*. Comparing the two, we see with a shock how cunningly the Joyce of *A Portrait* has lulled us into accepting without remark a revolution of form and style, for, however interesting its content, *Stephen Hero* is stylistically and formally orthodox enough. Its charm, as I have already implied, lies in its appetite for notation: life, which chiefly means speech, is pinned down while it is still warm. What we read when we are not listening to voices is prose set solidly in the pre-Joycean era:

> As Stephen looked at the big square block of masonry looming before them through the faint daylight, he re-entered again in thought the seminarist life which he had led for so many years, to the understanding of the narrow activities of which he could now in a moment bring the spirit of an acute sympathetic alien. He recognised at once the martial mind of the Irish Church in the style of this ecclesiastical barracks. He looked in vain at the faces and figures which passed him for a token of moral elevation: all were cowed without being humble, modish without being simple-mannered.

This is assured, decent, and literary. It will serve for many a respected writer, but hardly for a Joyce. As for the youthful egoism of the book, this is not a fault to be softened or expunged in a reworking. Egoism is essential to the scheme; what is required is an approach more suitable to it—not the epic or the dramatic but the lyric. In the lyric form, as Stephen Dedalus is soon to tell us, everything is subordinated to the personality of the poet. It is appropriate, in the final phase of the artist's development, that he should not merely take to the air but dominate everything on the earth beneath him.

In certain countries of the Far East, American films—even the most bizarre and fanciful—are taken for actuality, not fiction. Readers of Joyce in the West are sometimes no more sophisticated: they are more concerned with the biography of *A Portrait* than with the art, and they welcome *Stephen Hero* as a source of elucidation and gap-filling. This is desperately wrong. If we want a Joyce biography, we had better go to Gorman or Ellmann or Stanislaus Joyce's *My Brother's Keeper*. If there are ellipses in *A Portrait* we can be quite sure that they are integral to the scheme and that *Stephen Hero* is not to be welcomed as a gloss. Apart from all that, we ought to remember that Joyce's novels are only approximately autobiographical: he was a shaping artist not a faithful recorder, though *Stephen Hero* comes closer to being an actuality film than any other of his works. A comparison between *A Portrait* and its first draft, then, should be of interest only to the student of literary method. A style was adopted and later abandoned; *A Portrait* shows us why.

In *Stephen Hero* the egoism is, paradoxically, pointed because the young artist is seen on the same level of objectivity as the other characters: Stephen is a bumptious young man bumping against the foils of members of his family and of the University. In *A Portrait* Stephen has become godlike, containing everybody else, and his superiority is established by a sort of *lex eterna*. Similarly, events which are presented fully and dramatically in *Stephen Hero* become oblique, peripheral, rumours or whispers in the maturer book. Maurice has almost entirely disappeared in *A Portrait*; in *Stephen Hero* he is, as was Stanislaus in real life, a partner in dialectic. Dialectic has no place in a lyrical soliloquy, and so various of the white-hot arguments of *Stephen Hero*—particularly the one between Stephen and his mother about his refusal to make his Easter duty—appear in *A Portrait* only as the tiresome battering, reported with weary brevity, of a position the artist-hero has no intention of relinquishing. In the last chapter of *A Portrait* there are no more conclusions to reach: the hero knows the strength of his own wings; all that remains to do is to trumpet his position from the heights and then take off.

The element of this final chapter is, then, air, but the viaticum for the air-journey is made out of the lowlier elements. Stephen drains his third cup of watery tea; the dark pool in the dripping-jar reminds him of 'the dark turfcoloured water of the bath in Clongowes'. Water now serves him: his mother gives him a ritual washing before he leaves the house to go to his lectures at the University. She is shrunken to a mere faceless servitor, as are his living sisters (the death of Isabel, so terrible in *Stephen Hero*, has no place here):

59

—Fill out the place for me to wash, said Stephen
—Katey, fill out the place for Stephen to wash.
—Boody, fill out the place for Stephen to wash.
—I can't, I'm going for blue. Fill it out, you, Maggy.

Stephen's morning walk to the University recapitulates briefly his long training for flight. He shakes off, in 'loathing and bitterness', the voices that assail the pride of his youth—the screech of a mad nun, his father's shrill whistle, his mother's mutterings. He picks his way through the mounds of damp rubbish in the waterlogged lane, but wetness becomes the property of leaves and tree-bark, lifting his heart. He hears other voices—Hauptmann, Newman, Guido Cavalcanti, Ibsen (the god of the Stephen of the other book, and of the real-life undergraduate Joyce, here serves humbly, 'a spirit of wayward boyish beauty': the Stephen of *A Portrait* defers to nobody), Ben Jonson, Aristotle, Aquinas. He has absorbed a heterogeneity of influences. Add Blake, Bruno, Vico and you have very nearly the entire Joyce library.

He is late for his lectures, but the poet soars above time. He soars above other things too. He thinks of MacCann (nicknamed 'Bonny Dundee' in *Stephen Hero*: 'Come fill up my cup, come fill up MacCann'), and of what this progressive fellow-student said to him:

—Dedalus, you're an antisocial being, wrapped up in yourself. I'm not. I'm a democrat and I'll work and act for social liberty and equality among all classes and sexes in the United States of the Europe of the future.

He thinks also of Davin, the peasant student who worships 'the sorrowful legend of Ireland' and once told Stephen about what happened to him while he was walking home late at night from a hurling match. He called at a cottage for a glass of water and was offered richer hospitality by a half-naked young woman who said her husband was away for the night. The woman symbolises Ireland for Stephen, 'a batlike soul waking to the consciousness of itself in darkness and secrecy and loneliness and, through the eyes and voice and gesture of a woman without guile, calling the stranger to her bed'. In this final chapter there is a fusion of female images—Emma, Stephen's mother, the Virgin Mary, girls seen on the street or coming out of Jacob's biscuit factory, Ireland herself—into a single figure, an *Ewig-weibliche* that has completed the task of bringing forth the artist's soul but whose demands for worship—from son and lover—must be resisted. A different image of the eternal womanly has to be created—the giver and renewer, not the taker and eater—

and this must be one of the Homeric tasks of the mature artist, no longer a young man.

Stephen will serve neither MacCann's world nor Davin's, but the ensnarers of his soul are cunning. There is the dean of studies practising the 'useful art' of fire-lighting in the physics theatre, an English Jesuit, 'a humble follower in the wake of clamorous conversions', one easy to pity or despise. Stephen and he discuss aesthetics, but they are at cross-purposes: Stephen's metaphorical lamp provided by Aristotle and Aquinas, light-givers to the young aesthetic theorist, becomes Epictetus's lamp to the dean. Soon the dean, useful artist, is talking about the filling of this literal lamp. He uses the word 'funnel', whereas Stephen knows this only as a 'tundish'; 'tundish' is a word the dean has never met. And then Stephen feels 'a smart of dejection that the man to whom he was speaking was a countryman of Ben Jonson'. English belongs to the dean before it belongs to Stephen:

–The language in which we are speaking is his before it is mine. How different are the words *home*, *Christ*, *ale*, *master*, on his lips and on mine! I cannot speak or write these words without unrest of spirit. His language, so familiar and so foreign, will always be for me an acquired speech. I have not made or accepted its words. My voice holds them at bay. My soul frets in the shadow of his language.

Sooner or later it will become necessary for the artist to kill English by driving it to the limit, to put in its place a created language of his own. Meanwhile he must fret at the incompleteness of his emancipation: Ireland he may use in his art, but English will still use him.

Stephen sits through the physics lecture, 'fascinated and jaded' by the involutions of formula and calculation, a paper-borrower who has brought no notebook, distracted, superior, no model student. It is a brief marking-time before his encounter with MacCann in the entrance-hall. MacCann is collecting signatures for a testimonial in favour of general disarmament. Stephen, of course, refuses to sign. His antlers flash: 'Do you think you impress me when you flourish your wooden sword?'; dramatically jerking his shoulder in the direction of a picture of the Tsar, he says: 'Keep your icon. If you must have a Jesus, let us have a legitimate Jesus.' He is in good form. His fellow-student Temple admires him ('He's the only man I see in this institution that has an individual mind') but his friend Cranly, dark, coarse, saturnine, has nothing to say. Cranly's function in this scene is to play handball; he bounces and bounces his ball and says to Stephen: 'Your soul!' His true office appears later. After rejecting MacCann's ideals, Stephen now disposes of Davin's. He makes harsh and definitive pronouncements about Ireland: 'When the soul of a man is born in this country there are nets flung at it to hold it back from flight. You talk to me of nationality, language, religion. I shall try to fly by those nets.' Ireland is no poor old woman seeking the recovery of youth and beauty: she is 'the old sow that eats her farrow'. And now Stephen goes off with Lynch, not Cranly, to expound the articles of his true faith, art.

Stephen's theory of aesthetics is original, logical, and totally uncompromising. It is delivered with such brilliant eloquence that it reminds us of another lengthy and authoritative piece of propaganda—Father Arnall's sermon on hell, which this peripatetic discourse exactly balances. It is illuminating to contrast the techniques of presentation. The sermon is given whole, uninterrupted, statically—an unedited tape, its capacity to shock and harrow needing no enhancement from the artist. We are riveted, as young Stephen is, because we are scared. The aesthetic lecture has a purely intellectual appeal, and novel-readers, rightly, cannot bear very much intellectuality. Joyce, knowing this, orchestrates the long expository solo with comedy, coarseness, the everyday, the vapid. When he begins by saying, 'Aristotle has not defined pity and terror. I have. I say . . .' Lynch immediately interrupts with 'Stop! I won't listen! I am sick. I was out last night on a yellow drunk with Horan and Goggins.' The reader takes courage at this and is able to swallow the neat definitions that come after. It was a stroke of genius to exchange Cranly—Stephen's interlocutor in the corresponding section of *Stephen Hero*—for Lynch. Cranly is, for all his Wicklow coarseness, a deep and disturbing character full of Freudian obsessions. Lynch is a lighter foil, and Joyce is to use him again to accompany Stephen into another unknown region, that of the Circean phantasmagoria of Nighttown in *Ulysses*. Lynch's low comedy here in *A Portrait* highlights perfectly Stephen's intellectual shafts, but he will not do for later—the final nervous spiritual unburdening for which Cranly is the only proper recipient.

Stephen does what Aristotle did not do, and now follows his definitions of pity and terror with a strict delimitation of the term 'tragic'. People die in street accidents, but we cannot, like newspaper reporters, properly call such deaths tragic: 'the tragic emotion . . . is a face looking two ways, towards terror and towards pity, both of which are phases of it. You see I use the word *arrest*.' (Both terror and pity, he has said, arrest the mind 'in the presence of whatsoever is grave and constant in human sufferings'.) 'I mean that the tragic emotion is static.' Joyce is really defining his own kind of art, proper art. The arts which excite desire or loathing are improper, kinetic: they are pornographic or didactic. With the 'static' aesthetic emotion –which we cannot feel in relation to real-life events–'the mind is arrested and raised above desire and loathing'. This, of course, is why proper art cannot be popular, why *Ulysses* and *Finnegans Wake* met either fury or indifference. Your list of best-sellers always includes the pornographic (the arousers of desire) and the didactic (the books which tell you what to do). Combine the didactic and the pornographic, as in some Hindu sex-manual, and you have your best best-seller. The aesthetic emotion is no more generally wanted than is the mystical state. The average reader does not want to get outside life, to view it detachedly and indifferently; he requires the illusion of being more deeply involved in it.

We are already in deep philosophical water. Stephen's general definition of art requires setting off with memories of Cranly who, recalls Lynch, 'told us about them flaming fat devils of pigs'. The pigs snort about Stephen's lucidity: 'Art is the human disposition of sensible or intelligible matter for an aesthetic end.' But what is the aesthetic end, what is beauty? Stephen goes to Aquinas, who says: 'That is beautiful the apprehension of which pleases.' This is a starting-point. Truth and beauty Stephen, like Keats, recognises to be akin. If we want to know more about truth we must study the intellect which tries to perceive it, we must 'comprehend the act itself of intellection'. Similarly, to understand the nature of beauty we must 'understand the frame and scope of the imagination, . . . comprehend the act itself of aesthetic apprehension'. Before we can go further we must meet the fat student Donovan on Lower Mount Street. He announces examination results and goes off to eat pancakes. Lynch is scornful and envious of Donovan: 'To think that that yellow pancakeeating excrement can get a good job, and I have to smoke cheap cigarettes!' We have had our breather; we are ready for '*integritas, consonantia, claritas*': how far do these, Aquinas's conditions for beauty, correspond to 'the phases of apprehension'? Stephen translates them as 'wholeness, harmony and radiance'. He now proceeds to define them.

A butcher's boy has a basket on his head. Stephen asks Lynch to look at it; to do this he must separate the basket from the rest of the visible universe. 'You see it as one whole. You apprehend its wholeness. That is *integritas*.' Immediate perception is synthetic (many parts bound up into the sense of a whole); after this first phase comes analysis: 'Having first felt that it is *one* thing you feel now that it is a *thing*. You apprehend it as complex, multiple, divisible, separable, made up of its parts, the result of its parts and their sum, harmonious. That is *consonantia*.' Lynch says that if he will tell him what *claritas* is he wins the cigar. Stephen tells him, eloquently. We have heard about *claritas*, or 'radiance' before, in *Stephen Hero*—it is the *quidditas*, the 'whatness', shining out of the perceived object. Then we heard much about epiphanies, now the word is not mentioned: Stephen prefers terms like 'the luminous silent stasis of aesthetic pleasure, a spiritual state very like to that cardiac condition which the Italian physiologist Luigi Galvani . . . called the enchantment of the heart'.

Stephen ends his discourse with succinct definitions of the three main literary forms—the lyric, in which the artist presents his image in immediate relation to himself; the dramatic, in which he presents it in immediate relation to others; the epic, in which he presents it in mediate relation to himself and others. But these forms interpenetrate, or rather form a natural continuum, so that the personality of the artist starts as the lyrical centre, then passes into the epic narrative, and finally refines itself out of existence in the dramatic form.

–The artist, like the God of the creation, remains within or behind or beyond or above his handiwork, invisible, refined out of existence, indifferent, paring his fingernails.
–Trying to refine them also out of existence, said Lynch.

Much of this aesthetic theory, despite its strange and limited provenance, goes on making admirable sense; but it is of greatest value when considered in relation to Joyce's own work. *Ulysses* and *Finnegans Wake* look like epics but are really dramas: Joyce achieves the divine aim of invisibility and indifference by handing over the task of narration to unsympathetic or even inhuman agents—a pub cadger, a woman's magazine, a fugue, a scientific catechism, a dreaming mind. That chapter of *Ulysses* which is couched in dramatic form is not necessarily the most truly dramatic part of the book. The stage directions of the brothel scene are written in highly mannered prose, so that—as with the reading of Shaw's plays—we are aware of the dramaturgist breathing down our necks. Is this dramaturgist Joyce, 'mediately' presented, or is it some specially introduced play-writing agent who enables the true creator to remain in the background, invisible impresario, paring his fingernails? There is no doubt that we are listening to the Joyce voice, voice of Shem, and that this piece of drama is really a piece of epic. Joyce is his own Proteus, and he is never more dramatic than when not using the outward shapes and machinery of drama.

The discourse ends – in rain, shelter, the sight of the girl who has become nameless under the arcade of the National Library. 'Your beloved is here', whispers Lynch. Stephen feels a twinge of bitterness seeing her standing there silently among her companions – 'She has no priest to flirt with' – but his mind takes on a listless peace – the druidical 'cease to strive' peace he is to know again when, having emptied his brain of his *Hamlet* theory, he is to stand in sunlight on this very spot, Bloomsday halfway through. The peace engenders charity now:

And if he had judged her harshly? If her life were a simple rosary of hours, her life simple and strange as a bird's life, gay in the morning, restless all day, tired at sundown? Her heart simple and wilful as a bird's heart?

Having talked of the enchantment of the heart, Stephen is now to experience it. He wakes to a morning inspiration, the beat of a villanelle passing from his mind to his lips:

Are you not weary of ardent ways,
Lure of the fallen seraphim?
Tell no more of enchanted days.

Reading the poem, we cannot but feel a little let down. After the waves of eloquent aesthetic theory, after the wonderfully moving description of the dawn rapture – 'In the virgin womb of the imagination the word was made flesh. Gabriel the seraph had come to the virgin's chamber' – we have the formal perfection of Fleet Street rhymesters, followers of Austin Dobson, and the stale Swinburnianism of '. . . languorous look and lavish limb'. Stephen is as small a poet as his creator. The interest of the section lies, as always, in the prose with its subtle rhythms, the evocation of subtle moods. What formed solid narrative in *Stephen Hero* – the parties, the classes in Erse, the coy dark-eyed girls – becomes here a lyric memory. Stephen may despise the composite image of Irish womanhood he has formed, he may be angry with the girl whom Lynch has called 'your beloved' – 'He had done well not to salute her on the steps of the library. He had done well to leave her to flirt with her priest, to toy with a church which was the scullerymaid of christendom' – but the strength of his feelings is a kind of homage. And here now is the poem for her–what in *Stephen Hero* is called 'The Villanelle of the Temptress'. He sees her shorn of her Irish piety, or pseudo-piety, and yielding to him, the priest of the imagination. The poet is also magician and can turn a trim-booted colleen, equipped with Irish phrasebook, into eternal woman.

The priest of the imagination draws a good deal of his villanelle's imagery from the rite practised by the lowlier, despised priests of the Church. Blasphemy? The temptress is praised in a eucharistic hymn, sacrificial hands raise the chalice. If it is blasphemy it is also a kind of homage, a homage to be accorded back-handedly again and again throughout the major works. Stephen says, in the penultimate section we now approach, that he fears 'the chemical action which would be set up in my soul by a false homage to a symbol behind which are massed twenty centuries of authority and veneration'. He will not make a sacrilegious communion; he is under no delusion as to the incompleteness of his emancipation. But, perhaps without knowing it, he will best free himself from the Church's domination by secularising the emotions attached to her rites and symbols. Stephen, secular Jesuit, heretic Franciscan, is less mixed-up than he seems.

The final narrative section begins in a flurry of birds. Stephen, in *fin de siècle* weariness, leans on his ashplant watching them wheeling 'about a temple of air' in Molesworth Street. The bird motif is fullest developed here–Cornelius Agrippa on bird-auguries, Swedenborg on the correspondence of birds to things of the intellect. Stephen's stick becomes that of an augur, the image of ibis-headed Thoth, god of writers, appears to him; in a sort of fear he sees Daedalus himself, 'soaring out of his captivity on osierwoven wings'. The actual birds of Molesworth Street he cannot identify–are they swallows? It is the word 'swallow' that conjures the thought of his own impending migration, also–through the line 'I gaze upon them as the swallow gazes'–the remembered opening of the new National Theatre with Yeats's *The Countess Cathleen*, the hissing and catcalling of his fellow-students–'A libel on Ireland!' and 'Blasphemy!' and the rest. Cathleen had sold her soul to the devil to buy bread for her starving people; the audience was not willing to wait for her redemption, God's ways exhibited as stranger and more compassionate than the Dublin Catholics would allow. Everything points to Stephen's leaving.

The time for exaltation, for really taking to the air, must wait till the very last. Stephen must clear his mind in the presence of Cranly, make a final confession and a final avowal. We are very much earthbound again; the text is full of dragging-down symbols—the priest in the library reading-room who closes his copy of *The Tablet* with an angry snap; Cranly's book, *Diseases of the Ox*; the Scott-reading dwarf who is said to be the product of a noble but incestuous union (Stephen sees this act in an unbidden visionary flash, matching that earlier one of the *Foetus*-carving student in Cork—the rainy park, the swans, the embracing brother and sister); the coarse banter of the students under the colonnade; his own awareness of a lousy body and of thoughts that are 'lice born of the sweat of sloth'; his ambivalent bitterness towards his 'beloved'. But Temple, like an oracle, makes mad and prophetic pronouncements. He says that Giraldus Cambrensis celebrates Stephen's people as *pernobilis et pervetusta familia*. He quotes the last sentence of the zoology textbook: 'Reproduction is the beginning of death.' The Church, he says boldly, is cruel like all old sinners. Stephen at last drags Cranly away from the student-crowd. Dixon whistles the bird-call from *Siegfried* after them: we must not forget the mystery of flight.

Stephen tells Cranly that he has had a quarrel with his mother (the quarrel that is presented as a painful and lengthy narrative in *Stephen Hero*): he refuses to make his Easter duty. 'I will not serve', says Lucifer-Stephen, giving meaning to the line he has just now misquoted to himself—'Brightness falls from the air.' He is, as the protomartyr, doomed, but his damnation may be more than a metaphor. It is one thing to fall as Icarus (the father-son identification theme of *Ulysses* is emerging at the end of *A Portrait*: 'Old father, old artificer, stand me now and ever in good stead'); it is another to fall as Lucifer. Siegfried-Stephen, who understands the song of the birds and brandishes the sword Nothung at visions of hell, may yet have to go to hell; but he says that he is willing to make mistakes, that he is not afraid to make even 'a great mistake, a lifelong mistake and perhaps as long as eternity too'. Cranly does not respond to all this as Lynch might have done; Stephen could not say to Lynch what he now says to Cranly:

—I will tell you what I will do and what I will not do. I will not serve that in which I no longer believe, whether it call itself my home, my fatherland, or my church: and I will try to express myself in some mode of life or art as freely as I can and as wholly as I can, using for my defence the only arms I allow myself to use—silence, exile, and cunning.

This is, despite the brave words, a scene lacking altogether the fine, uncompromising, blade-bright confidence of that peripatetic lecture.

There is desperation in the defiance, a sense that what is being abandoned is being abandoned through pride as much as vocation, that a 'malevolent reality' may well reside in the bit of consecrated bread Stephen will not take, as well as in the whole absurd coherence and logicality of the Church. Above all there looms the terrible image of loneliness, incarnated in the cold sadness of Cranly's face.

–And not to have any one person, Cranly said, who would be more than a friend, more even than the noblest and truest friend a man ever had.

Stephen says he will take the risk.

Here the action of the novel ends. We must mark time a little before Stephen's mother puts his 'new secondhand clothes in order' and the self-doomed, unafraid young artist prepares to embark. We need a brief epilogue in which the mood of excitement at the prospect of flight can be restored, in which the spirit of the great comic novel to come can be hinted at, in which a new literary technique can be foreshadowed. The diary entries which close *A Portrait* anticipate, in their clipped lyricism and impatient ellipses, the interior monologue of *Ulysses*. But they also look back to the very opening, the baby Stephen coming to consciousness in flashes of discrete observation. This is right: the cutting of the physical omphalic cord is matched by the cutting of the spiritual. 'Welcome, O life!' says Stephen, going forth 'to forge in the smithy of my soul the uncreated conscience of my race'.

A Portrait is, by any standard, a remarkable novel, though *Ulysses*, which carries on Stephen's story, overshadows it and makes both its candour and its technical innovations seem less considerable than they really are. To the young, discovering it in paperback, its modernity may, since it is the spring of a whole contemporary mode of writing, seem unremarkable; the free-loving, drug-taking, agnostic undergraduate may wonder what the fuss could ever have been about. The type of student whom Stephen Dedalus represents, poor, treasuring old books with foxed leaves, independent, unwhining, deaf to political and social shibboleths, fanatically devoted to art and art only, is no longer to be found in the cities of the West: he disappeared in 1939. He is the traditional student, as old as Chaucer, and literature, as life, must be poorer without him. The rebels of the post-1945 novel rebel against everything on behalf of nothing– against coherent theories of art as much as against the authority of church, state and family. They are closer to Lynch than to Stephen, grumbling about having to smoke cheap cigarettes or no cigarettes at all. But at least Lynch listened to Stephen's aesthetic and even asked for some of the definitions to be repeated. *Stephen Hero*—that abandoned title is a proud one and a just one: Stephen Dedalus is the last of the artist-heroes of bourgeois fiction. The concept of the young man as comic Hamlet or ineffectual rebel remains, but he derives more from Eliot's Prufrock than from Joyce's Stephen—the innocent blushing butt of a hard world assured of certain certainties. As Denis in Huxley's *Crome Yellow* he shambles shamefully out of the picture; as Paul Pennyfeather in Waugh's *Decline and Fall* or William Boot in the same author's *Scoop*, he achieves his triumphs through a kind of trickery or the intervention of the god from the machine. But the rounded portrait of a young man who sins, suffers, and develops a noble fanaticism is hardly to be found after Joyce: Stephen Dedalus is both an end and a summation.

The book is not just the character: it is also itself—a lyric meditation which is also highly organised, in which symbolism is cunningly planted and even the most casual record of seemingly pointless speech or action proves (and this is even more true of *Ulysses*) to have its place in the intricate scheme—there is no slack, no irrelevance. The symbolism under the naturalism is not there for the glorification of Stephen, but for the glorification of art. If it were not for this perpetual feeling that every word, every act means more than it says or does, the name Stephen Dedalus would be a mere bit of pretentious decoration. As it is, the final image of Stephen as a priest of the imagination holds. Like a priest of the Church, he is bigger than himself by virtue of the power of which he is an agent. The egoism is not self-aggrandisement: it is the god inside the priest saying '*Om*—I, myself.' And finally the artist, the maker, is himself a creation of unknown arts—the *ignotae artes* of the epigraph: he is enclosed by a mystery. It is because of the presence of this mystery that our final response to *A Portrait* is one of wonder.

6: 'You Poor Poet, You!'

'COUSIN SWIFT,' SAID JOHN DRYDEN, 'YOU WILL NEVER BE A POET.'
Stephen Dedalus, walking on the beach in *Ulysses*, thinks of Swift—
one of his literary ancestors–and even, for a brief moment, identifies
himself with the great Dean. But he says to himself: 'Cousin Stephen,
you will never be a saint.' He resists literary condemnation but will
gladly enough accept the other kind. Joyce must have been aware of
the slenderness of his poetic talent, but it is essential to the Stephen
Dedalus image that it be haloed with great poetic promise and even
achievement. The only verses that Stephen makes in *Ulysses* are
poor Rhymers' Club stuff; the villanelle in *A Portrait* is, after the
loftiness of the artist's claims, very disappointing. The poems that
Joyce published in two separate volumes–*Chamber Music* and
Pomes Penyeach–make no great pretensions: they are not to be read
in a Stephen Dedalus context. They are charming, competent,
memorable, but they would never, on their own, have made the
name of their author. The 'poetic' side of Joyce (using the term in
its narrowest, most orthodox sense) had to be enclosed in the irony
of the great prose books for it to be effective. His verse talent is, in
fact, close to that of Swift (Dryden was, of course and as always,
right), and this is appropriate for the second man to draw great prose
out of Ireland. Joyce the versifier is best in lampoons and in the
occasional parodies and private satires he wrote for his friends.

We can take *Chamber Music* in good heart when we have taken its
title. There are coarse undertones: Joyce read the poems to a woman
who interrupted the recital to relieve herself, audibly, behind a
screen. This oracle named the book. When the book first appeared,
in 1907, it brought Joyce into association with the Imagist poets. But
the artist who drew his aesthetic philosophy from Aristotle and
Aquinas was not one to derive his poetic inspiration from contemporary modes of versifying, and there is as little of the Imagists
in the poems of *Chamber Music* as there is of Yeats and the Celtic

Twilight. These slight lyrics go back to the Elizabethans, and they are meant to be set to music and sung. Joyce the tenor knew what was needed in words for music–plenty of long vowels, simple stanzaic forms, no great length, unity of mood, conventional imagery and so on. These poems sound better than they read and they come into their own in Elizabethan-type settings (the ear shudders at the notion of their being done as *Lieder*), like those of E. J. Moeran:

> Strings in the earth and air
> Make music sweet;
> Strings by the river where
> The willows meet.

The poems are always being freshly set and are regularly sung, and one could, if they were not by Joyce, leave them at that. But there is always more to even the simplest Joyce creation than meets the eye or ear. *Chamber Music* is not a mere collection of verses; it is a sequence, a selection made from the large amount of verse Joyce wrote in Dublin and arranged to suggest a story. It is a love story, but no mere conventional one, such as the Elizabethan sonneteers might have devised: it is autobiographical, like everything Joyce wrote, but the autobiography is heightened, turned into myth. His love affair with Nora Barnacle lasted all his life; here love has to end. A real-life transient mood of loneliness has to be turned into a final, irreversible, state. It is the shaping of art.

The arrangement is as cunning as we might expect from the Great Shaper. The three opening poems are a tiny preludial suite, setting the mood. The scene is suburban rather than rural–there is an avenue and a lamp and a girl is playing the piano–and this homely actuality keeps the 'harps playing unto Love' in check. In the fourth poem the lover-poet sings at the gate of his beloved, then in the fifth he spoils everything by apparently invoking a different girl altogether in one of the most atrocious lyrics ever penned by a great writer:

> Lean out of the window,
>   Goldenhair,
> I heard you singing
>   A merry air . . .
>
> . . . I have left my book:
>   I have left my room:
> For I heard you singing
>   Through the gloom,

> Singing and singing
> A merry air.
> Lean out of the window,
> Goldenhair.

Soon it is true country matters, flavoured with genuine Elizabethan locutions like 'Welladay' and stiffened with harder words like 'plenilune' and 'epithalamium'. The beloved unzones her girlish bosom to, louder than the earlier strings and harp, 'the bugles of the cherubim'; the language becomes biblical: 'My dove, my beautiful one, / Arise, arise!' and the lover waits by a cedar tree (Dublin is far). Consummation is achieved, then stings follow the honey. The lover's friend grows jealous (the biographical roots are easily uncovered: Oliver St John Gogarty–Buck Mulligan in *Ulysses*–is the friend) and the beloved's name is dishonoured. An antique dignity enters the verse:

> He who hath glory lost, nor hath
> Found any soul to fellow his,
> Among his foes in scorn and wrath
> Holding to ancient nobleness,
> That high unconsortable one–
> His love is his companion.

The proud young poet flashes his antlers, unafraid but not alone.

But love has seen something of the rottenness of life, and the speck touches the apple. Shakespeare, whose songs were, after all, not all of pretty ringtime, is invoked, bequeather of mad tales 'at ghosting hour conjurable'; we hear a couplet too solid for love poetry:

> . . . And all for some strange name he read
> In Purchas or in Holinshed.

Love is coming to an end. Rain falls, 'the year is gathering', then winter cries at the door. The three postludial poems are the best of the sequence, and the last two–with the noise of waters, the desperate call of the forsaken lover who hears 'an army charging upon the land'–approach the achievement of Yeats, though they are essentially Joycean.

'You poor poet, you!' The words are Cranly's, and if we too want to use them of Joyce-Stephen we must borrow Cranly's intonation–mocking but affectionate and even reluctantly admiring, though not too much. For though the greater part of *Chamber Music* withers under criticism we are still left with two things–the sense of a small but powerful narrative structure; awareness of an almost shameful potency that Noël Coward authorised our finding in 'cheap music'. Some of these lyrics–and not the best ones either–call up the image of a young man genuinely in love, mooning about suburban avenues in 'cheap dusty mourning'. They are a commentary on an aspect of Stephen Dedalus that neither *A Portrait* nor *Ulysses* allows us to see. And if, as some of us did, we first read these poems when we ourselves were poor students and also in love, we find that the old uncomplicated emotions hang about them, like the cheap perfumes that were all our mistresses could afford. I know that this has little to do with literary criticism. A character in William Golding's *The Brass Butterfly* says that when he re-reads Virgil he is not transported to the Virgilian world but back to his own childhood: 'I am a boy again reading Virgil.' That is perhaps no tribute to great poetry, but to minor love-lyrics it might well be the best of all.

Joyce produced his other volume of verse–slighter even than *Chamber Music*–in 1927, when *Ulysses* had been out five years and the agonies of *Finnegans Wake* were under way. *Pomes Penyeach* cost a shilling, so that there should be twelve poems, but Joyce– like the old milkwoman at the beginning of *Ulysses*–adds a 'tilly', and 'Tilly' is the name of the first poem in the book. There seems little advance, either in language, rhythm or organisation, on the slender craft of the earlier volume: there are weary apostrophes to love, sighs of nostalgia and regret, and a sufficiency of thou-and-thee. Only occasionally does the prose-experimentalist peep out, as in 'A Memory of the Players in a Mirror at Midnight':

> They mouth love's language. Gnash
> The thirteen teeth
> Your lean jaws grin with. Lash
> Your itch and quailing, nude greed of the flesh
> Love's breath in you is stale, worded or sung,
> As sour as cat's breath,
> Harsh of tongue . . .

When we are moved it is often for the wrong reasons. We read into 'A Flower Given to My Daughter' not only the devotion of Joyce the father but the tragedy of Lucia Joyce's madness yet to come; in 'On the Beach at Fontana' the 'ache of love' felt for his son illuminates the facts of biography–we are perhaps too interested in what the poems tell us of Joyce (compare, if this be allowed, the Sonnets of Shakespeare) and too little interested in what the poems are capable of saying about ourselves. Yet could any lyric be less

73

general, more particular, than 'Ecce Puer', which Joyce wrote in 1932? His grandson Stephen was just born; his father had just died:

Of the dark past
A child is born;
With joy and grief
My heart is torn.

Calm in his cradle
The living lies.
May love and mercy
Unclose his eyes!

Young life is breathed
On the glass;
The world that was not
Comes to pass.

A child is sleeping:
An old man gone.
O, father forsaken,
Forgive your son!

In these poems of the mature Joyce we espy a deliberate limitation, and if we think about this we allow the old gloomy and indigestible questions about the nature of poetry to rise up again – questions which it is better not to ask. For it is the two big publications of 1922 – *Ulysses* and *The Waste Land* – which show how far the poetic and the non-poetic can interpenetrate, and how little significance terms like 'verse' and 'prose' really possess. How are we to classify the following? –

. . . If you don't like it you can get on with it, I said. Others can pick and choose if you can't. But if Albert makes off, it won't be for lack of telling. You ought to be ashamed, I said, to look so antique. (And her only thirty-one.) I can't help it, she said, pulling a long face. It's them pills I took to bring it off, she said. (She's had five already, and nearly died of young George.) The chemist said it would be all right, but I've never been the same. You *are* a proper fool, I said. . . .

. . . Wombed in sin darkness I was too,
Made not begotten.
By them, the man with my voice and my eyes and a
Ghostwoman with ashes on her breath.
They clasped and sundered, did the coupler's will.
From before the ages He willed me
And now may not will me away or ever.
A *lex eterna* stays about Him. Is that then
The divine substance wherein
Father and Son are consubstantial?

The first passage is, of course, from *The Waste Land* and the second is from *Ulysses*. There is no doubt as to which contains the more poetic intensity. But *The Waste Land* remains a poem and *Ulysses* a novel. Eliot's passage of flat colloquial is a deliberately administered glass of cold water to wash away the rich fruit-cake taste of the preceding Keatsian section; it also prepares our palates for a different, tarter, richness to come. The *Ulysses* passage is pure Stephen Dedalus interior monologue: we shall be all the readier for Leopold Bloom's grilled kidney when we have read it. The total structure is all.

That complexity and suggestiveness of language that we call poetical flourishes in Joyce not in the isolated lyric but in the enclosed lyric passage—he needs the flat setting for his flights just as Eliot needs the intense setting for his flatness (in *The Waste Land*, anyway). And, in general, it would be true to say that Joyce is most sure of himself in all the non-novelistic branches of literature he wished to practise when he is safely encastled in a great prose structure. The dramatic skill of *Ulysses* maddens adaptors into dragging pieces of it on to the stage; the 'Nighttown' episode is one of the great closet-dramas of all time; but Joyce as a playwright for the theatre is as little a success as Henry James.

It was inevitable that, having chosen Ibsen as his liberating saint, Joyce should early on have seen himself as a poet-dramatist. His first play, *A Brilliant Career*, has been remembered, however, only for the arrogance of its dedication (to the author's own soul) and for the interest that William Archer showed in it. The more mature effort, *Exiles*, belongs to the *annus mirabilis* 1914, when *A Portrait* had been completed and *Ulysses* was about to be started and when the first tendrils of recognition and help were putting forth. *Exiles* was published in 1918. It has been much read but little acted. Its interest is less artistic than biographical: we tend to approach it with the wrong motives.

Exiles does, in fact, illuminate a phase of Joyce's personal development and, since it is set in Dublin, 1912, this phase is far closer to the actual time of writing than is usual with him—except, of course, for the epiphanies of *Stephen Hero*. In other words, Joyce seems concerned with making a final declaration about his relationship with the world of his own past before getting down to the task of creating two huge myths out of that world. This is the last important bit of clearing up before the beginning of the real exile. Not that *Exiles* is all autobiography. Joyce returned to Ireland in 1912, just

75

like his writer-hero Richard Rowan. Buck Mulligan in *Ulysses* talks about 'hellenising' the island; Richard, eight years later, wonders whether he should accept a professorship of Romance languages at his old university and leaven dull doughy Dublin with the quick spirit of Europe. It is his friend Robert Hand who brings the offer of the appointment from the Vice-Chancellor, saying that his past 'act of folly' will be forgotten: Dublin is ready to do him honour as 'a scholar, as a literary personality'. The 'act of folly' was Joyce's own, only it is sharpened here into something like melodrama:

ROBERT: . . . Here is how the matter stands, Richard. Everyone knows that you ran away years ago with a young girl . . . How shall I put it? . . . With a young girl not exactly your equal. (*Kindly*) Excuse me, Richard, that is not my opinion nor my language. I am simply using the language of people whose opinions I don't share.
RICHARD: Writing one of your leading articles, in fact.

It is in this connection of a wife who is too desirable to be thought of as a lady and the husband's masterful yet masochistic attitude to her that the play, starting as near-autobiography, takes off into very interesting but very non-dramatic regions. All this business of the wounded artist will do very well for a self-portrait of Joyce in 1912 ('You have that fierce indignation', says Robert, 'which lacerated the heart of Swift'). But the triangular torments which give the play what action it has have little to do with Joyce and Nora Joyce and anybody else: Joyce is soaring into the fantasy zone which, more comically, Bloom is to reach in the nightmares of the brothel episode of *Ulysses*. He is here indulging a delicious dream of cuckoldry.

Robert says he loves Bertha, Richard's wife. At the peak of the second act Richard confesses how one part of his mind has longed for betrayal by the two people who mean most to him–his wife and his best friend: '. . . in the very core of my ignoble heart I longed to be betrayed by you and by her–in the dark, in the night–secretly, meanly, craftily. By you, my best friend, and by her. I longed for that passionately and ignobly, to be dishonoured for ever in love and in lust, to be . . . to be for ever a shameful creature and to build up my soul again out of the ruins of its shame.' Robert also has his big moment of eloquence. He wants a sort of duel between himself and Richard:

A battle of both our souls, different as they are, against all that is false in them and in the world. A battle of your soul against the spectre of fidelity, of mine against the spectre of friendship. All life is a conquest, the victory of human passion over the commandments of cowardice. Will you, Richard? Have you the courage? Even if it shatters to atoms the friendship between us, even if it breaks up for ever the last illusion in your own life? There was an eternity before we were born: another will come after we are dead. The blinding instant of passion alone–passion, free, unashamed, irresistible–that is the only gate by which we can escape from the misery of what slaves call life. Is not this the language of your own youth that I heard so often from you in this very place where we are sitting now?

This sounds like highly dramatic language, but dramatically it does not come off at all. This is partly because nobody, not even Stephen Dedalus, speaks like that; it is also because Robert Hand, for all the careful blocking in of his background, for all his high feeling and epigrams, never comes to life in his own right: he is merely an aspect of Richard. Bertha, with her 'O, my strange wild lover, come back to me again!', sparks into occasional life because a sort of Ibsen-heroine intensity is, when Joyce-Richard can spare the time from gesticulating at his other self, deliberately imposed on her; but the whole play resolves itself into a very static portrait of the wounded artist liking, rather than licking, his wounds. Bertha very sensibly asks him: 'In what way are you wounded?' And Richard talks of the deep, deep wound of doubt in his soul. Bertha could well say that, with his perverse desire for betrayal, he has brought the wound on to himself. And so he has, but he still seems to want pity and a kind of foetal cosseting. Bertha really comes out of it very well: we gain a fleeting glimpse of Nora Joyce as one of the great heroines of our time.

This is by no means an ill-constructed, amateurish play. It is very well put together, but it is a piece of pure morphology. It is the classic example of what a close student of Ibsen can do if he lacks talent for the stage. For much of the time we have the strange sensation that we are reading a rather stilted translation of Ibsen– there is a great lack of colloquial raciness, of even the normal contractions that we expect in everyday speech. Yet the stiffness and grandiloquence do not suggest poetry. The language is as special as the language of *Finnegans Wake*, but it is not rooted in actuality: it seems to be a grotesque attempt to make something dramatically viable out of the dead pedantic correctness of the hack translator.

Of all the plays of Ibsen which find echoes in *Exiles*, perhaps one of Ibsen's least successful–*When We Dead Awaken*–sounds out the strongest: it has a wounded artist and his wife who are contrasted, in neat symmetry, with a couple whose temperaments are less intense

77

(as Richard is contrasted with Robert, so Bertha–the awakened woman–is set against the mild virgin Beatrice Justice, Robert's cousin). The young Joyce wrote an article on *When We Dead Awaken*–his first published prose–and, going back to his other early writings on drama, one is able to toy with the notion of Joyce as a proleptically very sound drama critic, one who needed the experience of creating even a bad play to qualify him for the making of judgements on other men's works. But it went the other way round with him: after the essays 'Drama and Life' (not to be confused with the identically titled paper read in *Stephen Hero*), 'Ibsen's New Drama' (both written in 1900) and 'The Day of the Rabblement' (1901) the great dramaturgical act was long in coming, and Joyce persisted most of his life in considering *Exiles* a play well worthy of performance. He could be very obstinate about his own work.

Joyce practised dramatic and literary criticism in a somewhat distracted manner for most of his life, but we cannot regard his critical writings as 'professional'–he is not a critic in his own right as, say, Eliot is. *The Sacred Wood* helps us to understand the poetic aspirations of the author of *Gerontion*, but if Eliot had never written a line of verse he would still take his place among the great twentieth-century critics. When we read Mason and Ellmann's edition of Joyce's reviews and lectures and letters of protest (*The Critical Writings of James Joyce*, Faber and Faber, 1959) we do so not to learn about the authors Joyce deals with but to understand better this particular author. Thus the essay on James Clarence Mangan (1902) is concerned with blue-printing an aesthetic theory (the one delivered in the *Stephen Hero* paper 'Drama and Life') and in stating what kind of poet is needed by renascent Ireland–one not merely romantically mournful but also precise, Augustan, even joyful. The paper on William Blake–originally given as the second of two evening lectures in Trieste in 1912, delivered in Italian and called '*Verismo ed idealismo nella letteratura inglese*'–points a powerful affinity between the creator of the Giant Albion and the creator of Finnegan. The superficial resemblances between Blake and Joyce begin with their both marrying women of inferior education but blessed with the 'lineaments of gratified desire' and continue with the working of the details of daily life into eternal myth–the soldiers who were so rough with Blake become giant symbols of evil; the civil servants who annoyed Joyce ended up as the rough soldiers who disrupt Nighttown. The deeper resemblances are only to be seen long after the giving of the Blake lecture, but Joyce must have had his own great organic visions in mind when he said:

Eternity, which had appeared to the beloved disciple and to St Augustine as a heavenly city, and to Alighieri as a heavenly rose, appeared to the Swedish mystic [Swedenborg] in the likeness of a heavenly man, animated in all his limbs by a fluid angelic life that forever leaves and re-enters, systole and diastole of love and wisdom . . . Armed with this two-edged sword, the art of Michelangelo and the revelations of Swedenborg, Blake killed the dragon of experience and natural wisdom and, by minimizing space and time and denying the existence of memory and the senses, he tried to paint his works on the void of the divine bosom.

Ulysses is full of references to Blake, but it is also itself a sort of Blakean Prophetic Book, based on the Swedenborgian revelation of reality as a heavenly man which Blake was the first to turn into art, Joyce being the second and last. *Finnegans Wake* is even closer to poems like *Jerusalem* and *Milton*, very much a work that minimises space and time and is painted on the void of the divine bosom.

As Eliot has written of theology and the music-hall, as well as of literature, so Joyce has written of Bruno ('the Nolan') and of Home Rule and even (1912) of 'Politics and Cattle Disease'–an essay which leads us straight to the 'bullockbefriending bard' of *Ulysses*. Unlike Eliot, though, he has been less willing to speak directly of his own work than we could wish. His methods of easing our way into the labyrinth were always oblique–it was a matter of suggesting to other men (Stuart Gilbert, for instance) that they might possibly write this or that about his books and might conceivably take this or that approach and regard such and such a book as perhaps capable of throwing light on this or that problem. But, in an article published in *The New Statesman and Nation* and (in America) *Hound and Horn* in 1932, Joyce went some way towards making the technique of *Finnegans Wake* seem human, amiable, and approachable.

The article is called 'From a Banned Writer to a Banned Singer' and it takes up the cause of the Irish-French tenor John Sullivan who, Joyce was convinced, had received less than his due from the world of musical promotion. Sullivan's voice was, on the singer's own admission, past his best at this time, but Joyce heard, in his stubborn way, only its primal vigour and phenomenal range. This piece of writing, being part of a general programme of advocacy, is not obscure: its virtue as propaganda lies in its freshness, humour and ingenuity. It did little good, but it presents an unbuttoned and generous Joyce, and it is the best introduction to the linguistic difficulties of *Finnegans Wake* that we possess:

79

Just out of kerryosity howlike is a Sullivan? It has the fortefaccia of a Markus Brutas, the wingthud of a spreadeagle, the body uniformed of a metropoliceman with the brass feet of a collared grand. It cresces up in Aquilone but diminuends austrowards. It was last seen and heard of by some macgillicuddies above a lonely valley of their reeks, duskening the greylight as it flew, its cry echechohoing among the anfractuosities: *pour la dernière fois*. The black-bulled ones, stampeding, drew in their horns, all appailed and much upset, which explaints the guttermilk on their overcoats.

That is the second paragraph. Its difficulties are rather less than those of 'Jabberwocky', most of the portmanteau-words being self-explanatory—it is clear, for instance, that Sullivan comes from Kerry, land of the mountains known as Macgillicuddy's Reeks, that he is not only physically big (he could be a policeman; his feet are like those of a Collard grand piano) but big in voice, fit for the Metropolitan Opera. Some of the other references are more abstruse—the quotation from the French version of *William Tell*, for instance, in which Arnold's last visit home is paralleled by Sullivan's last visit (recent when the article was written) to Ireland. One cannot understand all at a first reading, and one is not meant to: as with *Finnegans Wake*, the general picture is filled out by experience, by chance discovery rather than deliberate study. Thus, it is enough at first that 'Aquilone' should suggest the north wind; later we may learn that Sullivan's nose was aquiline and that Mount Eagle is in the west of Kerry. But the first impression is always a valid one, and the image of a great-bodied, broad-chested, big-booted, vast-voiced hero comes through at once.

We find Joyce the poet and Joyce the dramatist at their most impressive and original in the two great novels. The same can be said of Joyce the critic. One of the great events of Bloomsday is Stephen's presentation of a new theory of *Hamlet* in the National Library. While describing the meeting of Bloom and Stephen, first in the newspaper office and later in the maternity hospital, Joyce gives us, as free gifts, a history of newspaper prose and of headlines, a critical textbook on rhetoric, and a parodic survey of English literature. *Finnegans Wake* completes the work begun in *A Portrait*—the work of demonstrating that literature is not just a commentary on life but an integral part of it. The poor poet, the indifferent dramatist and the casual critic take on greatness in the context of life, which is the context of the novel.

PART TWO
THE LABYRINTH

1: Ways into the Labyrinth

THE ODYSSEY OF *Ulysses* MAKES VERY PAINFUL READING. AFTER the seven-year labour of writing the book–poverty, eye-disease, the disruption of a European war–came the hell of trying to get it into print. (Even, for that matter, into typescript: much of the 'Circe' episode was burned by the disgusted husband of a volunteer typist.) When, printed at last in France and published by a Paris bookshop, all the regular British and American channels having turned it down, *Ulysses* appeared in its handsome colours of the Greek flag and full of misprints (on Joyce's birthday, 1922), it began an unbelievable career of suppression, vilification, adulation, piracy, public and private burning, smuggling. (As a schoolboy I sneaked the two-volume Odyssey Press edition into England, cut up into sections and distributed all over my body.) When, in 1933, Judge Woolsey pronounced in the United States District Court that *Ulysses* was not obscene and might legally be bought and sold in America, England still had to wait three years for its own edition. It had taken a long time, all too long, for the legal recognition of a masterpiece. Now we are past being shocked by *Ulysses*. We can take it calmly from the shelves of the school or public library and marvel at other things than dirty words and descriptions of bodily functions. There are a lot of things to marvel at but, first, a lot of questions to ask. Most of these questions are assumed in one fundamental question: Why did Joyce write the book at all?

Ulysses is a big book (933 pages in the 1960 Bodley Head edition), and its bigness is one answer. Every novelist wishes to prove to himself and to others that he can tackle a large canvas. The great novels of the past–*Don Quixote*, *Tom Jones*, *War and Peace*, for example–have all been very long, and it is only in great length that novelists can fulfil their blasphemous urge to rival God. To create a few human beings in a segmentary context of life is well enough for the minor artist, but the major writer wants a whole cosmos and the

83

whole of mankind. He cannot really have all this–Joyce, like Blake, was only able to achieve it by making one character play many parts– but he can at least create a big human community which is a sort of reduced image of the cosmos.

Starting with this vague and general and traditional intention, Joyce then (or simultaneously, or before) conceived another ambi- tion–to make a modern novel not merely rival classical achievement but contain it. Classical epic was expansive; classical drama was contractive. Homer covers heaven, earth, the sea and a great slab of time; Sophocles stays in one small place and confines the time of his action to twenty-four hours. And so Joyce stays in Dublin on June 16th, 1904, but also uses delirium and imagination to encom- pass a great deal of human history and even the End of the World. Greek epic and Greek drama are both contained within the frame- work of a modern bourgeois novel.

Epic length and the strictures of dramatic form can be reconciled not merely by imaginative 'loops' but by a more detailed examination of the characters' acts and motives than traditional novelists thought either necessary or decent. Bloom must not only eat but defecate; Molly Bloom must meditate not only on her lovers but also on what her lovers are like in bed. With so large a canvas, no human detail may be left out. But the traditional techniques for expressing un- spoken thoughts are bound to be insufficient. Hence the 'stream of consciousness' or the 'interior monologue'–an endless commentary from the main characters on the data thrown at them by life, but unspoken, often chaotic, sometimes reaching the thresholds of the unconscious mind. This device had been used before–by Dickens and Samuel Butler, even by that great primitive Jane Austen–but never on the scale or to the limits employed by Joyce. Joyce, after all, lived in the psycho-analytic era: he liked to joke about his name's having the same etymology as Freud's.

There are two artistic problems raised by the extensive use of interior monologue. The first is concerned with characterisation: how does one make one person's interior monologue sound different from another's, so that we instantly recognise which character is thinking without tiresome mechanical pointers like 'Stephen thought' or 'Bloom thought'? Part of the problem here lies in the fact that the 'stream of consciousness' is essentially pre-verbal: we do not say to ourselves: 'Where's light-switch? Very dark in here. Must be careful. Chair over there, I know. Damn. Barked shin on it'–rather we react without words to stimuli and memories, and any attempt to set down such a process in words is highly conventional. Joyce solves the problem by assigning a characteristic rhythm to the thought-stream of each of his three main personages. Stephen's is lyrical, subtle, somewhat clotted, and, since Stephen is a poet, his interior monologue is much more aware of words–not words as conventional signs for images but words as data for meditation–than that of either Bloom or his wife. Bloom's own rhythm is quick, jaunty, jerky, darting, clipped–appropriate for a man more given to pub-talk than to aesthetic disquisitions, expressive of the very soul of an intelligent, but not over-educated, advertising canvasser. As for Molly Bloom's rhythm, it somehow combines the practical and the poetical, short words organised into long flowing phrases which–as we are made to take her mind all in one piece, not in instalments–coalesce into a single mammoth sentence which makes up the last chapter of the book.

The other problem is concerned with what the characters shall think about. The mind naturally strays and wanders, holding to nothing very long, coming back frequently to the same point again and again but rarely staying there. A naturalistic representation of the human mind monologuising to itself may be of scientific interest, but it has nothing to do with art. Themes must be imposed on the three main minds of the novel, and these themes must move in towards each other, suggesting purposeful movement and the unity proper to a work of literature. The main subject of the book–the creative relationship between spiritual father, spiritual son, and non-spiritual mother-wife–will clamp the consciousness of each member of the main trio down, preventing over-much free flight, but–in so spacious a book–more than that is needed. We have to consider not only the theme of the book but its structure.

We are back to Joyce's epic intention. He is not only emulating Homer but taking him over. The title *Ulysses* is no mere ironical reference to the decline of the heroic as exemplified in the emergence of the bourgeois novel from the original epic form: the title is the key to the structure. Bloom is Ulysses having his little adventures in Dublin; Stephen Dedalus is Telemachus in search of a father; Molly Bloom is both the beguiling Calypso and the faithful Penelope. These identifications would be merely fanciful if there were not a more solid parallel with the Odyssey built into the structure of the work itself: a little study shows the parallel to be both profound and detailed. Each episode of *Ulysses* corresponds to an episode of the Odyssey, and the correspondence proliferates in a mass of subtle references.

85

When, for instance, Bloom strolls by Sir John Rogerson's Quay in glorious summer-morning weather, he is re-enacting the lotus-eating episode of the Odyssey. Everything–the warmth, the thought of a leisurely bath, the communicants in the church he visits, the odours of a chemist's shop, conduce to a mood of 'letting go', and the chapter ends with a vision of Bloom in the bath, lapped in a 'womb of warmth'. This motif controls the direction of Bloom's loose meditations, gives them form, shapes them to art. It even conditions the vocabulary which provides the symbols for his interior monologue: if we look carefully we see that this vocabulary is a true anthology, a mass of flower-references. It also modifies the rhythm of the monologue to something more relaxed and passive than we are normally to associate with Bloom.

But the Homeric parallel is only the beginning. Shape and direction are primarily imposed on each chapter by means of an Odyssean reference, but that reference suggests related references, sub-references, and these have much to do with not only the direction and subject-matter of the interior monologue but the action itself, and even the technique used to present that action. Thus, a Dublin newspaper-office is a reasonable parallel to the cave of Æolus–the god of the winds whose enmity Ulysses earned–and, so that the scriptures may be fulfilled, Bloom goes to the office of the *Freeman's Journal and National Press*. It is appropriate that the scene should be wind-swept, galleys flying about the place, but also appropriate that wind should suggest the lungs, the windiness of newspaper rhetoric, the art of rhetoric itself, the wind-swift transmission of news, the history of the art of the presentation of news (expressed in headlines which punctuate the text) and the technique through which the action, talk, and thought are presented. We end up with a formidable battery of clamps–the scene, the art, the presiding physical organ, the technique. Above everything puffs and blows the wind-god himself–the Editor. If we look deepest of all we shall find that the episode even has a predominant colour–red. Red is right for the art of inflaming passions through words and the journalistic cult of the sensational.

What applies in this chapter applies nearly everywhere in the book: to the Homeric parallel we add a presiding organ, art, colour, symbol, and an appropriate technique. The characters cannot think what they want to think nor do what they want to do: they are bound in a *lex eterna*, disciplined to the making of a work of art, and yet– such is the author's silence and cunning–they appear to have free-will. By the time we have finished the book they have presented us not only with a serio-comic re-telling of the Odyssey but also with a complete conspectus of the arts and sciences, a working model of the human body, a spectrum, and a textbook of literary techniques. These are gifts which we can accept or ignore, just as we wish: they are primarily there in the service of a story. As Joyce himself said, they make a bridge for the marching across of his eighteen chapters; when the chapters have achieved their passage the bridge can be blown sky-high. But the bridge is an astonishing piece of pontifical architecture in its own right.

So far we have answered the question about Joyce's purpose in writing *Ulysses* purely in terms of a kind of technical ambition. There is always the danger that, bemused by the sheer skill of the book, we may ignore what the book is about. It is difficult in any work of art to fillet subject-matter from the presentation of subject-matter, and we may find in Joyce's attempt to make a sort of encyclo-paedia with a heart, as well as a rainbow, a sufficient artistic, as opposed to technical, intention. The fundamental purpose of any work of art is to impose order on the chaos of life as it comes to us; in imparting a vision of order the artist is doing what the religious teacher also does (this is one of the senses in which truth and beauty are the same thing). But the religious teacher's revelation is less a creation than a discovery, whereas the artist feels that—God rather than God's servant—he is the author of order. I have already said that the creation of a human community in fiction is the closest the novelist can get to the creation of a cosmos, but Joyce is ambitious enough to want to create a human body (chapter by chapter, organ by organ) which is a sort of configuration (as in Blake or Sweden-borg) of the ultimate celestial order. This is perhaps less blasphemous than it looks: it may even be taken as a gesture of piety. It may cer-tainly be taken as Joyce's attempt to build for himself an order which is a substitute for the order he abandoned when he abandoned the Church.

But we must not forget that Joyce is, as well as a cosmic poet and apocalyptical epiphanist, a writer of stories. *Ulysses* is a story, and a simple story at that. It is a story about the need of people for each other, and Joyce regards this theme as so important that he has to borrow an epic form in which to tell it. The invocation of the Odyssey may reduce Ulysses to Bloom, but it also exalts Bloom to Ulysses. It is time to look at the nature of this invocation.

2: Taking over Homer

'ULYSSES' AND 'ULIXES' ARE, AS EVERY SCHOOLBOY USED TO KNOW,
Latin forms of the Greek 'Odysseus'. Odysseus was, even quite
early in life, Joyce's favourite epic hero, and, knowing something of
Joyce's temperament, one can see why. Most primitive poetry is
about fighting, and the ancient epic naturally extols fighting qualities, making its heroes out of heavyweights gifted with blind courage,
brute strength, and a garnishing of conventional virtue. Physical
violence was repugnant to Joyce – there is very little of it in his
books – but he responded readily enough to more intelligent ways of
overcoming an enemy – organisation, coolness, tact, cunning. These
qualities are all to be found in Odysseus, and to them we can add
various endearing imperfections of character. He longs to get home
to his wife, but he is not averse to fornication with nymphs and goddesses. This wife is a second-best to Helen, whose hand he failed to
win, and it is good loser's decency on his part to persuade all the
suitors to join him in swearing an oath to protect Helen from
violence. Yet when Helen is carried off to Troy he tries to evade his
obligations by pretending to be mad. Still, once launched on the
expedition he proves wise and cunning in counsel and prudently
brave in war. He is more likeable than Achilles and Ajax and Æneas;
he is more human, more Bloom-like. The Iliad gives us a sharp
picture of him.

Odysseus's qualities call for celebration in a separate epic poem,
and the Odyssey is devoted entirely to his adventures after the fall
of Troy. It covers the ten years between his demobilisation and his
arrival home in Ithaca to wrest the little island kingdom from the
suitors of his presumed widow Penelope. Most of the adventures
which fill the ten years are related in retrospect, the actual events of
the poem taking about six weeks. Before we meet Odysseus we meet
his son Telemachus (this opening section of the poem is called the
Telemachia). Telemachus, like Hamlet, is sick at heart. Various

island princes are seeking the hand of his mother, but she has–with
a cunning perhaps learned from her husband–been putting them
off by promising to come to a decision when she has finished
weaving a winding-sheet for Laertes, Odysseus's father. What she
weaves during the day she unravels at night, but, at the opening of
the poem, this trick has been discovered: she must choose her
husband now. It becomes urgent for Telemachus to get news of his
father. He faces the prospect of having a stepfather whom he hates
(he hates all the suitors, but Antinous, the candidate with the
shortest odds, is the worst of them all); moreover, these insolent
princelings are wasting the substance of the little kingdom of
Ithaca very fast. Telemachus goes off to consult Nestor at Pylos and
Menelaus and his wife Helen at Sparta: they may have news of his
father. Meanwhile, the suitors prepare an ambush against his return.

We come now to the Odyssey proper. Odysseus has been living
for seven years on the island of Ogygia, detained there by the
goddess Calypso. He wants to go home, but she will not let him. But
Zeus, father of the gods, steps in and orders his release, and Odysseus builds himself a raft. He sails on it for seventeen days and
comes within sight of Scheria, where the Phaeacians live, but then
Poseidon, the sea-god, blows up a storm and destroys the raft.
Odysseus, as we shall hear, put out the one eye of Poseidon's giant
son Polyphemus, and he will not be allowed to forget it. Odysseus
floats for two days on the sea, buoyed up by a scarf which Ino, sea-
goddess, has given him, and at length he is cast ashore on the coast
of Scheria. Nausicaa, daughter of the king Alcinous, finds him and
looks after him. In the palace the bard Democodus sings to him
about his own exploits–including that of the Trojan Horse–and
Odysseus, who has up to that moment concealed his name, now tells
the Phaeacians who he is and recounts his perilous story.

He tells of the raid on the Cicones at Ismarus, then of the land of
the Lotus-Eaters, where so many of his men succumbed to the will-
destroying, home-forgetting fruit. After that we hear about the one-
eyed giant cannibals called Cyclopes and how Odysseus put out the
eye of one of them–Polyphemus–with a red-hot stake. Then comes
the account of his stay with the wind-god Æolus, who gave him the
adverse winds tied up in a bag as a farewell present; his men, thinking that the bag contained treasure, released the winds, doing themselves and their leader little good. After that, the Laestrygones,
another giant race of cannibals, destroyed eleven of his twelve ships
and ate their crews. The forlorn remainder reached Æaea, where the

witch-goddess Circe turned them all into swine–except, of course, Odysseus, who was protected from enchantment by the herb moly, a gift from Hermes. After a year with Circe (during which he begot a son on her, Telegonus, who was eventually to destroy his father unwittingly) he left–his men having been restored to human shape– to consult the seer Tiresias in Hades about his prospects of returning to Ithaca. In Hades he saw the ghosts of many dead heroes and their womenfolk and talked with his own mother, Anticlea. Back on the sea again, he resisted the lethal song of the Sirens (himself tied to the mast, his men with wax in their ears) and steered between Scylla– a mariner-eating monster in a cave–and the whirlpool Charybdis. After so many lucky or cunning escapes, his men now did for themselves by killing the cattle of the Sun-god Helios on Thrinacia: such sacrilege earned them a thunderbolt, though Odysseus–who had warned them against their crime–escaped on the wreckage of the ship to Ogygia and the arms of Calypso.

Now comes the homecoming or *Nostos*. The Phaeacians take Odysseus back to Ithaca (for their pains their ship is turned, by Poseidon, into a rock on its return) and now the crafty Odysseus has to encompass the destruction of the suitors. The goddess Athene disguises him as a beggar, and the faithful swineheard Eumaeus tells him of the behaviour of the suitors. He shows himself to Telemachus (who escapes the suitors' ambush) and together they plan a massacre. Meanwhile, two others learn that this beggar is Odysseus– his nurse Eurycleia and his dog Argus. After insults from the suitors and a fight with the beggar Irus, our hero learns that Penelope is to marry the man who can string the bow of Odysseus and shoot an arrow through twelve axe-heads. Needless to say, only Odysseus can bend the bow and shoot the arrow, and now he stands revealed in his glory and all the suitors quake–with justice, as it turns out, for Odysseus, Telemachus and Eumaeus kill them all, starting with Antinous, and even hang their women. Penelope knows that this must be her husband, since he can tell her what their bedstead looks like, and so all ends, though bloodily, happily. That is how Homer tells the story.

Joyce tells it rather differently. He has eighteen chapters to Homer's twenty-four books; he misses out some of Homer's material but inserts an adventure of the Argonauts–that of the Symplegades, or clashing rocks, expanding a reference to the Planktai, or wandering rocks, in the twelfth book (line 61) of the Odyssey. Also, he changes the order of Odysseus's exploits and presents them all in dramatic immediacy, not in epic narration-within-a-narration. The Joycean Odyssey runs as follows:

Telemachus, like Hamlet, is sick at heart. His mother is dead, and he feels guilty about her; he has left his father's house to dwell with two companions. One of these is a foreigner, member of a race that has usurped the kingdom of his people; the other is a fellow-country-man who perpetually mocks him, demands money from him and even the key of the tower where they live together. He is dispossessed, bitter at the presence of the usurper. From Nestor–a sage, garrulous and reminiscent prince–he can learn nothing that will lead him back to lawful possession of his rights. He–not Mene-laus–consults the sea-god Proteus, but this god changes his form perpetually, slipping out of the grasp of Telemachus. Oracular hints have been flashed at him about his need for a spiritual, as opposed to a biological, father, but he cannot formulate this need to himself. Now, after this *Telemachia* of three episodes, we are ready for Odysseus. Joyce's hero is both an exile and at home. He has his dwelling in the west, but his heart is tugged by ancestral memories of the east, wherefrom his people have wandered. Thus his wife Penelope can take on the properties of a goddess who has seduced him into staying in exile: this is her kingdom, and her name is Calypso. Odysseus goes forth, having fed her with ambrosia and nectar, and at once finds himself among the Lotus-Eaters. He passes safely through their land and proceeds, with his companions, to Hades, where he meets the ghosts of the fabled dead. Next he makes windy contact with Æolus and nearly meets Telemachus, in whom–his own son being dead–he sees the lineaments of another son. He wanders next among the Laestrygonians, filthy gorgers all, but is himself uneaten.

On the way to Scylla and Charybdis, a necessary passage of his journey, he espies Antinous, whom he knows to be a suitor of his wife Penelope. He does not offer fight: he is solitary; he has no son to help him. But now he sees Telemachus himself taking on with courage the perilous passage between the monster's cave and the whirlpool. Telemachus, steering through, sees this sonless father in his turn, and recalls a dream in which such a man seemed to visit him. And now both pseudo-father and pseudo-son have to face new perils: they become Argonauts and venture among the clashing rocks which hide one from the other. Then we are with Odysseus alone once more, and he is not lured by the Sirens' song away from his purpose–to do the work the gods have set him to do and, at length, return safely to Ithaca. But he ventures into territory where the Cyclops Polyphemus lurks, and Polyphemus attacks him. Odysseus gets away, but the giant hurls a heavy missile after him. It is time to seek brief shelter from the hostile world before continuing the journey. He rests in sight of the sea.

On the seashore the king's daughter Nausicaa is playing with her companions. She falls in love with the mature and weary stranger and, in a dream of abandon, gives herself to him. In a dream Odysseus takes her, but, in the convalescence of after-love, he comes to the realisation that, while he is thus dallying away from home, the suitor Antinous has prevailed in Ithaca. It is a bitter moment. Still, ever more mindful of others than himself, he sails to the island where the Oxen of the Sun-god bellow their song of fertility: the island is full of women in labour, and he knows that the wife of a companion is soon to give birth. He lands on the island, enquires about her, and is told that the hour is at hand. He sees that the young Telemachus is there, revelling with drunken companions, and Odysseus is shocked to hear blasphemy spoken against the divine gift of conception: is not this a symbolic slaughtering of the holy oxen? But Zeus hears and, as a warning, launches terrifying thunder.

Odysseus sees that Telemachus has drunk too much wine; what dangers worse than blasphemy may not befall him? He appoints himself the young man's protector and follows him to the island of Circe, where men are turned by magic into swine. The prudent Odysseus is in no danger himself, for the god Hermes has given him the protective herb moly. He sails through terrifying apparitions and phantasmagorias unscathed. As for the young hero towards whom his attitude grows ever more paternal, he too resists gross transformation and is only in danger of attack from rough men whom lust and drunkenness have turned into beasts. He is struck in the face and falls. And now it is Odysseus's duty to take this new-found son back to Ithaca, to heal him, give him opportunity to recover, and offer him the freedom—as to a true son—of his palace.

But the return to the kingdom must be made with caution. They rest awhile, taking food and drink, in the rude shelter of Eumaeus. Then they take courage and walk to the Palace, imbibing there a sacramental cup of nectar, a pledge of paternality and filiality. The young man leaves, no stranger now. Odysseus seeks his couch—he is weary; he has travelled far—and his wife Penelope finds in him a masterfulness she has not known before. The suitors may have tasted of her body, but they have not prevailed as Odysseus has prevailed:

they cannot draw his long bow of cunning and knowledge of the world and the deathless gods that govern the world. And Odysseus has brought her a son to replace the true son they lost long ago to the gods of the underworld. This son, not being of her body, stands in the potential relationship of messiah and lover. She sleeps, well content.

That, briefly, is Joyce's own version of the Odyssey. All we have to do now is to dress these characters in modern clothes and make them live through their adventures in a modern city, expanding these adventures to epic length but imposing on them the tight rules of unity found in the classical drama. Let us go back to the beginning again but this time take it more slowly.

3: Telemachus

DAZZLED BY THE MOST GLITTERING ASPECT OF *Ulysses* – ITS display of literary techniques and its ingenuities of symbolism – we find it easy to regard each chapter as a separable item to be marvelled at, the whole book as a loose collocation of *tableaux*, like an exhibition, and to forget that its fundamental concern is with the telling of a story. A plain summary of this story is not very enlightening, but the theme on which the story is based is potent, suggestive, and compelling. It is the mystery of the relationship between nonbegetting father and unbegotten son.

What sounds like nonsense or, at best, a paradox becomes clear only in a context of theology. At the end of *A Portrait* we are puzzled by an identification which we did not expect. Stephen Dedalus has been seeing himself as the fabulous inventor of human flight and creator of the Labyrinth. But in his last diary entry he invokes Daedalus as a father. 'Brightness falls from the air' and '*Non serviam*' are for Lucifer but also for Icarus, the son of Daedalus whose wings failed him. Stephen is both Daedalus and Icarus, both father and son. How can this mystery be resolved? Only in the mystical terms of Christian theology, in which Father and Son are, though separate Persons, really aspects of each other.

And so the branch of learning (art or science) which presides over the first chapter of *Ulysses* is theology. This justifies the liturgical opening, with Buck Mulligan intoning the beginning of the Mass – *Introibo ad altare Dei* – and carrying a lather-bowl on which a cross is made by a razor and mirror. The scene is that Martello Tower on the Dublin coast where Joyce and Oliver St John Gogarty (the original of Buck Mulligan) lived for a short time (it is now a Joyce museum), and the hour is eight o'clock on the morning of June 16th, 1904. We enter the story without difficulty. The technique is a straightforward narrative one in which all the characters save one are young. Suddenly, though, the interior monologue of Stephen

94

Dedalus begins. Mulligan's teeth glisten with gold fillings, and the detached word 'Chrysostomos' is thrown at us. It means 'golden mouth' and it refers us back to a Saint John so called. The reference is ironically apt when we remember that Mulligan is Oliver St John Gogarty. Here the worries that accompany us when we read Joyce's major books begin – worries about real-life references which, properly, should have no place in the reading of a work of fiction. Time and time again obscurities only become clear when we consult the biographical background of *Ulysses*.

'Chrysostomos' – the word links the two worlds of the chapter and, for that matter, the book itself. It suggests Christian hagiography and, being a Greek word, it suggests the Greek myth which, underlying the whole work, must be established at once. Mulligan sees himself as a Greek. He will teach Stephen the language. They will go to Athens together. They will try to 'Hellenise' the island. He recognises that Stephen's surname is Greek, though this is absurd, since Stephen is a 'jejune jesuit'. Mulligan is a great mocker – of Stephen's poverty (he has given him some cast-off clothes), of the Jesuit strain in Stephen's make-up which cannot be eliminated. At once we start to see Mulligan as a kind of Antinous to Stephen's Telemachus. Stephen is patronised and bullied. He has, we learn, paid the rent for this tower where they are living; soon Mulligan will demand the key as well as 'twopence for a pint'. To make matters worse, an English friend of Mulligan's – Haines – is staying with them, and Haines serves to remind Stephen of his, and all Ireland's, servitude to the British state. The key symbol to this episode is 'Heir', and Stephen feels himself to be disinherited: there is nothing he can call his own.

Mulligan addresses the sea in Greek – '*Thalatta! Thalatta!*' – and says it is a 'great sweet mother'. This brings in a new and important theme – Stephen's guilt in relation to his own mother, recently dead. The exile foreshadowed at the end of *A Portrait* was fulfilled: Stephen went to Paris to study medicine. But a telegram stating that his mother was dying summoned him home again. At his mother's bedside he refused to kneel and pray for her – *non serviam*. The sea, a 'dull green mass of liquid', now reminds him of the bowl of sluggish bile 'she had torn up from her rotting liver by fits of loud groaning vomiting'. Pity for her rests with him and he wears mourning as its outward sign, but he would not kneel and pray, nor does he regret that he did not. His mother remains as a symbol for a Church he both despises and fears, since it is the temporal voice of a hateful

95

butcher God. And yet, in temperament, he is still what Mulligan says he is—a 'jejune jesuit'.

If you reject family—which a mother holds together—as well as the ties of Church and State, is there anything left for you? There is art, but art has to be nourished, and Irish art is 'the cracked looking-glass of a servant'. Stephen, so totally disinherited, does not yet know where he will find security and material for the great literature he must create. He despises his father, though he does not fear him: it is his mother, not his father, who is to be associated with the bearded monster called God ('Nobodaddy' to William Blake). What he needs, though he has still to recognise this, is a spiritual or mystical father, a father who is not 'consubstantial'. This father will be a mother as well, and we are given a hint as to where he lies. Mulligan, a medical student, sees bodies cut up in the dissecting-room of the Mater. The Mater is at the top of Eccles Street, where Leopold Bloom lives. '*Et unam sanctam catholicam et apostolicam ecclesiam*' rings through Stephen's head. 'Eccles'[1] is there. Bloom will take on the function of both a mother and a church.

Once this opening chapter is under way the father-son theme is presented obliquely but vigorously. Haines has heard of Stephen's theory of *Hamlet* and wants it expounded at once. Mulligan says: 'He proves by algebra that Hamlet's grandson is Shakespeare's grandfather and that he himself is the ghost of his own father.' Haines points to Stephen and says: 'What? He himself?' And then Mulligan mocks Stephen with 'O, shade of Kinch the elder! Japhet in search of a father!' Haines says: 'I read a theological intepretation of it somewhere. The Father and the Son idea. The Son striving to be atoned with the Father.' And then Mulligan, blasphemous as well as mocking, recites some of his own (that is, Gogarty's) verses—'The Ballad of Joking Jesus'.

The mockery is apt:

> —I'm the queerest young fellow that ever you heard.
> My mother's a jew, my father's a bird.
> With Joseph the joiner I cannot agree,
> So here's to disciples and Calvary.

Stephen broods on heresies about the relationship between God the Father and God the Son. In his own case, we realise, 'Photius and the brood of mockers of whom Mulligan was one' speak a salutary warning. If we are to turn Stephen into a kind of Christ we have to

[1] In *Finnegans Wake*, *Ulysses* is called 'The Blue Book of Eccles'.

remember that the word can only be made flesh through the mediacy of a mother. For Bloom to be father-mother is well enough in the world of the spirit, but the flesh remains: the physical mother is inescapable. Hence another symbol in this chapter—the omphalos. Stephen first speaks it to himself, in Matthew Arnold's words: 'To ourselves . . . new paganism . . . omphalos.' Mulligan, talking of the Martello Tower, says: 'Billy Pitt had them built when the French were on the sea. But ours is the *omphalos*.' We are linked to our mothers by a navel-cord, and so back for ever and ever. And so the image of his mother must remain, a potent symbol, with Stephen all day. Also he is linked through her to two other mothers—Ireland and the Church. He cannot really escape to an empyrean where the son and heir knows only mystical family ties.

I have said that the opening chapter concentrates, with one exception, on young people, sons and heirs. The exception is the old woman who comes to deliver the milk. She is Ireland, poor and dispossessed. Haines, her lord and master, speaks Irish; she does not; she has not even her own language. She goes off, uncomplaining, with her milk-bill not fully paid (the twopence that should go to her goes to Mulligan 'for a pint'). Though her Homeric analogue is Athene—who appears in the likeness of Mentor and tells Tele-machus to be wise and courageous like his father—she neither serves as a messenger nor upbraids like a goddess. And yet the sacramental potion of the day's beginning cannot be taken without her: Haines and Mulligan want milk in their tea; Stephen, though, significantly, is willing to take it black.

The last word of this section is 'Usurper', and it applies equally to Mulligan and Haines. Mulligan, as Antinous, is actively a usurper, here and now, mocking, patronising, taker of Stephen-Telemachus's goods as well as chider of his spirit and chiller of his courage. Haines's usurpation lies further back, the work of his ancestors, and Haines blames history for what he recognises as England's unfairness to Ireland. History is what Stephen is now to brood on in the following chapter. The morning marine colours of white and gold are changed to brown. The technique is that of a catechism, perpetual question and answer, and this is fitting for a scene laid in a school.

The school belongs to Mr Deasy, and Stephen is employed as a teacher there. As the chapter opens he is asking his class questions about Pyrrhus ('Another victory like that and we are done for'), but his interior monologue is obsessed with the nightmare of history in general. History is so very much *there*, an incubus on living man, as inescapable as the umbilical link with one's own mother. Was there ever any element of choice back there in history, anything which could have made events turn out differently?

Had Pyrrhus not fallen by a beldam's hand in Argos or Julius Caesar not been knifed to death? They are not to be thought away. Time has branded them and fettered they are lodged in the room of the infinite possibilities they have ousted. But can those have been possible seeing that they never were? Or was that only possible which came to pass? Weave, weaver of the wind.

His pupils too are oppressed by history. They ask their teacher for a story, a ghost story, the release through the imagination from the incubus of the past. Instead, Stephen hears their recitation from Milton's *Lycidas*, which they have been given to learn by heart. 'Sunk though he be beneath the watery floor': a 'drowned man' motif initiated in the preceding chapter (Mulligan saved a man from drowning) is continued here; it has its obvious Homeric parallel in the many drowned companions of Odysseus, but it has another function as well—it calls up an aspect of that world of the dead which, like history itself, oppresses the world of the living. The boy Talbot stumbles over the line 'Through the dear might of Him that walked the waves', and Christ suddenly overshadows history. 'Here also over these craven hearts his shadow lies and on the scoffer's heart and lips and on mine. It lies upon their eager faces who offered him a coin of the tribute. To Caesar what is Caesar's, to God what is God's.' But Stephen mocks the image away:

> Riddle me, riddle me, randy ro.
> My father gave me seeds to sow.

It is Thursday, a half-holiday (without that half-holiday the book would not have been possible), and the boys get ready to dismiss and then reassemble for hockey. First, though, Stephen gives them a riddle:

> The cock crew,
> The sky was blue:
> The bells in heaven
> Were striking eleven.
> 'Tis time for this poor soul
> To go to heaven.

They cannot answer it, and Stephen's own answer disappoints them: 'The fox burying his grandmother under a hollybush.' But Stephen means neither a fox nor a grandmother. The mother motif has reappeared and, when young Sargent comes to Stephen to be helped with his algebra ('He proves by algebra that Shakespeare's ghost is Hamlet's grandfather'), it is developed for the length of a whole paragraph. In Sargent Stephen sees the eternal son–'ugly and futile: lean neck and tangled hair and a stain of ink, a snail's bed'–protected from the world that would crush him by a mother's love. 'With her weak blood and wheysour milk she had fed him and hid from sight of others his swaddling bands.' In face of the dreadful nightmare of history is perhaps *amor matris* the only true thing in life? But, while he is asking this question, Stephen traces the symbols of an algebraic equation for Sargent, and Oriental images are suggested by these 'imps of fancy of the Moors'–Averroes and Moses Maimonides, 'flashing in their mocking mirrors the obscure soul of the world'. Leopold Bloom, too, at this moment, is drawn towards an ancestral East, as we shall see when we come to the Joycean Odyssey proper. Stephen's mind and Bloom's mind are tuning up for the eventual meeting.

Stephen and Mr Deasy have a session together in the old school-master's study, full of stale air, old coins and shells, pictures of horses on the walls. Mr Deasy is old, and his room stands for history. He himself stands for Nestor, the wise tamer of horses whom Telemachus first consulted about the whereabouts of his father. He can tell Stephen nothing that will bring him closer to the repossession of his heritage. 'You think me an old fogey and old tory', he says, rightly. He knows of wrongs committed in the past–'a woman brought sin into the world': Helen, for whom the Greeks made a ten years' war on Troy, MacMurrough's wife who brought the strangers to Ireland, the woman who 'brought Parnell low' (here one Homeric parallel is set, like a clue, before us). But history still 'moves towards one great goal, the manifestation of God'. To Stephen 'history is a nightmare from which I am trying to awake' and God is 'a shout in the street'. The young dispossessed heir and the man of ancient wisdom can meet at few points, and Mr Deasy shrewdly guesses that Stephen will not stay long in his school.

But Mr Deasy gives Stephen money–his month's salary–and Stephen, through his journalistic contacts, can do Mr Deasy a good turn. Nestor's castle stood near the mouth of the river Alpheus, the river which Heracles deflected to clean out the Augean stables. Around this river cluster a whole host of bovine associations (the Semitic letters alif, lam, pa form a root meaning 'ox'; the letter alpha is derived from a simple representation of an ox's head). It is appropriate, then, that Mr Deasy should be much concerned about foot-and-mouth disease in Ireland and a threatened embargo on Irish cattle. He is writing a letter on the subject for newspaper publication, and he wants Stephen to place it with one of the editors he knows. This ox motif is important. Through its associations with the Oxen of the Sun, which stand for fertility, it suggests a way out of the treadmill of history – the perpetual renewal presented in Vico's theory of history (the basis of *Finnegans Wake*), already prefigured here in a reference to Vico Road, Dalkey. The young poet dubs himself 'bullockbefriending bard': the ancient knight has given him a potent symbol.

Only here, though, do Nestor and Telemachus come together. Mr Deasy thunders his false prophecies, particularly about the ruin that the Jews will bring upon England. Ireland is safe, however, both from Jewish conspiracy and guilt about Jewish persecution. His last words explain why: 'She never let them in.' He apparently does not know of that man in Eccles Street. The fact is that Mr Deasy sees history as a march towards glory, the eventual vision of God, and blames the errors of history on bad women and on Jews. To Stephen, as to Blake, history is barren, 'fabled by the daughters of memory'. The symbols of history which are contained in Mr Deasy's study, neatly arranged like facts in catechisms, are shells and coins. To Stephen coins are to spend, not hoard; shells are mere sounding hollows. Telemachus leaves Nestor unenlightened, except for the possession of that bull-image, symbol of a renewal of life not to be found in shelled, coined history.

The third section of this *Telemachia* is a lengthy monologue and our first encounter with the really 'difficult' Joyce. The scene is the seashore, the colour is green, the symbol the tide, the hour approaches noon. The Homeric parallel is only indirectly concerned with Telemachus. Menelaus, whom Telemachus consults immediately after his visit to Nestor, himself seeks to consult Proteus, the old sea-god who is unwilling to be consulted and will only prophesy if captured. But he is hard to catch, being adept at changing his form, and it is only with the aid of Eidothea, Proteus's daughter, that Menelaus is able to hold him down and question him. Evidently Proteus, in his very name, suggests some primal force, the very stuff of life, capable of expressing itself in many forms. Man's most fundamental questions – about the nature of life, the heavens, the universe – are posed to a mess of shifting, elusive phenomena; he must learn the gift of reading the signs, of understanding the language in which life expresses itself. It is philology, the science of language, that presides over this episode of *Ulysses*.

Stephen is his own Menelaus, walking along Sandycove shore, enquiring into the nature of reality, straining the resources of human language in the process. The signatures he must learn to read are all about–'seaspawn and seawrack, the nearing tide, that rusty boot. Snotgreen' (so Mulligan described the sea in the first chapter) 'blue-silver, rust: coloured signs'. Aristotle is invoked, *'maestro di color che sanno'* ('master of them who know') according to Dante, to tame and classify the elusive world of matter. Stephen provides his own definitions of the elements in which this world lives and moves. Time is the *Nacheinander*–one thing coming after another; space is the *Nebeneinander*–one thing coming next to another. These subsist in the dark (Stephen shuts his eyes) when the world of visible matter has been shut out. Is the world of phenomenon dependent, as Bishop Berkeley thought it was, on the perceiver? Stephen opens his eyes and sees that everything is still there 'all the time without you: and ever shall be, world without end'. But he had a moment, his eyes closed, of wondering whether everything might vanish in that dark interlude. One cannot really trust the world of matter.

A couple of *Frauenzimmer* (Joyce is entitled, in a chapter devoted to philology, to draw on languages other than English) come down to the beach, one of them 'swinging lourdily her midwife's bag'. Stephen is at once back to the motif of the omphalos, a telephone which will bring one ultimately in touch with 'Edenville'–'Aleph, alpha: nought, nought, one.' Mr Deasy's bull has reappeared, next to a grosser symbol of fertility. At the end of the line is naked Eve, navelless, 'a belly without blemish'. If the metaphysical path leads Stephen to the 'ineluctable modality of the visible', the navel cord leads him back eventually to Eve's sin, original sin. Out of original sin came the generation of life not by miracle (Adam anaesthetised; the removal of a rib) but in pain. Stephen ponders his own making by two strangers–'the man with my voice and my eyes and a ghost-woman with ashes on her breath'–and is soon back on theology, the relationship between Father and Son, the lifelong war of the heresiarch Arius on the 'contransmagnificandjewbangtantiality'–a mysterious God-Christ identification which, in this grotesque term, anticipates the melting of Bloom into Stephen ('Stoom'; 'Blephen') and Stephen into Bloom.

'Airs romped around him, nipping and eager airs.' This chapter is full of *Hamlet* references, looking forward to the scene in the National

Library where this whole father-son theme shall be hammered out.
Stephen hears in imagination his 'consubstantial father's voice'
mocking his in-laws, the Gouldings (this is John Joyce himself with
his 'O weeping God, the things I married into . . . Highly respectable gondoliers . . . Jesus wept: and no wonder, by Christ').
Stephen cannot decide whether to visit his uncle Richie Goulding
or not, but a fine comic picture of him prepares us for an eventual
meeting with him—though the meeting is Bloom's, not Stephen's.
The Goulding house is in decay, like the Dedalus house. Man
brings things to decay, and it was a great Dublin brain that went
mad with viewing man's wretched folly. Stephen broods on Swift,
and the horse motif of the preceding chapter, as well as the 'equine'
length of Buck Mulligan's face (noted in the Martello Tower), re-
emerges out of the image of the Houyhnhnms. At once the 'furious
dean' and a memory of a priest whom, in *A Portrait*, 'some of the
boys called Lantern Jaws and others Foxy Campbell' bring in a
mocking reference to the Mass and, set in it, the 'imp hypostasis'—
hypostasis being the technical term for the doctrine of the common
substance of Father and Son.

The speed with which Stephen's mind rushes from subject to
subject, the links of association often being well-submerged, is appropriate to a chapter celebrating the quicksilver elusiveness of
Proteus: Proteus is the mind, as well as the phenomenal world
which the mind seeks to comprehend. An obscure Swiftian reference
(Dryden's 'Cousin Swift, you will never be a poet' becomes 'Cousin
Stephen, you will never be a saint') leads on to a self-examination
which cuts through the usual self-delusions put out by the Protean
ego. How stupid were his old ambitions—the epiphanies left to all
the great libraries of the world, to be read 'after a few thousand
years, a mahamanvantara' (we have met that mahamanvantara—the
Indian 'great year'—before: in *The Holy Office*. It is one of the
motifs that draw us to the East. In a chapter ruled by the sea-tide it
is proper to be reminded of the manvantara and the pralaya—the
human periods of waking and sleeping which find analogues in the
rhythms of the seasons and of the sea itself).

Stephen walks on, past the Gouldings' decayed residence, and
turns north-east towards the Pigeonhouse. This makes him think of
a lewd French joke about the Virgin Birth—'*C'est le pigeon, Joseph*':
we cannot be long away from the Divine Incarnation. But this is also
a way into a lengthy and elliptical reminiscence about his time in
Paris among the other Irish 'wild geese' (the exile theme which

matches Bloom's sense of estrangement). The literary technique is brilliant here with its evocation of 'Paris rawly waking, crude sunlight on her lemon streets'. We can, if we wish, fill out the ellipses with biographical references. As I have already indicated, so much of the remembered, as opposed to enacted, life of *Ulysses* touches the region of actuality. There is a penumbra surrounding the book, full of signs which lead us out to Joyce's own experience. Fiction itself is Protean, a disguise of real life. Often the interior monologues of both Bloom and Stephen seem like the iceberg surface, with submerged mountains of references we can only reach by forgetting that *Ulysses* is a work of art and using it as an encyclopaedic guide to real history. Does this invalidate the novel as literature? I think not. True naturalism calls for shadows and mysteries and clues which may or may not be taken up, just as we please. If we cannot understand everything in *Ulysses*, nor can we understand everything in real life.

Stephen thinks of Kevin Egan, the revolutionary wild goose forgotten. 'Remembering thee, O Sion.' A faint image of Bloom, that other exile, beckons here. Looking south to the Martello Tower, Stephen reaffirms his loneliness. 'He has the key. I will not sleep there when this night comes . . . Take all. Keep all.' The dispossessed heir is also the dispossessed father: he sees himself an instant as the ghost in Elsinore, King Hamlet as well as Prince Hamlet. But now the exterior world asserts itself again, though the language in which it is described is no diaphanous veil: 'He climbed over the sedge and eely oarweeds and sat on a stool of rock, resting his ashplant in a grike.' The language draws attention to itself and, as we see at once, rightly. Stephen reminds us that philology is the science which presides here: 'These heavy sands are language tide and wind have silted.' The emphasis is back on reading the signs of nature, looking through nature's symbols, her disguise, for nature's own self. A dog runs across the sand, and Stephen–who, like his creator, fears dogs–comforts himself with 'I have my stick. Sit tight.' The prose becomes highly contrapuntal, a vision of the Vikings landing ('bark/barque' is an inaudible enharmonic chord) leading Stephen to think of that Northern blood that flows hidden in him, the invaders of history, the pretenders of history (the Irish pretend to be 'all kings' sons'), the collapse of his own pretences when he finds himself shaking 'at a cur's yelping'. Behaviour, like history, is all disguises, gifts of Proteus. He tries to be honest with himself: could he, like Mulligan, have saved a man from drowning? No, nor could he save his mother: 'Waters: bitter death: lost.'

The disguise theme enfolds the dog, which seems to turn into a hare, a buck, a horse, a wolf, a calf, a fox, a panther (the waves, under the dog's influence, turn for an instant into 'herds of seamorse', Proteus's own flock). A panther. Haines had wakened Stephen the previous night with a shout in his sleep about a black panther. Afterwards, as a kind of soothing ointment, Stephen was granted a dream in which, on a street of harlots, an Oriental offered him hospitality. He remembers that dream now. Some hundreds of pages later it will come true.

Cockle-pickers on the sand, trudging with their bags, appear to Stephen as 'red Egyptians' and flavour his monologue with the speech of the gipsies, language ready with a new disguise of reality:

> White thy fambles, red thy gan
> And thy quarrons dainty is.
> Couch a hogshead with me then.
> In the darkmans clip and kiss.

But the monologue has been steadily thickening with strange speech – the sea's own language, the giant words of 'Sir Lout' ('*laut*' is the Malay word for the sea): 'I'm the bloody well gigant rolls all them bloody well boulders, bones for my steppingstones. Feefawfum. I zmellz de bloodz odz an Iridzman.' All the chief European tongues blend, as they are to do later, and more spectacularly, in *Finnegans Wake*. The terms of heraldry brighten Stephen's imagery, trying to hold down the Protean spectrum in fixed and formal colours. And then the welter of language breaks in a poem which Stephen, lacking other paper, writes down on a torn-off end of Mr Deasy's letter for the press. It is a symbol of control, of taming Proteus: 'Put a pin in that chap, will you? My tablets.' (*Hamlet* is never very distant.) A kind of content comes: Stephen lies at full length on the pointed rocks, his 'Hamlet hat' –the wide-brimmed hat he brought back from Paris–tilted over his eyes. 'Pain is far.' He recalls a line of Fergus's song, the poem of Yeats which Stephen-Joyce set to music and sang while his mother lay close to death, weeping for the sadness of the words: 'And no more turn aside and brood.' The image of the drowned man washed up seems to lose some of its terror ('Seadeath, mildest of all deaths known to man'). *Hamlet* makes its last appearance in the chapter with a recollection of Ophelia's song for a dead father. Stephen, having achieved a sort of victory over Proteus, is ready for a drink (he is supposed to meet Mulligan and Haines, flush with his salary, in the Ship at twelve-thirty). He leaves the tribute of a little dry snot on a rock-ledge. Before quitting 'the burning scene' he notes a ship sailing into harbour–the returned wanderer. An old sailor, emblem of completed exile, will preside over his meeting with Bloom at day's end.

I say 'a sort of victory over Proteus'. This is no mere fancy. The chaos of primal matter, of the phenomenal world, is figured in the chaos of language, ever-changing, hard to pin down. But language, despite the chaos, has, in a manner, pinned down the world outside. It remains for the poet to impose order on language and, by using the to-and-fro rhythms of the tide, to create an image of organic order, achieve the ultimate pinning-down. Already, at the end of the *Telemachia*, Stephen has come some way towards regaining his inheritance: he rules through words, and even Mulligan fears the lancet of his art, while the sea's ruler, Haines, has a mind to make a book of wisdom out of Stephen's sayings. But Stephen, though a prince of words, is not yet big enough to write *Ulysses*. He needs Leopold Bloom.

4: Beginning of the Journey

THE 'PROTEUS' EPISODE WE HAVE JUST CONSIDERED IS A *tour de force* of linguistic virtuosity. Besides presenting the bewildering Protean variety of the world of matter, and of the resources of language which are able to tame it, it exhibits the learning and intellectual subtlety of Stephen Dedalus so richly that we are forced to accept him as a sort of Homeric hero of the mind. He seems to enclose the universe of words and ideas; yet, ironically, he does not enclose the lowlier Bloom. Undernourished, dressed in cheap mourning and cast-off shoes, his teeth bad, a nose-picker because he has no handkerchief, he transcends the limitations of the body. He needs, and the book needs, to be brought down to earth. As we commence the Bloom Odyssey proper, we are aware that Stephen stands for the spirit and Bloom for the flesh. The opening of the *Telemachia* – the narrative of young men – was celebrated with the inaugural words of the Mass; when we first meet Mr Bloom – the mature man's narrative – it is in terms of 'the inner organs of beasts and fowls', the thought of kidneys for breakfast.

This consultation of viscera is a kind of ritual, but it does not lead to high-flown Dedalus themes like those of theology and philology. The science which presides over No. 7 Eccles Street is economics – the useful art of household management. A kidney is the symbol which controls the chapter – a utilitarian, unpoetic organ which, nevertheless, is to provide the shape of the New Bloomusalem when it is built, later on in the book. The glorification of the body starts now: physical organs have not been celebrated in the *Telemachia*. As for Bloom's own name – an anglicisation of the ancestral Hungarian Virag, which means a flower – it sums up pretty well what its owner stands for: something remarkable but unpretentious springing out of common earth. The comparative contentment of Bloom in his domestic surroundings, organising breakfast for his wife, giving the cat milk, contrasts with Stephen's divine dissatisfactions and aspirations. Bloom is, nevertheless, at a higher stage of development in certain respects than the young poet: he is close to the mature Joyce in having achieved paternity (a loved daughter, a son who died in infancy), tolerance, the quiet wisdom of a man who has seen the world. Unlike Odysseus and like Joyce, he prefers cats to dogs.

His wife is Madam Marion (Molly) Tweedy, professional singer. 'Tweedy' suggests the weaving of Penelope, whose counterpart she is; it also suggests the double thread of her fabric, for she is part Irish and part Spanish Jewess, born in Gibraltar–where her military father was stationed. We are to meet Molly as Penelope only in the final chapter; here she appears as Calypso, nymph of an island with a great cave at its navel (Gibraltar too has its caves). Now, and throughout the book, her place is bed.

In a sense, Bloom is detained in her abode. As soon as he goes out to buy his breakfast kidney he is preoccupied with visions of the East, the far ancestral home. But, as Stephen is unconsciously moving towards him, so he is moving towards Stephen, for Turko the Terrible appears in his thoughts–the very pantomime character whom, so Stephen remembers, his mother used to love. Bloom is an exile, with a certain emptiness inside. The science of economics temporarily fills the emptiness–speculations about money in beer, exiles from the county Leitrim blossoming as brewery kings. The butcher's shop he now visits is run by an exile of his own kind–Dlugacz. A girl is ahead of him, buying sausages; Bloom picks up a cut sheet from a newspaper, and he is East again: 'The model farm at Kinnereth on the lakeshore of Tiberias. Can become ideal winter sanatorium.' The economics of farming fill his mind for a space. Then the sensual, earthy Bloom flowers again quickly: he wants to get his kidney at once, to follow the girl down the street and admire her moving haunches. But he is too late and he tells himself–'Soda-chapped hands. Crusted toenails too'–that the morning desire is marginal.

Walking back home he reads his piece of cut newspaper. There is a planter's company–Agendath Netaim–which, for eight marks, will plant you a dunam of land with Oriental fruits. The East calls again, symbolised in an orange or citron, a tiny rising sun. But we are also concerned with economics: 'Can pay ten down and the balance in yearly instalments. Bleibtreustrasse 34, Berlin, W.15.' The name of the street–'Staytrue'–reminds us, if not Bloom, that he has not stayed true to the religion of his fathers. In both senses he is an exile from Jerusalem. And the kidney he takes home is a pork kidney.

'Citron' recalls other Jewish exiles like himself—the fruit's very namesake of Saint Kevin's Parade, and cither-playing Mastiansky. Then the sun goes in for a moment, the moment when the sea turns into a bowl of bitter waters for Stephen (it is just after eight). Bloom, in a grey horror which sears his flesh, sees the Dead Sea and the dead cities of a wandering people, his own: 'the grey sunken cunt of the world'. The image is suggested by the sight of an ancient hag clutching a noggin bottle; Stephen, in complement, is reflecting on the dry shrivelled breasts of a woman who gives milk that is not her own. Bloom's depression lifts as the sunlight returns, running towards him like a gold girl, a nymph (nymphs, in deference to Calypso, rule this chapter). He relates such blue phases to the dysfunctioning of the body ('Morning mouth bad images'). Bright colours return and the post has come. There is a card for his wife from their daughter Milly, but for himself (she is daddy's girl) there is a letter. There is also a letter for Molly, and he knows who its sender is: 'His quick heart slowed at once. Bold hand.' Stephen has faced his Antinous; Bloom's Antinous seems already to have conquered without the bending of a bow.

Bloom reads his daughter's letter. Again we find a link with Stephen's world. At the end of the first chapter a young swimmer tells Mulligan that a certain Bannon (with whom Mulligan's brother happens to be staying in Westmeath) has 'found a sweet young thing down there. Photo girl he calls her.' The photo girl is Milly. She mentions Bannon in her letter and says that he sings Boylan's song about 'those seaside girls'. Bannon is a link between the two incarnations of Antinous—Mulligan's brother on one side, on the other Blazes Boylan, the 'hairy chap' whose letter Molly is at that moment reading. Bloom smiles 'with troubled affection' at the evidence of Milly's growing up. She is another nymph—'slim legs running up the staircase'—who holds him here on the island of caves.

Molly's bedroom is a cave, all 'warm yellow twilight'. He serves her with bread and butter and tea and sugar and cream—nymph's food—and learns that Boylan is bringing the programme for the concert tour he is organising. '*La ci darem*' (from *Don Giovanni*—an appropriate opera in Boylan's connection) is one of the songs that Molly is to sing; the other is 'Love's Old Sweet Song', an ominous title. But almost at once Bloom gives proof of a superiority that, without his having to draw out a single arrow, is eventually to reduce Boylan and all such suitors to a heap of ashes. Molly has a book called *Ruby: the Pride of the Ring* (Ruby is another nymph, naked and being lashed by the ringmaster, hidden in an illustration among smudged pages); she has met the word 'metempsychosis' there and wants to know its meaning. Bloom knows and tries to explain: 'It's Greek: from the Greek. That means the transmigration of souls.' Molly says: 'O, rocks! Tell us in plain words', and then Bloom, like Mulligan, starts Hellenising wild Irish, seeing in Molly something like a reincarnation of the nymph in the picture above the bed ('Given away with the Easter number of *Photo Bits*: Splendid masterpiece in art colours'), but not getting very far with his lesson on the true meaning of 'metempsychosis'. There is a smell of burning: the frying kidney calls: he returns to internal organs. But, of all the Dubliners who exemplify the call of the flesh, he shows himself to be the most rarefied, almost an intellectual. He is the most meet to be foster-father to a poet.

He is a meat-eater, but no cannibal. He is kind to his cat, he deplores the cruelty to performing animals that *Ruby: Pride of the Ring* brings to mind, he is off this morning to witness–mourning on, like Stephen–the ceremonial interring of the flesh of poor dead Dignam. He is wise in the limitations of the body, tolerant. The body is a garment that the soul can change, following the laws of metempsychosis–the nymph Syrinx into a reed, the nymph Daphne into laurel. The body is a cave for the soul. But, even before the soul can migrate, change goes on, uncheckable. Bloom sees the Protean in his daughter, who is changing into her mother: 'Will happen, yes. Prevent. Useless: can't move.'

Bloom, in the cave of his body, his body in the cave of its black suit for funerals, moves out to the cave of the outside jakes, taking with him–appropriately, since he has recently been suffering from constipation–a copy of *Titbits*. Defecation is nothing to be ashamed of: dung is a fertiliser. 'Dirty cleans.' Calypso, cave-nymph, follows him even here; he never has his wife long out of his thoughts. He remembers the bazaar dance when the band played Ponchielli's *Dance of the Hours* (it was there that Molly had first met Boylan): 'Evening hours, girls in grey gauze. Night hours then black with daggers and eyemasks.' Time is a procession of nymphs, all veiled, metempsychosed from morning into noon into evening into night, then ready to renew the cycle of change. But, so the bells of George's church remind him, leaving the closet with his work done, time sometime must have a stop. The bells toll for thee, as well as for poor dead Dignam.

In the second chapter we meet Bloom on Sir John Rogerson's Quay. He has moved south from Eccles Street, towards the sun, giver of life (the presiding organ is the genitals) but taker-away of energy (the Homeric parallel is the Lotus-Eaters). It is about ten o'clock, and the day is warming up nicely. The preceding chapter was concerned with the vigorous arts of money-making, but now the vegetable kingdom rules. The text is crammed with references to flowers, herbs, and the decoctions that the druggists make from these: the sciences of botany and chemistry join languid hands. Everywhere there is a sense of listlessness, of *dolce far niente*, and the gentle drag towards the East–here primed by the window of the Belfast and Oriental Tea Company–is renewed. At the same time there is a pull towards the earth's centre: 'Thirtytwo feet per second, per second. Law of falling bodies: per second, per second.' Bloom saunters to Westland Row post office–ever further south–and, countering the morning's lassitude with a phallic symbol, rolls up his copy of the *Freeman* into a baton.

In the post office there is a letter for him–addressed to 'Henry Flower, Esq.' Like Odysseus, he is a cunning name-changer, though, unlike Odysseus, he will not move too far from the truth: 'Bloom' and 'Flower' are still 'Virag'. The recruiting posters show soldiers who look half-baked, hypnotised: the lotus eats up even the vigour of the military. The letter is from a woman, but he cannot read it yet. A character from *Dubliners*, McCoy, accosts him. (In the preceding chapter we have already re-met, in name only, another *Dubliners* character–Gretta Conroy.) McCoy's wife is a singer, like Bloom's, but she is only a 'reedy freckled soprano', apt for little ballads but not for '*La ci darem*'. McCoy, as *Dubliners* tells us, is always borrowing valises for his wife's concert tours, and Bloom's interior monologue refers to this habit. Bloom does not want to talk; he wants to read his letter and he wants to feast his eyes on a high-class woman who has come out of the Grosvenor. His sexuality is passive: he likes to look. We learn later that he no longer has normal sexual relations with his wife (the guts went out of this side of marriage when their son, Rudy, died) and that he practises onanism. The genital image and the lotus image fuse into passivity.

Nevertheless, it is time for the father-son theme to make an appearance in Bloom's Odyssey. It comes, as with Stephen, out of *Hamlet*. Bloom sees a poster announcing that Mrs Bandman Palmer will play in *Leah* tonight; last night she played the prince of Denmark–'Male impersonator. Perhaps he was a woman. Why Ophelia committed suicide?' Bloom sees nothing odd in such a theory; later, in fantasy, he himself is to appear as the 'new womanly man'; the *yin* and *yang* elements cohere in him as the *yoni* and *lingam*, the phallus and the flower, meet as joint rulers of this chapter. Is not Bloom himself, a man, also a flower? And now the paternity theme is presented in its filial aspect–Nathan, 'who left the house of his father and left the God of his father', and Bloom's father's own comment on that affecting speech from *Leah* (Mrs Palmer's two plays have equal relevance in the father-son situation): 'Every word is so deep, Leopold.' An almost female tenderness wells up now in the son whose father sought the ultimate lotus, dying by his own hand.

But the lotus of the living calls again. Bloom passes gelded horses, all passion spent; reflects, going by the cabman's shelter, on the life of the 'drifting cabbies, all weathers, all places, time or setdown, no will of their own'. At last, watched by 'a wise tabby, a blinking sphinx', he is able to read his letter in peace. It is from a certain Martha Clifford, a passionate pen-friend whom he has never met, a slushy letter with an odd mistake in it: 'I called you naughty boy because I do not like that other world.' At least one edition of *Ulysses* silently corrected 'world' to 'word', thus ruining that scene in Nighttown where Stephen's mother, risen from the dead, unconsciously quotes Martha: 'I pray for you in my other world.' It is one of the minute devices for drawing Stephen and Bloom together.

Enclosed in the letter is Bloom's own rebus–a flower, dried and with almost no smell. Bloom re-reads, 'weak joy' opening his lips, and Joyce, seeking a direct means of conveying the act of re-reading without actually repeating the whole text of the letter, throws flowers at us: 'Angry tulips with you darling manflower punish your cactus if you don't please poor forgetmenot how I long violets to dear roses when we soon anemone meet all naughty nightstalk wife Martha's perfume.' Botany is with us all the time, but now the specific lotus-eating motif, with Oriental orientation, is renewed through the very name Martha. 'Martha, Mary . . . He is sitting in their house, talking.' Bloom, a Jew, is not willing to mention the holy name, but he unconsciously recognises that Christ is a lotus-symbol: 'Long long long rest.' Thus he is led to the church of All Hallows, weaving a little fantasy about missionaries, opium, Buddha, joss-sticks,

Christ's thorns, St Patrick's shamrock, religion lapped up like milk. Mass is being said, and the Eucharist emerges for Bloom as the supreme lotus. He is sceptical about all religions, but he concedes a value to this 'bread of angels'–'there's a big idea behind it, kind of kingdom of God is within you feel'. As for the believers, they are partly summed up in an old man asleep near a confessional: 'Blind faith. Safe in the arms of kingdom come. Lulls all pain. Wake this time next year.' Other lotus themes appear–music, liquor (Benedictine and Green Chartreuse), eunuchs ('one way out of it'), women, flowers, incense. When the priest prays: 'Blessed Michael, archangel, defend us in the hour of conflict', we are reminded of what the Church still means to another non-believer, Stephen. Stephen will no longer even go through the forms of faith, but Bloom openly admires the strength and organisation of Catholicism.

It is ten-fifteen, and the funeral is at eleven. After botany, chemistry, or at least a chemist's shop. Bloom has to get a lotion made up for Molly, but he realises that he has left the recipe, as well as his latchkey (hence no easy homecoming if he is late) in his other trousers. In Sweny's shop on Lincoln Place his thoughts naturally turn to herbs, electuaries, simples, love-philtres while the chemist looks up Molly's prescription in his book. Sweet perfumes lull his senses to a mood of sexual abandon. He will go and take a bath in the mosque-shaped Hammam (the East again) and, while in the bath, he will masturbate. In his very first two chapters Bloom, after the burnt offering of the kidney, seems concerned with a total cleansing and a total evacuation of the body's secretions. A clean Jew, he is a nice contrast to the dirty Christian he will make his son. (Stephen rarely washes and never baths: after all, 'all Ireland is washed by the Gulf Stream'.) Bloom buys some lemon-scented soap.

Today is the day of the Ascot Gold Cup, and Bantam Lyons (another *Dubliners* character) sees Bloom's newspaper as Bloom leaves the shop. 'I want to see about that French horse that's running today', says Lyons. 'Where the bugger is it?' Bloom decides to give him the newspaper to get rid of him. But, generous and good as he is, some of the gods are against him. He says: 'I was just going to throw it away.' Lyons knows and we, who have looked up our copies of Cope's *Racegoer's Encyclopaedia*, also know that a horse called Throwaway is running in the Ascot Gold Cup. We know, and all Dublin will eventually know, that Throwaway won that race at 100–5. Lyons thinks he has been given a tip: Bloom is a dark horse himself, innocent-seeming but full of guile and secret knowledge.

The cunning of Odysseus led to the planting of a dark horse in the Trojan camp: this horse is the means of gaining the exile further hatred from a community that already both fears and despises him. Bloom is prudent and does not gamble; but, when the time comes for spending winnings in bars, who will believe that?

So, through 'heavenly weather' which Bloom, philosophical about change, knows cannot last, the wanderer proceeds to his bath. The stream of life can be halted for a moment, be tamed to warmth and the service of cleansing. The image of the Eucharist hovers: 'This is my body.' He foresees it and, at its nub, his flaccid penis – 'the limp father of thousands' – turned into a 'languid floating flower'. But all this is an interlude, with time and history and destiny suspended, his navel not connecting him with the past (remember Stephen and the omphalos) but a mere harmless 'bud of flesh', a lotus. After the rest and the cleansing he must engage the dirt and the rewards of life.

5: Hell, Wind, Cannibals

JOYCE DESCRIBED THE TECHNIQUE OF THE LOTUS-EATING CHAPTER as 'narcissistic', and this explains its occasional references to water—not just the water of Lethe which is cognate with the juice of the lotus–but water as a stroker, warmer and flatterer. So far we have looked at the world, and at the man himself, from out of Bloom's own flesh and guts: 'This is my body.' What we have learned of Bloom does him credit. He has not hidden himself from us with veils and masks, for his author has not given him that opportunity. He is revealed wholly as a man of average fleshly appetites, kindly curiosity, an optimism tempered by long knowledge of the world (though he is only thirty-eight), strong family feeling, considerable general benevolence. It is time to meet him in the company of his fellow-citizens, but, before launching him on a journey to and through Hades, we ought to note what bodily organ rules over his next adventure. It is the heart. The heart is a pump, so Bloom matter-of-factly notes, that grows rusty and faulty and breaks down. In the graveyard, while Dignam's body is being committed to the earth, he is aware of death as that and no more–the failure of a pump. It is not the opening of a door on to ultimate reality. Though religion is the study woven into this chapter, it is not religion as it was presented in the first episode of the *Telemachia*, the terror and majesty of theology. Religion to Bloom is priests and prayers, conventional ceremonies performed when the human pump fails and the body is buried, a parcel of useless rubbish.

But we remember that the word 'heart' has another connotation, and that this fits Bloom very well. He is body, opposition and complement to Stephen Dedalus's intellect, but he is also feeling, warmth, love. Soon we shall see that this is the very quality which marks off Bloom from the rest of weak, irresponsible, cadging Dublin, and which–as with so many other great fictional heroes–earns him contempt and something like fear. At the moment, stepping into a carriage of the funeral cortège, he is with men who are reasonable enough citizens, though weak, who may not altogether understand Bloom but who are tolerant of him and his foreignness. His three companions bring *Dubliners* and *A Portrait* together: Simon Dedalus, Stephen's consubstantial father, irascible, pungent of speech, very much the man we have met before, though older, a widower, far advanced in decay; Martin Cunningham, from 'Grace', a good-natured and intelligent man, as close to Bloom's quality as anyone in the book; Mr Power, youngish, insipid, given to debts, another of that businessmen's retreat congregation in 'Grace'.

The Homeric parallel is Odysseus's voyage to Hades, the land of the dead. Death is in Bloom's thoughts right from the start–his son's death, his father's. But, the first hint of a new son to fill the vacarcy, Stephen Dedalus–'a lithe young man, clad in mourning, a wide hat' –is seen passing Watery Lane. Mr Dedalus snarls briefly about 'that Mulligan cad' and his wife's people, the 'drunken little costdrawer and Crissie, papa's little lump of dung, the wise child that knows her own father'. They come to the Dodder, one of the four waterways of Hades, the others being the Liffey and the Grand and Royal Canals. Mr Dedalus resumes his diatribe on Mulligan–'a counter-jumper's son'–and Bloom, reflecting that a father is right to be full, as Mr Dedalus is, of his own son, brings the name of the dead child, 'little Rudy', to the surface of his interior monologue. His need for a son remains but, young as he and his wife still are, the philoprogenitive urge is gone (we anticipate the Shakespeare of Stephen's discourse– his son Hamnet dead at eleven, but no second–second-best–son).

They go past the Dogs' Home–a whiff of the Cerberus motif to come–and Bloom remembers his dying father's wish: 'Be good to Athos, Leopold . . . We obey them in the grave. A dying scrawl. He took it to heart, pined away. Quiet brute. Old men's dogs usually are.' The name 'Athos' suggests 'Argus', Odysseus's dog, and, for a moment, Bloom seems identified with Telemachus. This father-son confusion is germinal to the book. But so, of course, is the suitor theme, and it is not long before Blazes Boylan goes by, 'airing his quiff'. Bloom's interior comment is direct: 'Worst man in Dublin.' But our present business is with getting to Hades, and we are already seeing ghosts of great dead men in the form of public statues–Sir Philip Crampton, Farrell, Smith O'Brien, 'the hugecloaked Liberator's form'. A story about the son of Reuben J. Dodd, the money-lender, and his comic attempt at suicide in the Liffey brings a reference to a boatman (Charon) to whom Dodd gave the obol of a florin for saving his son by fishing him out with a pole. And when Mr Dedalus and Mr Power eulogise dead Paddy Dignam, Bloom remembers that he died of drink – 'Blazing face: redhot. Too much John Barleycorn' – and we remember that this also happened to Odysseus's companion Elpenor, who fell from the roof of Circe's palace dead drunk. We are approaching the gates of Hell.

A child's coffin recalls dead Rudy, and at once – father motif following the son – Mr Power talks about the disgrace of having a suicide in the family. Martin Cunningham sees the indiscretion of this in Bloom's presence. When Mr Dedalus says that suicide is cowardice, he is quick with 'It is not for us to judge.' Bloom inwardly appreciates this – 'Always a good word to say' – and is led on to pity the hellish torments-in-life that Cunningham undergoes. It is his wife who leads him 'the life of the damned', pawning the furniture every Saturday, drunk, singing 'They call me the jewel of Asia' (a useful Oriental theme for later development in Bloom's fantasy life). Poor Cunningham is both Sisyphus, pushing a colossal burden uphill only to see it fall down again ('Wear the heart out of a stone, that'), and Ixion ('Shoulder to the wheel') tied to his burning circle. Then we are back with Bloom's own tormented father, 'the redlabelled bottle on the table'.

We are given, still rolling hellwards, plenty of reminders that life has to go on, in spite of other people's deaths – the Gordon Bennett race in Germany, a barrel-organ playing 'Has anybody here seen Kelly?' But the Mater Misericordiae, at the top of Bloom's own street, brings death back to mind with its ward for incurables: Bloom temporarily forgets that a hospital's function is to heal. He thinks of old Mrs Riordan dying in Our Lady's Hospice. She was, we remember, Stephen's governess Dante: another small stitch in the fabric of Bloom-Stephen *rapprochement*. And then when a drove of cattle appears – 'Roast beef for old England' – we know we are looking at the ghostly herd of Orion, Orion himself shouting 'Huuuh! Out of that!' as he cracks flanks with his switch (bronze mace in the Odyssey). Death and hell forever supervene on life.

The Royal Canal, and another Charon on his barge. The dead figures of the stonecutter's yard, mutely appealing to cross to the further bank. An old tramp, another Sisyphus, condemned to pounding Ireland's hills for ever. The house where Childs was alleged to have murdered his brother. More statues among the poplars of Prospects – 'white forms and fragments streaming by mutely, sustaining vain gestures on the air'. They have arrived at the doors of

Hades. A hawker is selling simnel cakes. Bloom thinks: 'Cakes for the dead. Dogbiscuits.' The dog Cerberus had to be fed with such dainties. Paddy Dignam's corpse, like the soul of Elpenor, has arrived in Hades before them. Here is a 'leanjawed harpy', one of the mourners. Bloom reflects, thinking of Dignam's widow, 'There are more women than men in the world'—a tag to be taken up later that day by the ghost of Stephen's mother. And now comes Cerberus himself, the priest who is 'bully about the muzzle', 'with a belly on him like a poisoned pup'. He shakes holy water over the coffin, the water of Lethe. The one word 'sleep' comes to Bloom's mind. And all the time he is aware of the city of the dead, of which Glasnevin Cemetery is but a suburb, taking in its fresh batches every day. As with Gabriel Conroy in 'The Dead', there comes this image of the other world as, paradoxically, having a life of its own.

Mr Kernan, an Ulsterman from *Dubliners*, tells Bloom that the vernacular is more powerful than any Latin in a service for the dead: '*I am the resurrection and the life*. That touches a man's inmost heart.' (That word 'heart' appears again and again.) The rationalist Bloom tells himself: 'The resurrection and the life. Once you are dead you are dead.' But still, central to the philosophy of Joyce's novels, the two worlds intermingle. John Henry Menton, the solicitor, whom Bloom once beat at bowls, praises Molly Bloom—'a finelooking woman'—to Ned Lambert, but asks: 'What did she marry a coon like that for?' When Bloom, at the end of this chapter, points out to him that his hat has a dinge in it, Menton snubs him. ('How grand we are this morning', thinks Bloom.) His haughtiness is the haughtiness of dead Ajax in the Odyssey. At the same time, the genuinely dead—Daniel O'Connell and Parnell—join the Greek fellowship as Heracles and Agamemnon. The lord of Hades is another O'Connell—John—who is very much alive: he has married a fertility goddess (like Persephone) who has given him eight children. Everybody wants to be on good terms with him: it would not do to get on the wrong side of Pluto. If we have been looking for Tantalus—hungering and thirsting amid sustenance that flies away or turns to dust as soon as he tries to snap at it—it is O'Connell himself who supplies his tortures. He makes love near the tombstones, and this must be 'tantalising for the poor dead'. As for Prometheus, whose liver was exposed to the eternal pecking of vultures, we must find his analogue in the statue of Christ pointing to his Sacred Heart, at which the sins of the world nibble.

The Homeric parallel is worked out at considerable length in this chapter, but it is no mere game. It lends a kind of sempiternal dignity to the naturalism of this cemetery scene; it binds together sundry broodings on death. Alone among the Catholic mourners, Bloom has no confidence in the doctrine of personal immortality. He faces up to the facts of death, proclaims to himself that there is still plenty of living to be done before the dark iron-cheeked god gets him. Still, every man yearns for immortality and Bloom has lost his chance of gaining it through a son of his own loins. The prophet Tiresias–whom Odysseus went to consult in Hades–says nothing to Bloom in his disguise as Robert Emmet. All that Bloom meets is death, the failure of a pump–death, death, and more death. Having meditated with him on man's inescapable tragi-comic end, there is little need for us to meditate again. The last drop has been wrung out of the subject, and the sensation of 'going under' has never so thoroughly been expressed: everything gapes and yawns (even a tramp's boot) and even the road is up, exposing the rusty pumps of the living city. Bloom comes through the dank confrontation, as he comes through everything, very well. Death is not going to get him 'this innings'. As for the future life, that is already in preparation for him: he will contrive his immortality through contact with the intellectual imagination–the poet who will, when he is Bloom's own age, start setting down this chronicle. In an age feverish for records, we have no record of the death of Bloom.

But, after the funeral, life calls again, the claims of the living and a living are reasserted. Bloom is an advertising canvasser, a job on the outermost fringes of the vocation of letters; Stephen, a poet, is at the very heart of literature. Both meet–or nearly meet–in the one area that will accept them both–journalism. After the dead colours white and black, the living colour red–colour of blood and sensationalism–gushes out in the scene set in the office of the *Freeman's Journal and National Press*. This is the home of Æolus, the wind-god. The presiding organ must be the lungs, and the built-in art the windy one of rhetoric. The chapter must move not by steps of logic but by the oratorical puffing device of the enthymeme–a type of syllogism (or logical statement) which suppresses its major or minor premise, assuming a truth rather than stating it. Joyce has laborious fun here. He crams the text with examples of rhetorical devices– figures of speech, puns, perversions of language; he also pins us down to the rhetorical craft of journalism by punctuating the action with headlines. These headlines provide a skeletal history of journalism. They begin stately–'IN THE HEART OF THE HIBER-

NIAN METROPOLIS'—and end facetious: 'SOPHIST WAL-
LOPS HAUGHTY HELEN SQUARE ON PROBOSCIS.
SPARTANS GNASH MOLARS. ITHACANS VOW PEN IS
CHAMP' (even the popular press is drawn into the surge and thun-
der of the Odyssey).

Bloom is concerned with arranging for a 'puff' for one of his
advertising clients, Alexander Keyes. 'WE SEE THE CANVAS-
SER AT WORK' (canvas–ship–wind). He can have a 'little par'
in the *Telegraph* (an evening paper managed by the *Freeman*) if he
will give a three months' renewal of his advertisement. The advertisement itself is to embody a rebus of two crossed keys, and
Bloom has seen a suitable design in a Kilkenny paper: his search for
this is, through the National Library, to bring him closer to Stephen.
First, though, Keyes himself has to be consulted about the proposed
arrangement: Bloom is caught up in a little gale of business. He
enters the *Telegraph* office to telephone, and he finds a number of
Dublin characters—Simon Dedalus, Ned Lambert, Professor Mac-
Hugh ('professor' very much a courtesy title: the small Latin teacher
has blown himself up)—laughing at a piece of windy rhetoric
('. . . 'neath the shadows cast o'er its pensive bosom by the overarch-
ing leafage of the giants of the forest'). Bloom's interior monologue
is full of Æolian references to bladder-bags, gale days, windfalls,
'what's in the wind', weathercocks, 'all blows over', and Professor
MacHugh calls the author of the rhetoric an 'inflated windbag'.
As though driven by violent blasts, all the characters act testily
or impatiently or move nimbly. The Editor, Æolus himself, is red
and harsh and loud. If, in all this wind, we miss some of the rhetorical
tropes, Lenehan the sports writer (one of the two gallants of *Dubliners*) is ready to give us easy spoonerisms. 'There's a hurricane
blowing', cries the Editor, and even language is blown and dis-
hevelled into 'I hear feetstoops' and 'Clamn dever'.

When Bloom goes off to see Keyes we have one of our rare opportunities of viewing him from the back, 'a file of capering newsboys'
in his wake. 'Look at the young guttersnipe behind him hue and
cry,' says Lenehan, 'and you'll kick. O, my rib risible! Taking off his
flat spaugs and the walk. Small nines. Steal upon larks.' This is a
typical reaction to Bloom. He can never be treated normally. He is
either a figure of fun or a foreign mystery to be admired, feared,
rarely trusted. Once he is gone, taking his interior monologue with
him, the world grows flatter. The gap can only be filled by another
interior monologue: it is time for Stephen, bullock-befriending bard,

to enter with Mr Deasy's letter for the press. He is accompanied by Mr O'Madden Burke: 'Youth led by Experience visits Notoriety.' Telemachus, young, blushing, has to hold his rhetorical own in the council of mature men, but the time is not yet. He must listen first, aware of his youth. When the Editor asks Stephen to write something for him, adding 'You can do it. I see it in your face', we are back to Conglowes and Father Dolan: 'See it in your face. See it in your eye. Lazy idle little schemer.'

Bloom tries to re-enter, remotely, by telephone, but the Editor, changeable as a wind-god should be, says: 'Tell him to go to hell', unaware that he has been there already. Stephen is on his own, great gales of oratory blown at him, though in that remembered eloquence of John F. Taylor Bloom's people are brought in as type of all oppressed nations, prototypical Irish. Stephen's thoughts are driven eastwards: 'By the Nilebank the babemaries kneel, cradle of bulrushes: a man supple in combat: stonehorned, stonebearded, heart of stone.' Stephen asserts himself, makes himself mature, though not with loud speech: he has money, he suggests a drink. 'Chip of the old block!' cries the Editor: Stephen is son of the wrong father. And yet the long anecdote he tells on the way to the pub has the 'Promised Land' theme in it—*A Pisgah Sight of Palestine or the Parable of the Plums*. It is a story of two elderly Dublin women who want to see Dublin from the top of Nelson's pillar. They climb up, provisioned with brawn, panbread, and plums, but then—'too tired to look up or down or to speak'—eat their plums and spit the stones out between the railings.

Bloom catches the Editor, himself 'caught in a whirl of wild newsboys', as he goes off to drink with Stephen and the rest. He has seen Keyes, and Keyes will give a two months' renewal of his advertisement if he can get his par in the *Telegraph* Saturday pink. But Æolus was inhospitable when Odysseus returned to him, all the adverse winds released from their bag. Now the Editor is rude. 'What will I tell him, Mr Crawford?' asks Bloom, and Mr Crawford replies: 'Will you tell him he can kiss my arse?' For good measure he adds: 'He can kiss my royal Irish arse. Any time he likes, tell him.' Bloom, the new Moses, is scorned. The bits of Irish nationalist oratory which have been re-delivered in Stephen's presence were ready enough to draw their analogies from the Egyptian bondage, but a living breathing Jew is rudely slighted. And Stephen is arm in arm with these shiftless Irish citizens who are all wind, off for a drink, having told a very Irish story about a Promised Land with plum-stones dribbled all over it. Rhetoric is nothing but an empty noise.

From the windy lungs to the windy stomach, or rather oesophagus. In the next chapter everybody goes to lunch. The Homeric parallel is to be found in the episode of the Laestrygonians, the cannibals who devoured so many of Odysseus's companions. Bloom and his fellow-citizens are all moved, peristaltically—as food is moved on the long road to digestion—through the great digestive tracts of the city; they are contained in a digestive system, and thus the cannibalistic motif holds well. Bloom's interior monologue is obsessed with food, often regurgitating with more disgust than gusto as he sees the one o'clock Dubliners gorging themselves like little Laestrygonians. And yet, in this welter of eating, we must hang on to some vestiges of human dignity. Bloom sees the ritual aspects of slaughtering and cooking, the blood victim and the burnt offering, and leads us on to the noblest of all human arts through considering the building of altars and the shedding of blood on the foundation of a public edifice. Architecture seems to blend strangely with eating, but Bloom finds a connection. These Dublin streets, coiling like intestines, are more than guts through which the citizen-gobbets are sluggishly impelled. They are a pretext for magnificent architectural erections.

But food, food as gutsy excess, dominates Bloom's thoughts—gormandising priests ('I'd like to see them do the black fast Yom Kippur . . . One meal and a collation for fear he'd collapse on the altar'), drunken rats floating on vats of porter ('Drink till they puke again like christians'), nuns frying everything in the best butter. Even the Liffey brings to mind Reuben J. Dodd's son swallowing 'a good bellyful of that sewage', while greedy gulls flap strongly over the water. Bloom, always kind to animals, buys a Banbury cake to feed them. The little rhyme he makes up about them—'The hungry famished gull / Flaps o'er the waters dull'—leads him temporarily to the *Hamlet* motif (awaiting its full development in the chapter that comes after): 'Hamlet, I am thy father's spirit . . .' He is not concerned about the meaning of the blank verse, however—only, and not with any great curiosity, the form. As for the gulls, they give him no thanks: 'Not even a caw.' They are typical Dubliners.

The river flows on, rowboat at anchor on its 'treacly swells', and the rowboat advertises *Kino's 11/- Trousers*. Bloom gives this his professional approval and thinks 'All kind of places are good for ads.' A quack doctor once stuck up clap-cure posters in public urinals;

Bloom catches the image of 'some chap with a dose burning him' and then refuses to give shape to a particular horrid thought:

If he . . .
O!
Eh?
No . . . No.
No, no. I don't believe it. He wouldn't surely?
No, no.

The hour is approaching for the knocking on the door of Blazes Boylan, the rehearsal of 'Love's Old Sweet Song'. Bloom escapes back into meditations on words–'parallax', Molly's folk-etymologising of 'metempsychosis' (met him pikehoses)–and, through seeing five men advertising H. E. L. Y. S. on their five tall white hats, the safe world of advertising, though food (Plumtree's potted meat under the obituaries, 'cold meat department') is never very far away.

He meets Mrs Breen, an old friend of Molly's, who tells him, among other things, that another friend, Mrs Mina Purefoy, is in the lying-in hospital in Holles Street –'Dr Horne got her in. She's three days bad now.' This is important, for it will send Bloom, ever kind-hearted, to visit the hospital and thus become irrevocably involved in Stephen's future: Stephen, drunken poet, temporarily moneyed, will be carousing there with medical students. Nor is this concern about Mrs Purefoy's confinement a mere plot-device. Bloom, in his womanly way, feels for women in labour: in the nightmare of the brothel scene he will undergo labour himself and give birth to grown-up sons. It is an aspect of his maternal paternality.

Food, food, food. Constables march from College Street, off to their beats, in goose-step, fat soup under their belts; others make their way, marching, to the station, 'bound for their troughs'. These constables stand for the digestive process–the march of the food down the gullet, the entry of the nutriment into the blood-stream, dispersed then–as these about the city–into the various organs of the body. The decay and renewal of the body's parts, already prefigured in some of the images of the graveyard scene, is given more general treatment here:

Things go on same; day after day: squads of police marching out, back: trams in, out . . . Dignam carted off. Mina Purefoy swollen belly on a bed groaning to have a child tugged out of her. One born every second somewhere. Other dying every second. Since I fed the birds five minutes. Three hundred kicked the bucket. Other three hundred born, washing the blood off, all are washed in the blood of the lamb, bawling maaaaaa.

History is presented to Bloom as a sort of cannibalism, time eating cities as well as citizens, architecture itself ('Pyramids . . . built on bread and onions') an eater of building slaves but also food for time, leaving the faeces of rubble and big stones. 'No one is anything.' Bloom is depressed: 'Feel as if I had been eaten and spewed': the Laestrygonians have got at him.

After seeing George Russell (AE) and reflecting that aesthetes eat ethereal food–'only weggebobbles and fruit'–Bloom works towards hunger for lunch through love, an acceptable form of cannibalism: 'Perfumed bodies, warm, full. All kissed, yielded: in deep summer fields, tangled pressed grass . . .' Joyce, according to his friend Frank Budgen, was fond of the fancy that the fermentation of food into alcoholic liquor derived from love-play. Bloom, a page or so later, is to recall a day with Molly on the hill of Howth: 'Yum. Softly she gave me in my mouth the seedcake warm and chewed. Mawkish pulp her mouth had mumbled sweet and sour with spittle. Joy: I ate it: joy.' But it is to the twitterings of generalised voices of love that he enters the Burton restaurant: 'Jack, love!–Darling!–Kiss me, Reggy!–My boy!–Love!'

We have now one of the most realistic evocations of disgust at the act of eating that literature has ever given us. Meat-eating is, after all, a species of cannibalism: a pig or a rabbit can be, in life, a member of the family. Here the horror is neo-Hogarthian:

A man with an infant's saucestained napkin tucked round him shovelled gurgling soup down his gullet. A man spitting back on his plate: half-masticated gristle: no teeth to chewchewchew it. Chump chop from the grill . . . Smells of men. His gorge rose. Spaton sawdust, sweetish warmish cigarette smoke, reek of plug, spilt beer, men's beery piss, the stale of ferment . . . Look on this picture then on that. Scoffing up stewgravy with sopping sippets of bread. Lick it off the plate, man! Get out of this.

Cannibalism brings men low: the Laestrygonians have frightful table-manners. Bloom again proves himself a Superior Person. He leaves, appalled, and goes to Davy Byrne's ('moral pub') for a glass of burgundy and a cheese sandwich. Cheese, 'the corpse of milk', can be disgusting when one thinks about it or ('the feety savour') separates smell from taste. Bloom eats with 'relish of disgust', Nosey Flynn's perilous dewdrop at his snout's end not helping. Flynn also, chatting to Bloom about Molly's concert tour and bringing in the name of Blazes Boylan ('O, by God, Blazes is a hairy chap') impairs digestion: 'A warm shock of air heat of mustard hauched on Mr Bloom's heart. He raised his eyes and met the stare of a bilious clock.

Two . . . Time going on. Hands moving.' (*La ci darem la mano.*)
'Two. Not yet.' But not long to go now.

Before Bloom leaves the bar to reply to the quiet message from his
bladder he allows the main themes of the chapter to coalesce. The
process of ingesting, digesting, excreting is low–'food, chyle, blood,
dung, earth, food: have to feed it like stoking an engine. They have
no. Never looked. I'll look today. Keeper won't see. Bend down let
something fall see if she.' The architecture of the Library Museum
is embellished by the statues of naked goddesses. Bloom thinks,
though he cannot be sure, that these immortals have no back passages. This afternoon he will know for certain. There is a world
beyond the endless peristalsis, the moving forward in circles, which
men have to suffer. 'Nectar, imagine it drinking electricity: gods'
food.' He yearns towards it through idealised forms of his own wife:
'Shapely goddesses, Venus, Juno: curves the world admires.'

While he is out he is discussed. Davy Byrne–a landlord, one who
must speak well of everyone–says that he is a 'decent quiet man. I
often saw him in here and I never once saw him, you know, over the
line.' Nosey Flynn gives Bloom the regular Dublin tribute of respect
(he is generous, prudent) and suspicion (he is a freemason, he will
never put anything in writing). And then Paddy Leonard and Bantam Lyons come in, accompanied by Tom Rochford who has (it is
high time somebody had it) dyspepsia. Talk about the Ascot Gold
Cup and Bantam Lyons's smug winking over the tip he has had
('I'm going to plunge five bob on my own') coincides with Bloom's
reappearance. 'That's the man now that gave it to me', whispers
Bantam Lyons. Though Paddy Leonard goes 'Prrwht!' in scorn we
can feel the tension between Bloom and his fellow-citizens beginning
to tighten.

But Bloom has now left the pub and we go with him. In the urinal
that busy internal monologue has been ticking away, unheard of us
and the author; we re-enter it *in medias res*: 'Something green it
would have to be: spinach say. Then with those Röntgen rays
searchlight you could.' A dog vomits 'a sick knuckly cud' and laps it
up again. 'Surfeit. Returned with thanks having fully digested the
contents.' Lunch is ended; it is the hour for digestion, rumination,
defecation (Bloom passes closestools in the window of a plumber,
William Miller–an appropriate grinding name). The next meal will
be supper. Bloom, his sound-track back on *Don Giovanni*, skips '*La
ci darem*' and moves on to '*Don Giovanni, a cenar teco m'invitasti*':
'Don Giovanni, thou hast me invited to come to supper tonight.'

He thinks that 'tonight' may possibly be the translation of '*teco*'. But '*teco*' means 'with you', and it is hidden from Bloom that he will be taking a late collation with somebody important. Still, Bloom is never far wrong about anything, and this meeting will, in fact, give the night its meaning.

Food moves down the gullet into darkness. The caecum is an intestinal sac with a blind end. It is appropriate that Bloom should try and make himself blind about what is going to happen that afternoon in Eccles Street ('Today. Today. Not think') and that he should help a blind young man across the road. But then he has to wrestle with an attack of seeing that sends him into frightful confusion. 'Straw hat in sunlight. Tan shoes. Turnedup trousers. It is. It is.' Blazes Boylan. Bloom turns his eyes up to the eternal glory of pseudo-Greek architecture, making for the Museum gate. He fiddles in his pockets fussily, trying not to see or be seen by Boylan. He enters the abode of learning and Greek goddesses, temporarily safe from the grinding and digesting and chewing and spewing of the gutsy world.

6: He Proves by Algebra

WE HAVE BEEN OPPRESSED BY GUTS, BY VISCERAL ORGIES. THE time has come for the brain to assert itself. To a writer the brain's greatest achievement is literature, and the greatest name in all literature is William Shakespeare. The most interesting–if not the greatest–play of Shakespeare is *Hamlet*. The afternoon hour has struck for Stephen's promised disquisition on the meaning of that play. The scene is the National Library and the technique is a dialectical one, a moving towards truth–or at least plausibility–through the Socratic method of question and answer or proposition and counter-proposition. The Homeric parallel is Scylla and Charybdis, the rock and the whirlpool. The lines hold by the loosest of threads, the classical reference is fanciful rather than imaginative. And yet, in a chapter dominated by Stephen Dedalus, imagination burns as it has burned only once before–in the 'Proteus' section. It is right to be reminded of that section and its presiding art–philology. Without language there is no literature; without a literature no language can survive its speakers. It is this fact in relation to the Irish revival that John Eglinton (the editor of *Dana*, presented here under his own name) implies at the beginning:

–Our young Irish bards have yet to create a figure which the world will set beside Saxon Shakespeare's Hamlet though I admire him, as old Ben did, on this side idolatry.

It is Stephen's cue.

But the Quaker librarian, Lyster, has already, in his vague way, opened the door to Shakespearian discussion and at the same time hinted at the Scylla-Charybdis motif. In Goethe's *Wilhelm Meister*– 'a great poet on a great brother poet'–the soul taking arms against a sea of troubles also comes to grief against hard facts: whirlpool and rock. George Russell (AE) is here too, full of swirling mysticism about 'formless spiritual essences' which, he says, it is art's function to reveal. Stephen is all for the hard basic rock of biographical fact: the solution to the problem of interpreting art lies in the life of the artist–at least, this is true of Shakespeare. Russell offers Plato's world of universals (Charybdis the whirlpool); Stephen prefers to steer close to hard rocky Scyllan Aristotle. What is wrong, his interior monologue seems to tell him, with the Irish art which Russell exemplifies is its wishy-washy whirly theosophical insubstantiality. When Best (another historical character) comes in, it is to state that English Haines, that precious stone set in a silver sea, is waxing enthusiastic about Hyde's *Lovesongs of Connacht*–swirling watery lyrics. But Russell's reference to Mallarmé (France's 'finest flower of corruption') leads Best to mention the Mallarmé prose-poem on *Hamlet*–'*HAMLET ou LE DISTRAIT*'–so a French provincial theatre advertised it–'*Pièce de Shakespeare*'. Stephen translates '*Le Distrait*' as 'The absentminded beggar'. Then he is off on the dangerous voyage of his Hamlet *theory*.

The whirlpool is figured in Stephen's interior monologue. He has been drinking, he has had no lunch: thoughts and sensations swirl. But his speech is incisive and his facts are rock-solid. It is only his conclusions from the facts which fail to convince his auditors. He says, in effect, that it is wrong to identify Shakespeare with Hamlet, 'ineffectual dreamer' (Lyster's words). Hamlet is Hamnet, Shakespeare's own dead son; Shakespeare is the ghost, the wronged husband, deposed king; Ann Shakespeare, born Hathaway, is the guilty queen. Russell, naturally, objects to this 'prying into the family life of a great man'. Stephen, steering by the rock of hard cash, remembers that he owes Russell a pound–'A.E.I.O.U.'–and does not contradict him. But when Eglinton says that Ann Hathaway has no place in Shakespeare's works, that 'she died, for literature at least, before she was born', Stephen is quick and rude with his retorts. Ann was a wife and a mother (he thinks an instant of his own mother and his own guilt–'Who brought me into this world lies there, bronzelidded, under few cheap flowers'), and if Shakespeare made an error in marrying her, then it was a volitional error, 'a portal of discovery'.

What, in fact, can an artist learn from a mother and a wife? Socrates, remarks Eglinton, had a shrew-wife like Shakespeare; what useful 'portal of discovery' could she be? Stephen at once replies that he may have learned dialectic from her and from his midwife mother how to bring thoughts into the world. Fanciful but brilliant. And then we are back in the schoolroom, Stephen teaching young Sargent algebra and reflecting how impotent is a mother's love to protect her child from the trampling feet of the world. Socrates was condemned to death, and 'neither the midwife's lore nor the caudlectures saved him from the archons of Sinn Fein and their noggin of hemlock'. Here is Stephen's reply to Mulligan's proposal to Hellenise Ireland–the Hibernicising of Athens. There was never any golden age in Greece and prophets and poets are always liquidated if they do not toe the party line. Hence Stephen's cynicism about the Dublin literary movement ('We are becoming important, it seems') and his inward sneers at Russell's false Orientalism–'Yogibogeybox in Dawson chambers . . . Crosslegged under an umbrel umbershoot he thrones an Aztec logos, functioning on astral levels, their oversoul, mahamahatma.' Like Bloom, Stephen is not really of this provincial Dublin. He gives another copy of Mr Deasy's letter to Russell, politely asking for its publication in the *Homestead*. Russell is offhand, not sure: 'We have so much correspondence.' He rejects the oxen, symbols of fertility, as the whole Irish literary movement rejects them.

But we have to return to Shakespeare. Stephen proposes the theory that a Stratford Adonis was seduced by a Shottery Venus, but that the beauty of his heroines derived from that girl he left behind him. Shakespeare steers between the rock of home and the whirlpool of London. Soon, though, he is unsure of solidity anywhere: Ann is unfaithful to him. Here is one of the most delicious 'set-pieces' in all *Ulysses*:

> Christfox in leather trews, hiding, a runaway in blighted treeforks from hue and cry. Knowing no vixen, walking lonely in the chase. Women he won to him, tender people, a whore of Babylon, ladies of justices, bully tapsters' wives. Fox and geese. And in New Place a slack dishonoured body that once was comely, once as sweet, as fresh as cinnamon, now her leaves falling, all, bare, frighted of the narrow grave and unforgiven.

And so back to *Hamlet* and the cuckolded ghost that is Shakespeare himself. But, says Stephen, 'through the ghost of the unquiet father the image of the unliving son looks forth'. The artist, like Penelope, weaves and unweaves his image. The crass world of time and space presents the father and the son *Nacheinander* and *Nebeneinander*, but the artistic imagination makes them one. Stephen's argument is not always easy to follow, mainly because it is so laced with literary allusion and coloured with deliberate Elizabethanisms and clotted with eye-distracting paradoxes. But we reach at length the image of a father who has steered beyond the whirlpool and the rock of passion to become a ghost, a shadow finding life in 'the heart of him who is the substance . . . the son consubstantial with the father'.

We approach the whirlpool of theology, as Buck Mulligan–loudly shouting 'Amen!' from the doorway–is quick to remind us. 'You were speaking of the gaseous vertebrate, if I mistake not?' he says to Stephen. Mulligan, as we remember, is of the 'brood of mockers', and Stephen's interior monologue at once embarks on a grotesque credo about 'He Who Himself begot . . . sitteth on the right hand of His Own Self.' But the librarian thinks that Stephen himself may be a mocker who has presented a mere paradox, though one can never be sure: 'The mocker is never taken seriously when he is most serious.' We are led away, through Mulligan, from Shakespeare to Synge and are ready to forget about the father-son hypostasis. And then the eternal father himself appears, offstage, Bloom asking for the files of the *Kilkenny People* to find that design for the House of Keyes. 'A patient silhouette waited, listening.' Suddenly all the literary brilliance echoes hollowly. We remember Bloom's warmth and solidity, a fatherly substance, no ghost.

The mocker mocks. Mulligan cries, 'The sheeny! What's his name? Ikey Moses?' Bloom has left his card; Stephen hears his name for the first time. Mulligan rattles on: 'Jehovah, collector of prepuces, is no more. I found him over in the museum when I went to hail the foamborn Aphrodite . . . He knows you, he knows your old fellow. O, I fear me, he is Greeker than the Greeks. His pale Galilean eyes were upon her mesial groove.' (Bloom, the dogged enquirer, has at last found out about goddesses' back-passages.) Mulligan has turned Bloom into a Greek, then, and it is appropriate that the name 'Penelope' should start off a resumption of talk about Ann Shakespeare. Bloom's wife is Penelope, no more faithful than Ann; he is a cuckolded father without a son–we, if not Stephen, are beginning to find him Shakespearian. Stephen is concerned only with his theory.

He paints a fine picture of Shakespeare in London, dallying 'between conjugal love and its chaste delights and scortatory love and its foul pleasures'–Scylla and Charybdis again. Meanwhile, in Stratford, Ann–'hot in the blood. Once a wooer twice a wooer'–is committing adultery. Back to *Hamlet*: 'Two deeds are rank in that ghost's mind: a broken vow and the dullbrained yokel on whom her favour has declined, deceased husband's brother.' There is a choice of three Shakespeare brothers for the adulterous act–Gilbert, Edmund, and Richard. Stephen will deal with that later. In the meantime, there is this question of Shakespeare's meanness to his widow: the man who lived richly in a rich town left her his second-best bed. At this point Joyce breaks into blank verse which ends up, like Shakespeare himself, in drunken feverishness:

> Leftherhis
> Secondbest
> Bestabed
> Secabest
> Leftabed.
>
> Woa!

Shakespeare was mean, a speculator, hoarder, usurer. 'He drew Shylock out of his own long pocket.' John Eglinton asks Stephen to prove that he was a Jew (a word spelt, throughout *Ulysses*, with a small 'j', as to point Dublin's contempt and suspicion of Bloom's race). Stephen, fulfilling the book's pattern, does so fancifully. The Christian laws forced the Jews to hoard affection as well as goods. No man shall covet Shakespeare's chattels, nor his wife. If Shakespeare was a Jew, he was a most un-Bloomlike one.

But Eglinton will not have this probing into family. He agrees with Russell: 'What do we care for his wife and father?' We are back on the old motif. Bloom comes unbidden into Stephen's thoughts: 'Your own? He knows your old fellow. The widower.' And then his mother in her 'squalid deathlair'. Stephen cannot throw off family so easily ('Agenbite of inwit: remorse of conscience') and does not see how Shakespeare could. Boldly but hopelessly he throws out definitions that are crucial to the whole conception of *Ulysses*:

Fatherhood, in the sense of conscious begetting, is unknown to man. It is a mystical estate, an apostolic succession, from only begetter to only begotten. On that mystery and not on the madonna which the cunning Italian intellect flung to the mob of Europe the church is founded and founded irremovably because founded, like the world, macro- and microcosm, upon the void . . . Paternity may be a legal fiction. Who is the father of any son that any son should love him or he any son?

To himself Stephen says: 'What the hell are you driving at?' The answer is not young Stephen's so much as middle-aged Joyce's: 'I know. Shut up. Blast you! I have reasons.' Stephen pushes on:

The son unborn mars beauty: born, he brings pain, divides affection, increases care. He is a male: his growth is his father's decline, his youth his father's envy, his friend his father's enemy . . . Sabellius, the African, subtlest heresiarch of all the beasts of the field, held that the Father was

Himself His Own Son . . . Well: if the father who has not a son be not a father can the son who has not a father be a son?

Riddles, but the image of that special paternity of the imagination is being etched out, defined in terms of what it is not.

Stephen deals with the rest of the Shakespeare family and finds that, though Gilbert—his soul filled with the playhouse sausage—does not lend his name to any of his brother's characters, yet Richard and Edmund (the one the eponym of *Richard III*, the other the villain of *King Lear*) figure notably in the depiction of evil. The theme of the usurping or adulterous brother is always with Shakespeare, as is the theme of banishment. Dispossession is Stephen's own cry: Shakespeare is a kind of Telemachus. But he is too great to be so diminished, turned into a moaning son. Stephen agrees with Eglinton's summing-up: 'He is the ghost and the prince. He is all in all.' (In other words, he is God.) But Stephen unwittingly brings him closer to Bloom: 'His unremitting intellect is the hornmad Iago ceaselessly willing that the moor in him shall suffer.' So, in the brothel scene to come, Bloom is to desire and see enacted his own utter humiliation. Joyce now makes Eglinton confuse father and son: 'When all is said Dumas *fils* (or is it Dumas *père*?) is right. After God Shakespeare has created most.' It is as near as we will get to the blasphemous identification.

But Stephen is led to blasphemy a different way. The opposites—whirlpool and rock—between which we steer may be illusion. Travel itself may be illusion: 'We walk through ourselves, meeting robbers, ghosts, giants, old men, young men, wives, widows, brothers-in-love. But always meeting ourselves.' It is God—'the playwright who wrote the folio of this world and wrote it badly (He gave us light first and the sun two days later)'—who, merging all forms into one, His own, 'is doubtless all in all in all of us'. The 'hangman god' invoked by Stephen's mother looms, the enemy, old Nobodaddy.

The scene ends with Stephen's denial of the validity of his own theory. Mulligan leads the way out with medical-student ribaldry which, once again, takes in Bloom—'A man passed out between them, bowing, greeting.' Mulligan notes that Bloom, like, appropriately, the Ancient Mariner, fixed his eye upon Stephen. This, to Mulligan, can mean only one thing: 'He looked upon you to lust after you . . . O, Kinch, thou art in peril. Get thee a breechpad.' But, with Stephen, Bloom has at last registered. He remembers his dream of last night. In that dream he came to full Daedalian stature, no falling Icarus: '. . . I flew. Easily flew. Men wondered.' And after that came the street of harlots, the Oriental man who held out 'a creamfruit melon'. Twice so far Bloom and Stephen have very nearly met – once in a place of newspapers, once – higher up in the literary scale – in a place of books. Stephen does not know that soon there will be a real meeting, and that his own dream has pointed to it. In Kildare Street a kind of peace comes over him – 'Cease to strive' – and, though he sees no birds there now (he remembers himself as he was at the end of *A Portrait*), he notices that 'Frail from the housetops two plumes of smoke ascended, pluming, and in a flaw of softness softly were blown.'

This is a difficult, subtle chapter, as befits its central character, its subject, its symbol, and the art it glorifies. It draws on more literary forms than anything we have met so far – the lyric, the dramatic (both verse and prose), and an interior monologue that contains (like a whirlpool) concentric layers of reference, touching the very verges of consciousness. The vocabulary is immense and the Shakespearian scholarship formidable. An apparently simple theme – the drawing together of brain and heart and senses in a father-son symbiosis – is dealt with on various interlocking levels, some of which seem to contradict each other. It is enough for us to see in it a second (and final) presentation of the intellectual and imaginative powers of an immature poet and to consider how much this whirlpool needs to look across at a rock, image of steadiness. After such a chapter it will be a relief to encounter once more the simple life of the city, be involved in action, however trivial, and to get on with the story.

7: Labyrinth and Fugue

WE NEED TO STAY OUT IN THE DUBLIN STREETS FOR A WHILE AFTER the close atmosphere of the National Library. It is three o'clock in the afternoon, the hour when the blood is most sluggish. Joyce whips up the blood, draws attention to the wonder of its circulation, and allows it to rule this near-central chapter of his book (there are eighteen episodes in all; this is the tenth). Bloom and Stephen are temporarily free from the encumbrances of work and theory; there is no reason why, Dublin being so small a town, they should not now meet. But Joyce must reserve their meeting to a time of greater magic and drama–the night; moreover, though we have taken Stephen's measure, we have not yet learned enough about Bloom: Bloom must show more of himself, and he needs the foil of the city, not of the poet, for this. And there is the question of his necessary cuckolding, timed for after four, a consummation in which the intellectual imagination is not involved. Joyce has to use great cunning now. Here are the streets, and here are Stephen and Bloom walking through them, but they must be stopped–however artificially–from achieving contact.

Artifice is the very blood of this chapter. The 'art' featured is mechanics; the engineer in Joyce erects a small labyrinth at the centre of the great one which is the whole book. In this labyrinth there is confusion, a need for steering at least as careful as in the Scylla and Charybdis episode just completed. The classical parallel is provided by those Symplegades, or Wandering Rocks, between which Jason and the Argonauts had so perilously to navigate. (We are outside the Odyssey for a space; we are looking down on a model of the total structure.) Those clashing rocks formed an archipelago which is traditionally located in the Bosphorus–Europe on one coast, Asia on the other. Joyce has to find civic parallels here, and he finds them in representatives of the Church and the State, calm, fixed shores between which the citizenry wanders.

This episode was conceived spatially, and it is in order for us to look over it with a surveyor's eye, as though it were a map (Joyce in fact wrote it with a map of Dublin and a stop-watch in front of him). Count the number of sections in it, and you will find eighteen, the number of chapters in the entire book. In the first section we meet Father Conmee S.J., or rather re-meet him, since we have already made his rather remote acquaintance at Clongowes Wood, in *A Portrait*. In the final section we meet Lord Dudley, Viceroy of Ireland, driving through the city in proud cavalcade. Church and State are well-separated, parallel powers. Place your street-wanderers between them, in neat little parcels, and you will seem to have done— an easy and ingenious synthesis, a sort of *Dubliners* without plots. But nothing in Joyce is ever exactly easy.

Our problems begin with Father Conmee. Nothing could seem more straightforward than this representation of serene priestly authority:

The superior, the very reverend John Conmee S.J., reset his smooth watch in his interior pocket as he came down the presbytery steps. Five to three. Just nice time to walk to Artane. What was that boy's name again? Dignam, yes. *Vere dignum et justum est.* Brother Swan was the person to see. Mr Cunningham's letter. Yes. Oblige him, if possible. Good practical catholic: useful at mission time.

He goes on his way, saluted and saluting, meditating mildly on what he sees, on providence and men's souls. Then he stops to read his office by Rathcoffey. Without warning we are told: 'His thinsocked ankles were tickled by the stubble of Clongowes field.' But, we know, he is no longer at Clongowes. We are brought up short, our smooth passage impeded by a little rock. We seem to have taken the wrong turning in a labyrinth. Confusion is deliberately wished upon us. Then we realise that this is no displacement of time, only a mere memory of a past sensation. We can go on our way again, but we must remember to go carefully.

We must remember also that Joyce is remembering, despite all these perverse-seeming ingenuities, to carry on with his story. Father Conmee is doing something to help a bereaved Dignam (so, as will soon appear, is Bloom himself). In Eccles Street the bare arm of Molly, who is awaiting her lover, throws out a coin to a singing one-legged sailor who is growling a song about the 'onehandled adulterer', Lord Nelson. Blazes Boylan, not yet due at Molly's, is buying fruit in Thornton's–'far pears' and 'ripe shamefaced peaches'. The story is moving gently towards its various climaxes, but the technique seems to be living a life of its own. Thus, right in the middle of Boylan's little scene, a line thrusts in, apparently from nowhere: 'A darkbacked figure under Merchants' arch scanned books on the hawker's car.' Who is this–Stephen or Bloom? We shall not know until we reach the brief section from which the fragment is displaced. Soon we become used to the trick. Each section of the chapter concentrates on a particular Dubliner–either deeply involved in the plot, or presented only to be discarded almost at once–and into each section a brief passage from another section intrudes. Wandering rocks bump into us if we are unskilful navigators, but we can learn our way through the maze.

More examples. In the course of a conversation between McCoy and Lenehan this sentence pushes in: 'A card *Unfurnished Apartments* reappeared on the windowsash of Number 7 Eccles Street.' Then back to the conversation, which happens to be about the charms of Molly and, with a kind of reluctance, the peculiar distinction of her husband: 'He's a cultured allroundman, Bloom is . . . He's not one of your common or garden . . . you know . . . There's a touch of the artist about old Bloom.' Bloom himself, in the following section, is borrowing *Sweets of Sin* from a bookshop specialising in near-pornography. The scene is interrupted by: 'On O'Connell Bridge many persons observed the grave deportment and gay apparel of Mr Denis J. Maginni, professor of dancing &c.' We are then at once sent back to Bloom: '*Fair Tyrants* by James Lovebirch. Know the kind that is. Had it? Yes.' Another section shows us Mr Dedalus with no money to give to his daughters. He berates them: 'An insolent pack of little bitches since your poor mother died.' A fragment from another section breaks in: 'Mr Kernan, pleased with the order he had booked, walked boldly along James's street'; then we are back once more with Mr Dedalus and his daughters. Thinking we have endured our ration of floating rock, we are not ready for another collision: 'The viceregal cavalcade passed, greeted by obsequious policemen, out of Parkgate.' And then Mr Dedalus is allowed to finish his episode in peace.

Wandering rocks are, though unique, a natural hazard; a labyrinth is a man-made device for causing confusion. Both, Joyce seems to be telling us, are puzzles soluble by human memory and human cunning. The booby-traps placed in this chapter are external, mechanical obstacles for which we must be on the look-out. When one of the Dubliners–Cashel Boyle O'Conner Fitzmaurice Tisdall Farrell–strides past the windows of a Mr Bloom who is a dental surgeon, we have no excuse for confusing this Bloom with our hero. The duplication of names is a mere mechanical hazard. When the Viceroy of Ireland goes grandly by, only ignorance convinces two old women that they are seeing 'the lord mayor and lady mayoress without his golden chain' and Gerty MacDowell that this is 'the lord lieutenant'. The chapter is crammed with fallible machines: at one end is the whole clockwork universe which Stephen thinks an act of imagination might bid collapse 'but stun myself too in the blow'; at the other is Master Dignam's collar-stud, too small for its hole, so that his collar springs apart in salute of the Viceroy; in the middle is news from America of an explosion on the *General Slocum* and consequent shipwreck. On the whole the cosmic machine works well and the apparent rock-clashing confusion is really an artful laby-rinth. At the same time, though, a machine whose parts interlock so wonderfully may really be as unpredictable as the Symplegades. Parnell's brother plays chess in a DBC teashop: how much is skill and how much is chance?

Surrounded by machines – racing bicycles, dynamos in the power-house, 'Mickey Anderson's all time ticking watches', Tom Roch-ford's latest invention (a device to show latecomers to the music-hall what turn is on and what turns are over) – we may think that living is merely a matter of learning certain mechanical tricks of control. But Bloom and Stephen are here to remind us of the imponderables, the uncontrollable manic forces which will not submit to a mechani-cal reduction. Bloom, at a bookstall, is set upon by images of con-cupiscence conjured by *Sweets of Sin*; he becomes a mirror of adulterous Boylan. Stephen, also at a bookstall, meets his sister Dilly, who has bought a second-hand French grammar, and he is overcome with regret and despair – the family is breaking up, he cannot save his kin who are drowning in poverty: 'Agenbite of inwit. Inwit's agenbite. Misery! Misery!' (It is typical of Stephen, inciden-tally, that he should describe this very privy prick of conscience in archaic terms. It is an attempt to push the pain back into ancient literature, make it remote. This does not work, however. The past is all too real.)

Meanwhile the band, like a well-oiled engine, marches along, its polished instruments discoursing 'My Girl's a Yorkshire Girl'. The viceregal cavalcade slides through the city: the State is sure of its mechanical ability to order life. But so is the Church: Father Conmee, his 'smooth watch' ticking in his pocket, goes his smooth parallel way. The Viceroy is going to 'inaugurate the Mirus bazaar in aid of funds for Mercer's hospital'; the priest is going to help the Dignams. Even the exercise of charity is drawn into the machine: the heart is a ticking watch. But the hearts of Bloom and Stephen keep more irregular, more human, time.

When can a machine be also a living organism? When it is a piece of music. In this 'Wandering Rocks' episode Joyce has been essaying a sort of counterpoint, trying to achieve a kind of simultaneity of action in a medium that, being time-bound, fights against it. The labyrinth is mechanical, however, timed with a stop-watch and measured with a slide-rule. But music has been trying to dominate the chapter. The band plays; there is a significant conversation in Italian between Stephen and his teacher, Almidano Artifoni, about the sacrifice of Stephen's (or Joyce's) voice; even Father Conmee thinks of a song about the joy-bells ringing in gay Malahide. The cavalcade and the loud band take us straight into the next chapter, which is dominated by music. The mechanical labyrinth has become a work of art – a fugue; the ear is the presiding organ; we have come to the bone-heaped island of the Sirens.

The way into the lair of Miss Douce and Miss Kennedy – barmaids at the Ormond – is not easy. The first thing we meet is a collection of unintelligible fragments:

Trilling, trilling: Idolores.
Peep! Who's in the . . . peepofgold?
Tink cried to bronze in pity.
And a call, pure, long and throbbing. Longindying call.

There are just over two pages of these. Having sailed successfully between the Wandering Rocks, we would be right in guessing that lines like 'Clapclop. Clipclap. Clappyclap' and 'Goodgod henev erheard inall' will make sense when we meet them in context. They are, in fact, displacements of the kind we have already met in the preceding chapter. But their function is different: they are the musical themes which are to be developed in the score to come. Joyce loves a puzzle, but he does not like us to have to wait too long for the solution. And so his second theme – 'Imperthnthn thnthnthn' – makes sense very quickly. The pageboy has brought tea to the two Sirens. He is cheeky, and Miss Douce complains of his 'impertinent insolence'. The young brat immediately deforms that, cheeky still, into 'Imperthnthn thnthnthn'.

We have two things to wrestle with – the detail of the Homeric correspondence; a technique which tries to turn words into music with onomatopoeic fidelity. The Sirens themselves are the less trouble. Both have musical names–Mina (a pun on 'minor) and Lydia (a reference to the Lydian scale–F major with B natural instead of B flat). Because their Homeric prototypes lived on an island, they must be surrounded by marine associations. They 'cower under their reef of counter'; Miss Douce has been on holiday and has lain on the beach all day–'tempting poor simple males', teases Mr Dedalus; to remind us what they are in their mythical aspect, Bloom is made to look at a poster which shows 'a swaying mermaid smoking mid nice waves. Smoke mermaids, coolest whiff of all.' Miss Douce is the only Siren who sings, and she does not know the words of her song very well: 'O, Idolores, queen of the eastern seas!'–meaning '*my* Dolores'. The singing in this chapter is reserved for the tempted males. As for tempting, there is not much of that: they are barmaids, and it is part of their office to flirt mechanically with the customers. The Sirens are swirled up into the whorl of a huge ear, caught in a web of music.

The technique of this episode is described by the author as that of a *fuga per canonem*–a strict form which words are not really competent to imitate. We need not take it too seriously, then, though we ought to note that the subject of the fugue–the theme, that is, on which the composition is based–is represented by the Sirens themselves; the answer (technically, the subject sounded in another voice, a fifth higher or fourth lower) is Mr Bloom, entering the Ormond and monologuising; the counter-subject–the contrapuntal accompaniment to the answer and, from then on, to every re-statement of the subject–is Blazes Boylan, taking a final drink before going to Eccles Street then jingling off. Between re-statements of subject and answer there have to be brief interludes known as 'episodes', and these are provided by the songs sung by Mr Dedalus (tenor) and Ben Dollard (bass). It is all rather fanciful, but Joyce's real achievement here–foreshadowed among the Wandering Rocks–is the creation of genuine counterpoint of action. While the Sirens are drinking their tea and gossiping, Bloom is buying notepaper so that he can write a reply to his pen-friend, Martha Clifford. A mere reference to his name ('But Bloom?') is enough to make us aware of his own music playing horizontally to that of the Sirens. As the chapter advances, the technique grows subtler, and we can take in three or four strands of counterpoint at the same time–Bloom's unspoken thoughts; the singing in the concert-room; the knocking of Boylan at the door of Number 7 Eccles Street ('with a cock with a carra') and the tapping ('Tap. Tap. Tap') of the stick of the blind piano-tuner (the one whom Bloom helped across the road earlier that day) as he comes back to the Ormond to recover his tuning-fork (left on top of the piano he has tuned). The quasi-musical technique enables Joyce to indulge fully in a daring but successful device–that of allowing a single word, like a musical note, to sound a whole world of harmonics. Thus the word 'jingle'–thrown into the text with neither preparation nor resolution–stands for Boylan's riding off to see Molly Bloom in a jaunting-car and, proleptically, for the bouncing of the adulterous springs.

Bloom has been gathering themes all day. His most recent is provided by the book he has borrowed for Molly–*Sweets of Sin*–and its adulterer-villain Raoul. Raoul he identifies with Boylan; 'sweets of' or 'sweet are the sweets of' is enough to sound the overtones of his own sensual imaginings, his awareness of what is happening in Eccles Street (the hour is four in the afternoon), and a kind of pleased acquiescence in his cuckoldry. Soon this technique will not merely serve a celebration of the art of music: it will be integral to the whole pattern of the Bloom or Stephen interior monologue.

Bloom comes to the Ormond for a meal–liver and bacon: he remains inner-organ-loving and still defies the taboos of his ancestral religion. Stephen's uncle, Richie Goulding, sits near him, eating steak-and-kidney pie. Bloom is cut off from the seduction of the Sirens in the bar; he is also cut off from the sight of Mr Dedalus and Ben Dollard singing in the concert-room. Still, a true Dubliner, vocal music affects him deeply, colours his musings, drives his moods from joy to sadness. We disentangle him from a mass of musical tricks–a tremolo, for instance: 'Her wavyavyeavyheavy-eavyevyevy hair un comb:'d'; a staccato triplet: 'I. Want. You.'; hollow fifths: 'Blmstdp'–in which the vowels are missing ('Bloom stood up') on the analogy of suppressed thirds in common chords. We have recapitulations, ornamented cadences, appoggiaturas, but above everything we have an exploitation of the musical possibilities of sheer sound which can only be matched by that ultimate word-symphony *Finnegans Wake*.

Does the virtuoso display obscure this latest phase of the story? No, since the essence of the whole book is Bloom and his qualifications for the spiritual fatherhood of a poet, and we must meet Bloom's inner world at all its levels. Every fresh stimulus brings to the surface a new aspect of the man, and music–in a city passionately devoted to it–is a stimulus of considerable potency. But Joyce does

not forget that a crucial event is taking place at this afternoon hour –
Bloom's cuckolding. Boylan enters the bar to the tune of Lenehan's
'See the conquering hero comes', counter-subject to 'Between the
car and window, warily walking, went Bloom, unconquered hero.'
Joyce means this latter. Boylan is smiled on by the barmaids (one
of whom snaps her garter for him – '*Sonnez la cloche*') and shines in
all the glory of a provincial Don Giovanni, but he is essentially
ridiculous, and the musical technique serves to bring this out:

By Bachelor's walk jogjaunty jingled Blazes Boylan, bachelor, in sun,
in heat, mare's glossy rump atrot, with flick of whip, on bounding tyres:
sprawled, warmseated, Boylan impatience, ardentbold. Horn. Have you
the? Horn. Have you the? Haw haw horn.

(He has been described as 'Boylan with impatience' by Lenehan,
who also asked: 'Got the horn or what? Wait.') Impatient, anxious
to put horns on Bloom, Boylan continues on his way:

Jingle by monuments of sir John Gray, Horatio onehandled Nelson,
reverend father Theobald Matthew, jaunted as said before just now. Atrot,
in heat, heatseated. *Cloche. Sonnez la. Cloche. Sonnez la.* Slower the mare
went up the hill by the Rotunda, Rutland square. Too slow for Boylan,
blazes Boylan, impatience Boylan, joggled the mare.

Soon he is near Bloom's kidney-seller:

This is the jingle that joggled and jingled. By Dlugacz' porkshop
bright tubes of Agendath trotted a gallantbuttocked mare.

('Bright tubes' of sausages and the advertisement for 'Agendath
Netaim: planter's company' refer us back to that morning excursion
of breakfast-buying Bloom – before the letter from Boylan had
arrived.)

Bloom, meanwhile, liver and bacon finished, is writing his letter
to Martha Clifford – a more subtle kind of infidelity than his wife's.
At last Boylan arrives:

Jog jig jogged stopped. Dandy tan shoe of dandy Boylan socks skyblue
clocks came light to earth.

And then:

One rapped on a door, one tapped with a knock, did he knock Paul de
Kock, with a loud proud knocker, with a cock carracarracarra cock.
Cockcock.

(Boylan has already been identified by Bloom with one porno-
graphical villain. Now he becomes the actual writer of certain spicy
romances beloved of Molly Bloom: 'Paul de Kock. Nice name he

has.') The ridiculous betrayer is heard periodically from now till the end of the chapter: 'Cockcarracarra . . . With a cock with a carra.' Music must end soon, since it has been debased into silly rhythms to match Boylan's silly lust. The tap of the stick of the blind piano-tuner is heard more frequently now–a mere noise, though it suggests the still centre of sound represented by the tuning-fork he is coming for. Noises are starting in Bloom's inner organs: 'Pwee! A wee little wind piped eeee. In Bloom's little wee.'

Bloom, in Hades that morning, did not meet the seer Tiresias, in his reincarnation as Robert Emmet. But now he sees Emmet's last words in Lionel Marks's window: 'When my country takes her place among. Nations of the earth. Then and not till then. Let my epitaph be. Written. I have. Done.' This is punctuated by new, more urgent noises (Bloom blames his flatulence on the noontime glass of burgundy): 'Prrprr . . . Fff. Oo. Rrpr . . . Pprrpffrrppfff.' We are reminded of Joyce's devotion to sheer sound, meaningful or otherwise–the cat's cry, the noise of the printing machines in the 'Æolus' episode, the squeaking of Stephen's ashplant as he trails its ferrule on the ground behind him. And so, after a stretto in which all the themes of the chapter are gathered together over a pedal-point ('Tap. Tap. Tap. Tap'), Bloom pushes on to his next adventure. The song of the cuckoo, which mocks married men, is to be deferred till nightfall, but 'Love's Old Sweet Song' is doubtless now jingling happily away.

8: Fireworks

WE MUST NOTE TWO CHANGES THAT TAKE PLACE IN JOYCE'S approach to his technique from about the middle of *Ulysses* on. First, the chapters grow longer, as if the author is trying to make the fictional time–the time required for the enactment of the fictional events–correspond exactly to the reading time–the time required to read about those events. Second, he makes far greater use of parody. We have met parody sporadically so far–the skits on newspaper headlines and on newspaper rhetoric in the 'Æolus' episode, the Elizabethan and Irish Renaissance pastiches in the National Library. Now we find it employed pretty consistently. Joyce leans to condensation when writing in his own person–never a word too many. It is natural, then, that he should choose for parody styles which are tedious, gaseous, inflated. The length of the chapters and the nature of the parodies thus become aspects of each other.

Bloom goes to Barney Kiernan's tavern at five in the afternoon, looking for Martin Cunningham. Martin Cunningham has his connections with Green Street Courthouse, and Barney Kiernan's– crammed with curiosities of crime (murder-weapons, rope, forged money)–is close to the Courthouse. Bloom wants to arrange for the payment of Dignam's widow's insurance money, and Cunningham knows all about that. His errand, then, is a charitable one, but he runs straight into hate and contempt. In this tavern there is a loud-mouthed, drink-cadging Irish Nationalist known as 'The Citizen', a jingoist who hates all foreigners, especially Jews. His Homeric prototype is the giant cannibal Polyphemus, one of the race of one-eyed Cyclopes, shepherds good to their sheep but always ready to dash a man's brains out and devour his body in a couple of gulps. Polyphemus ate most of Odysseus's companions who went ashore and into his cave, but Odysseus saved himself by his usual cunning. He gave his name as Outis or No-man, he introduced Polyphemus to wine. When the giant was vinously asleep he prepared a pointed stake of wood in the fire, then put out Polyphemus's one eye with it. Polyphemus yelled, his neighbours came near his cave to ask what the matter was: had anyone harmed him? He replied that No-man had harmed him. His neighbours concluded that he was dreaming or delirious and went back to their homes. Odysseus and his uneaten men got away by clinging to the fleecy bellies of the giant sheep and being driven out to pasture with them, but, once embarked, the hero could not resist boasting. In rage, Polyphemus hurled a huge rock at the ship but, naturally, missed. A near thing, all the same.

It is Joyce's main purpose to emphasise the absurdity of gigantism, especially when it is one-eyed. The Citizen's vision is limited to the trampled-on greatness of Ireland, the hopes of her re-birth when the foul foreigner shall be driven out. His patriotism, he considers, earns him many free drinks and, by extension, his dog Garryowen free biscuits. But he is also a hero in his own right, a once-great athlete, still a man of muscle. Muscle is the part of the body that rules here, and the art of politics—in its narrowest aspect of chauvinism—sits over everything like the Irish giant himself. Joyce lets the Citizen have his say, but is quick to inflate him in the mock-epic style, though on a scale of ridicule unknown to his picaresque forebears:

> The figure seated on a large boulder at the foot of a round tower was that of a broadshouldered deepchested stronglimbed frankeyed redhaired freely freckled shaggybearded widemouthed largenosed longheaded deepvoiced barekneed brawnyhanded hairylegged ruddyfaced sinewyarmed hero. From shoulder to shoulder he measured several ells and his rocklike mountainous knees were covered, as was likewise the rest of his body wherever visible, with a strong growth of tawny prickly hair in hue and toughness similar to the mountain gorse (*Ulex Europeus*).

Joyce, like Rabelais, dearly loves a catalogue pushed to intolerable length, and he spends a page listing the 'tribal images of many Irish heroes and heroines of antiquity' which are engraved on the stones that dangle from the giant's girdle:

> ... Cuchulin, Conn of hundred battles, Niall of nine hostages, Brian of Kincora, the Ardri Malachi, Art MacMurragh, Shane O'Neill, Father John Murphy, Owen Roe ... Henry Joy McCracken, Goliath, Horace Wheatley, Thomas Conneff, Peg Woffington, the Village Blacksmith, Captain Moonlight, Captain Boycott, Dante Alighieri, Christopher Columbus, S. Fursa, S. Brendan, Marshal MacMahon, Charlemagne, Theobald Wolfe Tone, the Mother of the Maccabees, the Last of the Mohicans, the Rose of Castille, the Man for Galway, The Man that Broke the Bank at Monte Carlo, the Man in the Gap, the Woman Who Didn't, Benjamin Franklin, Napoleon Bonaparte, John L. Sullivan, Cleopatra, Savourneen Deelish, Julius Caesar ...

And so on, not forgetting Patrick W. Shakespeare, Thomas Cook and Son, and Adam and Eve. This ubiquitous cataloguing derives from Homer himself, who is precise and detailed about the furniture of the Cyclops's dwelling. Here, finally, is Garryowen:

At his feet reposed a savage animal of the canine tribe whose stertorous gasps announced that he was sunk in uneasy slumber, a supposition confirmed by hoarse growls and spasmodic movements which his master repressed from time to time by tranquillising blows of a mighty cudgel rudely fashioned out of paleolithic stone.

Then comes deflation into demotic Dublinese:

So anyhow Terry brought the three pints Joe was standing and begob the sight nearly left my eyes when I saw him land out a quid. O, as true as I'm telling you. A goodlooking sovereign.

The straight narrative, as opposed to the gigantesque commentary, is put into the mouth of an anonymous Dubliner with no literary pretensions–indeed, no pretensions at all except to the unlimited imbibing of other men's beer-treats. Anonymity and pseudonymity are appropriate to a chapter in which Bloom ceases to be Odysseus and becomes No-man. Thus, some play is made with Bloom's ancestral name, Virag; the Citizen's name is never once mentioned; the narrator is not sure whether a character is called Crofton or Crofter; Garryowen becomes Owen Garry–and so on. There are two other Homeric motifs which are cunningly planted–mere decoration–in the narrative: the eye (always singular) and the stake which put out the eye. These appear at the very start of the chapter, together with another Homeric reference:

I was just passing the time of day with old Troy of the D.M.P. at the corner of Arbour hill there and be damned but a bloody sweep came along and he near drove his gear into my eye.

Later we find Bloom smoking a 'knockmedown cigar'–again, a purely decorative allusion, since Bloom does not use the cigar as a weapon. But Joyce seems to find it necessary to press home the classical parallel even if his references are mere fancy. At the end of the chapter Bloom's name is suppressed entirely to remind us that he is No-man and 'a loafer with a patch over his eye starts singing *If the man in the moon was a jew, jew, jew.*' But what really interests us is not the ingenuity of technique so much as the genuinely heroic qualities that Bloom shows when set among jingoists, cadgers, and Jew-baiters.

Bloom is feared because he is both Jewish and part-Hungarian–

144

doubly a foreigner and, moreover, a man allegedly given to un-Irish practices, such as selling Hungarian lottery tickets and buying cream for his wife. He is recognised as uxorious but is also called a 'pishogue – a half-and-half'. Unlike the Citizen, he does not believe in the use of force to settle arguments and – to a response of contempt which turns to outrage – he dares to preach the doctrine of love. The parodic technique seems to sneer along with the Citizen:

Love loves to love love. Nurse loves the new chemist. Constable 14A loves Mary Kelly. Gerty MacDowell loves the boy that has the bicycle. M.B. loves a fair gentleman. Li Chi Han lovey up kissy Cha Pu Chow. Jumbo the elephant loves Alice the elephant . . . His Majesty the King loves Her Majesty the Queen. Mrs Norman W. Tupper loves officer Taylor. You love a certain person. And this person loves that other person because everybody loves somebody but God loves everybody.

But Bloom finds himself in trouble for another reason. When he leaves the pub to look for Martin Cunningham in the Courthouse, Lenehan, prince of cadgers, says: '. . . The courthouse is a blind. He had a few bob on *Throwaway* and he's gone to gather in the shekels.' We remember that, quite by accident, Bloom gave Throwaway as a tip for the Ascot Gold Cup to Bantam Lyons, telling him that he could keep his newspaper: 'I was going to throw it away that moment.' Nobody doubts for one second that this man who is a dark horse himself, possessor of access to secret information ('He's the only man in Dublin has it'), has made a tidy win: it is clearly his duty to push the boat out. But when he comes back he makes no move to order pints all round. Everything is set for a pogrom, and the Citizen is ready to start it. The narrator sums up the general attitude:

Courthouse my eye and your pockets hanging down with gold and silver. Mean bloody scut! Stand us a drink itself. Devil a sweet fear! There's a jew for you! All for number one. Cute as a shithouse rat. Hundred to five.

The Citizen says: 'Don't tell anyone', and Martin Cunningham – who is the book's real model of prudence – gets Bloom away, aware of coming trouble. The Citizen bawls: 'Three cheers for Israel!' and Bloom courageously answers him back:

– Mendelssohn was a jew and Karl Marx and Mercadante and Spinoza. And the Saviour was a jew and his father was a jew. . . . Your God was a jew. Christ was a jew like me.

This leads to one of the two solitary acts of violence in the whole of *Ulysses*, though it is weak and ineffectual enough. The Citizen – 'By Jesus, I'll brain that bloody jewman for using the holy name. By

Jesus, I'll crucify him so I will'—hurls after Bloom the biscuit-tin from which Garryowen has been devouring crumbs. The sun is in his eyes (i.e., he is drunk) and so, like Polyphemus, he misses. But the prose at once explodes gigantically:

> The catastrophe was terrific and instantaneous in its effect. The observatory at Dunsink registered in all eleven shocks, all of the fifth grade of Mercalli's scale, and there is no record extant of a similar seismic disturbance in our island since the earthquake of 1534, the year of the rebellion of Silken Thomas. The epicentre . . .

And so on.

What emerges from this brilliant and extremely funny series of parodies is a sense of the falseness of the values that the public world tries to impose on the individual. Joyce gives us skits on all kinds of puffed-up writing, from provincial newspaper reportage to Wardour Street English, taking in also technical jargon, monstrous but vacuous catalogues, rituals from which the life has gone, and the sesquipedalian evasiveness of parliamentary answers. It is the language which the State uses to hide behind when aware of the corruption of its enactments (politics, we remember, is the pseudo-art ruling this chapter); it is also the language of romanticism gone bad and turned to sentimentality—pretending to feeling when feeling has fled; it is the postures of little men pretending to be big. The communication media inflate language because they dare not be honest and call a spade a spade; popular historical novels falsify the past and simplify the motives which make historical change. Men are influenced by big loud empty words, styes which swell the eyelids and impede vision of the truth. Low as the garrulous narrator is, we can still see him as a creature not really taken in by humbug and, perhaps, ultimately on the side of Bloom rather than the Citizen: his speech is all deflation.

Bloom himself is totally undeceived by the shouts and promises of the politicians. If the world is to be improved it must be by the exercise of individual charity (he has only entered this ambience at all because of his desire to perform a charitable act). He uses the word 'love' and is derided for it. He is also derided for seeming to use the very language of inflation which fills the bellies of his enemies—terms like 'phenomenon' and 'mortgagee'. But when Bloom uses a word he normally uses it accurately. He comes close to Stephen, if not in imagination or the poetic gift, at least in a desire to rule language, make it serve truth, and not be ruled by it. He is David against the Philistines as well as against Goliath. He is the real deflator.

He wins through at a price. We do not meet him again till nearly nightfall—eight o'clock—and then he has become passive, convalescent, resting alone among the rocks on Sandymount shore. The encounter with violence has shaken this man of peace. But an unexpected reward awaits him. He is to possess the heart of the king's daughter Nausicaa, and she, in imagination, is to give herself to him. A direct sexual encounter would be vulgar, fit only for lechers like Boylan; what is needed for Bloom is the dignity of ritual, the rite of Onan. By a fine irony his happiness is to be encompassed by the very forces of inflation that have struck at him in the preceding chapter, only this time we can call inflation by a new name—tumescence.

Nausicaa is changed, by metempsychosis, into Gerty MacDowell, a sweetly pretty girl given to dreams and the reading of popular trash for women. It is in terms of this trash that she is described:

The waxen pallor of her face was almost spiritual in its ivorylike purity though her rosebud mouth was a genuine Cupid's bow, Greekly perfect. Her hands were of finely veined alabaster with tapering fingers and as white as lemon juice and queen of ointments could make them though it was not true that she used to wear kid gloves in bed or take a milk footbath either. Bertha Supple told that once to Edy Boardman, a deliberate lie, when she was black out at daggers drawn with Gerty (the girl chums had of course their little tiffs from time to time like the rest of mortals) and she told her not let on whatever she did that it was her that told her or she'd never speak to her again.

The parallel with Homer's princess (who Samuel Butler believed was the authoress of the Odyssey) is maintained fairly closely through all the flat whimsy. Nausicaa's race was known for its cult of clean linen, and it was to hold a large wash-day that she went down to the shore where Odysseus, hidden from sight, slept off the weariness of his long sea-tossing. Gerty MacDowell washes no garments now, but references are made to her delight in spotless undies and her pride in her many sets. She has come down to the seashore with attendant nymphs, most unnymphlike—Cissy Caffrey and Edy Boardman, together with 'the baby in the pushcar and Tommy and Jacky Caffrey, two little curly-headed boys, dressed in sailor suits with caps to match and the name H.M.S. Belleisle printed on both'. Nausicaa and her attendants played with a ball after the clothes-washing, and it was this ball, over-thrown, that woke up Odysseus. So here 'Master Jacky who was really as bold as brass there was no getting behind that' kicks the ball towards the rocks and Bloom, who is lying there, throws it back. It is then that Gerty notices our dark hero, mature, in mourning, his face wan and drawn, and is strongly attracted.

She could see at once by his dark eyes and his pale intellectual face that he was a foreigner, the image of the photo she had of Martin Harvey, the matinée idol, only for the moustache which she preferred because she wasn't stage-struck like Winny Rippingham that wanted they two to always dress the same on account of a play but she could not see whether he had an aquiline nose or a slightly *retroussé* from where he was sitting.

Gerty is virginal but all woman, like 'Mary, star of the sea', whose church on Sandymount strand is holding an evening service ('. . . there streamed forth at times upon the stillness the voice of prayer to her who is in her pure radiance a beacon ever to the storm-tossed heart of man'). She is to be worshipped rather than possessed, gazed on in her pure radiance, but she knows that the eye–which, along with the nose, is the dominant organ of the chapter–can be the window which lets passion come raging in. When the Mirus Bazaar fireworks begin and her companions rush off to see them over the housetops, she remains on the beach and feasts Bloom's eyes on a dream of well-filled hose, a richer, more leisurely, meal than *sonnez la cloche*.

We know what happens to Bloom because the fireworks tell us so:

And then a rocket sprang and bang shot blind blank and O! then the Roman candle burst and it was like a sigh of O! and everyone cried O! O! in raptures and it gushed out of it a stream of rain gold hair threads and they shed and ah! they were all greeny dewy stars falling with golden, O so lovely! O so soft, sweet, soft!

Tumescence has reached its limit. Bloom, who did not, after all, masturbate in the bath that morning, receives the reward of his continence. The tumescent prose comes to an end with Gerty walking off 'with a certain quiet dignity characteristic of her but with care and very slowly because, because Gerty MacDowell was . . .' Bloom's interior monologue, taking over at once, completes the sentence: 'Tight boots? No. She's lame! O!' And now a long session of detumescent evening musings brings on night and the toughest, yet most magical, part of the book.

The colours of this chapter are blue (for the Blessed Virgin) and grey (for the bitter waters of the sea–this, remember, is Stephen's territory–and the falling dusk). The art figured here is painting, but this does not quite come off. Joyce's intention is to give the eye (put out in the preceding episode) more than a feast of frillies, but he is temperamentally incapable of being very interested in this organ. Little pictorial episodes follow each other, like lantern-slides, in the romantic dreams of Gerty: pictures are her substitute for thought. Bloom thinks of colours ('depend on the light you see') and re-enacts in memory the *tableaux* of party charades, but his author's heart is not in it. Joyce is happier with the other organ, the nose, and lets Bloom luxuriate in remembered perfumes, especially the perfumes of women. But all women lead home to one–the adulterous Molly.

Has Bloom himself been unfaithful here on Sandymount strand? Technically, no. But he has achieved a sexual conquest more satisfying than any enacted on a strange bed–pleasure without regret or recriminations, no fear of pregnancy, no weeping, no going back, in detumescence, on tumescent promises. 'For this relief much thanks.' (We can never get away from *Hamlet*.) He has done better than Boylan today–an adoring letter and a sort of surrender, and both from virgins. And this brief auto-erotic session is also an unpremeditated preparation for the taking up of his responsibilities later that night. He will follow Stephen to Nighttown, but, being spent of seed, he will not be tempted by female flesh: he will be stern with prostitutes, unseducible. Odysseus was saved from enchantment into a swine because he carried Mercury's gift, the flower moly. Bloom carries this flower in his trousers–'a languid floating flower', no rod to beat him to his knees, gibbering in beast's lust, in the house of Circe.

Bloom closes his eyes for a moment at the end of the chapter– 'just for a few'. The interior monologue swoops deeper than ever it did in full daylight; it touches the borders of dreams and anticipates the sleep language of *Finnegans Wake*:

O sweety all your little girlwhite up I saw dirty bracegirdle made me do love sticky we two naughty Grace darling she him half past the bed met him pike hoses frillies for Raoul to perfume your wife black hair heave under embon *señorita* young eyes Mulvey plump years dreams return tail end Agendath swoony lovey showed me her next year in drawers return in her next her next.

One is persuaded that this is how the mind receives its images (little pictures all separate, no gluing of ideas together into logical statements) when it approaches sleep. Any reader presented with this passage unprepared would be baffled by it. If we have read *Ulysses* without skipping up to this point we shall recognise every single motif–Molly's version of 'metempsychosis', for instance, and the villain of *Sweets of Sin*, Raoul, who is identified with Boylan; Molly's first lover, Mulvey; the bit of newspaper ('Agendath Netaim') Bloom picked up in the butcher's that morning. Bloom's own recent sexual abandon and his brief sensuality on the street before breakfast, Molly in bed reading her lover's letter, the phrase 'her heaving embonpoint' from *Sweets of Sin*—all are fused into a single emblem of desire and its fulfilment. It is a miracle of compression.

But the bats fly, seeing nothing, and Bloom will not come face to face with the fact of his cuckolding. It is left to the cuckoo-clock in the priest's house, where, evening service over, Canon O'Hanlon and Father Conroy and the Reverend John Hughes S.J. are eating mutton chops with catsup, to proclaim to the world what Bloom now is—*Cuckoo Cuckoo Cuckoo*, and on to the stroke of nine. The night in which, cuckold or not, he shall beget a son and conquer all the suitors, is now beginning.

9: Bullockbefrienders

SHEER GOODNESS OF HEART, AND A KIND OF VICARIOUS MASOCHISM, send Bloom to the Lying-in Hospital in Holles Street at an hour when the pubs are gay and the theatres playing. Mrs Purefoy is trying to give birth and, as Mrs Breen told Bloom at lunchtime, having a hard time of it. Bloom knows her well and, with his capacity for imaginative penetration into the sufferings of women, is anxious to know how long it will be before she delivers. This is his motive for going to Sir Andrew Horne's house of labour and joy, but what comes out of the visit is the first fruitful meeting between himself and Stephen Dedalus. There have been two abortive contacts earlier in the day, but now Bloom and Stephen are to sit at the same table. Admittedly there will be the distraction of noisy company, tipsiness and ribaldry, for Stephen is carousing with the medical students in their common-room, but at last the *rapprochement* between body and soul, common sense and imagination is ready for parturition, and this chapter is an important one. Typically, Joyce refuses to let us have too clear a view of what is happening; he flashes an almost intolerable technical brilliance into our eyes, though this is not sheer wantonness. The Homeric correspondence must be kept up, an art or science celebrated, and a fresh literary technique attempted. This, though, is the most consciously virtuoso of all the episodes of *Ulysses*, and for some readers Joyce will seem to go too far.

Before, as a schoolboy, I smuggled my own copy of *Ulysses* into England, I was lent the Odyssey Press edition by my history master. This was in two volumes, and he gave me the second volume first. The second volume starts with this maternity hospital chapter, and I was thrown into the most difficult part of the whole book without preparation. But it seemed pretty clear what Joyce was trying to do. He begins with three ritual statements, each intoned three times. 'Deshil Holles Eamus'–let us go to Denzille and Holles Street.

'Send us, bright one, light one, Horhorn, quickening and womb-fruit.' I took this to be an invocation to Hecate, goddess of the moon and patroness of women in childbirth, but I should have realised that the moon has nothing to do with the 'horhorn'–the phallic erection with which generation starts. The 'bright one' is the sun. The 'horhorn' (I could not know this till I had read the 'Sirens' chapter) goes back to Boylan, the musical-comedy presentation of his lust, but Sir Andrew Horne is in the picture too. Finally, we hear the joyful cries of the midwife when a son is born: 'Hoopsa, boyaboy, hoopsa!'–three times, of course. Then I plunged into the real difficulties:

Universally that person's acumen is esteemed very little perceptive con-
cerning whatsoever matters are being held as most profitably by mortals
with sapience endowed to be studied who is ignorant of that which the
most in doctrine erudite and certainly by reason of that in them high
mind's ornament deserving of veneration constantly maintain when by
general consent they affirm that other circumstances being equal by no
exterior splendour is the prosperity of a nation more efficaciously asserted
than by the measure of how far forward may have progressed the tribute
of its solicitude for that proliferent continuance which of evils the original
if it be absent when fortunately present constitutes the certain sign of
omnipollent nature's incorrupted benefaction.

Gibberish? Possibly, but Latin gibberish–an attempt to turn English into a limping, lumpish travesty of Latin. Why? The answer came after three ghastly paragraphs in this style, Bloom to the rescue:

Some man that wayfaring was stood by housedoor at night's oncoming.
Of Israel's folk was that man that on earth wandering far had fared. Stark
ruth of man his errand that him lone led till that house.

No Latin here–indeed, nothing but Anglo-Saxon. Joyce's purpose became clear. The Latin stood for the feminine element–here shapeless and unfertilised–in the English language; the Anglo-Saxon represented the masculine. One would have to fertilise the other before English as we know it could come to birth. From then on the technique explained itself: a sort of history of English prose from Anglo-Saxon to the present day seemed to indicate growth–surely, the growth of the embryo in the womb? Then the language of the future could be born–a hybrid giant.

When I eventually read Stuart Gilbert's commentary on *Ulysses* I discovered that I had not gone far enough. Now I know that it is Bloom himself who stands for the fertilising principle: he enters, phallus-like, the house of all-woman; even the taking off of his hat has its sexual meaning. As for the series of literary pastiches that follow they have cunningly embedded in them references to the various stages of the development of the embryo–here comes the eye, here the jawbone and so on. The growth of the embryo is not uniform; some parts lag behind others. Joyce symbolises this in a deliberate harking back to an earlier stage of the language when, in terms of historical progress, there seems no justification for it. Thus, in the course of an Elizabethan pastiche a passage of Anglo-Saxon suddenly appears.

Complexities enough, but we still have the Homeric correspondences to deal with. We are given a clue as to what part of the Odyssey finds its parallel here at the very beginning–'Send us, bright one, light one, Horhorn . . .' The 'bright one' is the sun, or rather the Sun-god, and 'Horhorn'–a duplicated form–refers to the two-horned oxen of the Sun-god. Odysseus and his men landed famished on the triangular island of Sicily, and–though they knew that this was a blasphemous act–the sailors slaughtered the holy oxen that were guarded there by the daughters of the god–Phaethusa and Lampetie, who find their correspondence in the two nurses of the Lying-in Hospital. All comes clear if we remember that the Oxen of the Sun stand for fertility, and that the medical students in Horne's house blaspheme against it, loudly expressing their belief in the separation of sex from procreation–'copulation without population'. Odysseus's men were struck down by the thunder of Zeus, and Stephen's companions are temporarily daunted by the thunder of the God of the Catholics.

References to triangles in this episode (the red triangle of the label of a bottle of Bass, for instance) keep the island of the Sun-god in our minds, and there are lengthy references to bulls. We remember that Stephen is a 'bullockbefriending bard', but, if we have forgotten, somebody comes in with an evening paper in which Mr Deasy's letter about foot-and-mouth disease appears. Bloom is a 'bullockbefriender' in that he is on the side of fertility. He is, after all, a father, and his protective paternalism towards the drunken Stephen is given full scope for expression in the pastiches of prose of a more pious, God-and-fertility-centred, age. The following is in the style of Malory's *Morte D'Arthur*:

But sir Leopold was passing grave maugre his word by cause he still had pity of the terrorcausing shrieking of shrill women in their labour and as he was minded of his good lady Marion that had borne him an only manchild which on his eleventh day on live had died and no man of art could save so dark is destiny. And she was wondrous stricken of heart for that evil hap and for his burial did him on a fair corselet of lamb's wool, the flower of the flock, lest he might perish utterly and lie akeled (for it was then about the midst of the winter) and now sir Leopold that had of his body no manchild for an heir looked upon him his friend's son and was shut up in sorrow for his forepassed happiness and as sad as he was that him failed a son of such gentle courage (for all accounted him of real parts) so grieved he also in no less measure for young Stephen for that he lived riotously with those wastrels and murdered his goods with whores.

Stephen himself, with Thomistic logic, insists on the right true end of sex:

Gramercy, what of those Godpossibled souls that we nightly impossibilise, which is the sin against the Holy Ghost, Very God, Lord and Giver of Life? For, sirs, he said, our lust is brief. We are means to those small creatures within us and nature has other ends than we.

Bloom and Stephen, however, are alone in according reverence to the sacred oxen.

This chapter has a function over and above stylistic display, symbolism, the slow pushing-on with the story. Joyce has amassed a great deal of material which has not been developed, and the time has come to use it. He is concerned here primarily with shapes, forms, styles of writing, but form cannot exist without content. The content, then, may as well come from the odds and ends, the slogans, songs, small obsessions of the day. Thus, when–in this historical survey of English prose–it becomes necessary to imitate the style of the Authorised Version of the Bible, the subject-matter is drawn from those early musings of Stephen on the beach, the wild geese, exiled artists and patriots whom Ireland has forgotten:

Look forth now, my people, upon the land of behest, even from Horeb and from Nebo and from Pisgah, and from the Horns of Hatten unto a land flowing with milk and honey. But thou has suckled me with a bitter milk: my moon and sun thou hast quenched for ever. And thou hast left me alone for ever in the dark ways of my bitterness: and with a kiss of ashes hast thou kissed my mouth.

Stephen's thoughts of the tied-up navel-strings of the world leading back to the ultimate telephone exchange find a reference in a pastiche of Sir Thomas Browne:

And as no man knows the ubicity of his tumulus nor to what processes we shall thereby be ushered nor whether to Tophet or to Edenville in the like way is all hidden when we would backward see from what region of remoteness the whatness of our whoness hath fetched his whenceness.

When Joyce reaches the age of romanticism he becomes more ambitious, making a rich De Quincey vision out of a word that Bloom has half-heartedly puzzled about all day ('Parallax stalks behind and goads them . . .'), that butcher's-shop slip of newspaper ('Agendath is a waste land, a home of screechowls and the sandblind upupa'), Bloom's pen-friend, daughter, and wife ('And lo, wonder of metempsychosis, it is she, the everlasting bride . . . Martha, thou lost one' – a reference to '*M'appari*', sung that afternoon by Simon Dedalus – 'Millicent, the young, the dear, the radiant'). At the same time Joyce keeps his eye on the fertility theme in its Homeric aspect – 'Alpha, a ruby and triangled sign upon the forehead of Taurus' (there is your Bass label) – and does not forget the 'moving moaning multitude, murderers of the sun'. It is a brilliant performance.

But the mere fact that Joyce has to find *static* material for his literary pastiches (ideas, images, motifs) in order to fill up the nine months of gestation and nine hundred years of linguistic history makes us doubtful about the validity of his technique. He seems to be forgetting about Bloom and Stephen; they have been subordinated to a mere display of ingenuity – that at least is what we are inclined to object. On the other hand, it is right that we see them both under as many social and mythical aspects as possible, and this can only be done by a kind of metempsychosis – Stephen and Bloom through the ages, wearing a whole museum of dress, using the whole of English speech as a sort of Oxtail Book of English Prose might present it, becoming the heroes of every major English writer from King Alfred to Carlyle. And yet the ghosts of these writers – as conjured in that drunken common-room – are not concerned at all with these heroes, only with the orts and offal of their thoughts and speech. The dress remains fancy dress, the whole thing is a pageant-charade. Joyce has to go to his bulls – tauric, papal, Irish – for the Swiftian climax of the chapter, and to concoct masterly dishes of mere kitchen scraps for the rest. When, at last, Mrs Purefoy's child is born (naturally, we have been bludgeoned by sheer technique into forgetting all about this) Bloom makes an important decision which it is all too easy to miss in the general flurry:

By heaven, Theodore Purefoy, thou hast done a doughty deed and no botch! Thou art, I vow, the remarkablest progenitor barring none in this chaffering allincluding most farraginous chronicle. Astounding! In her lay a Godframed Godgiven preformed possibility which thou hast fructified with thy modicum of man's work. Cleave to her! Serve! Toil on, labour like a very bandog and let scholarship and all Malthusiasts go hang. Thou art all their daddies, Theodore.

The point about fertility is well taken, but Bloom is more important than Mr Purefoy: *he* is supposed to be all their daddies. With difficulty, in a blaze of slang, neologisms, foreign loan-words, pidgin (the language of the future?), we follow Stephen and his fellow-drunks to Burke's pub, and we follow Bloom solicitously following after. Then we think we hear Stephen's voice:

Lynch! Hey? Sign on long o me. Denzille lane this way. Change here for Bawdyhouse. We two, she said, will seek the kips where shady Mary is.

We have to seek those kips ourselves before we can come into the clear light of sanity, and even then it is a drunken phantasmagoric sanity, the only kind available in Nighttown. It seems strange that we should have to go to the next chapter to find out what has happened in this.

And yet, of all the episodes of *Ulysses*, this is the one I should most like to have written, and there are many authors who would agree with me. It is an author's chapter, a dazzling and authoritative display of what English can do. Moreover, it is a fulfilment of every author's egotistical desire not merely to *add* to English literature but to *enclose* what is already there. Literary history is a line; Joyce wants to see it as a series of concentric circles, himself the outer ring. Again, it is heartening to be reminded that literary creation—in whatever century—is an act of homage to the oxen of fertility, that writers are the remarkablest progenitors of them all. But it is a pity that Stephen and Bloom have to get lost in the process of glorifying an art that is supposed to be their servant.

10: Men into Swine

THAT 'OXEN OF THE SUN' CHAPTER CELEBRATED FERTILITY, THE womb, the sober art of medicine. Now everything turns bad. Instead of a maternity hospital, a brothel; instead of mothers, whores. The locomotor apparatus–which syphilis can ruin with tabes dorsalis–and the wayward and dangerous art of magic rule in the land of Circe. In the last chapter rain fell on the earth; now all is mist, twisting the real into the fantastic. It is Mr Bloom's strangest territory and not one he would himself choose. But, we learn, he feels it a fatherly duty to follow out Stephen's night to its crapulous end. Stephen and Lynch–the peripatetic audience of theorising Stephen in *A Portrait*–have come to Mabbot Street by train from Westland Row; all other friends–especially Mulligan and Haines, who cadged drinks to the end–have deserted the drunken poet. Drunken poets do well in brothel districts, but Bloom fears disaster for the son he wants to adopt. He is well able to look after him, as well as himself. He has drunk little in Burke's. He carries the flower moly to protect him from sensual enchantment–his recent ejaculation on the beach, the spiritual presence of his wife (her name is very nearly 'Moly'). The potato he carries in his pocket, a homely talisman for warding off rheumatism, will serve as the outward sign of these inward graces: it is not romantic, it is something that, with its aura of home and normality, may well ward off a whore's advances. Bloom also has his soap, faithful back-pocket companion of the day's wanderings. To weigh down his pockets further, he buys himself a pig's trotter and a sheep's foot. These are also protective talismans, but they are drawn into the huge animal symbolism of Circe's island. Circe turned Odysseus's companions into swine. Here there is more a zoo than a farm–every form of beast, especially the lowlier forms, will swallow a man's soul. When man remains man he becomes twisted, stunted, drooling. Only Bloom remains the paragon of animals, Odysseus the untouched of any debasing wand.

157

This chapter is the longest in the book—142 pages in the 1960 Bodley Head edition. Structurally, it is the most important. We have seen, in the previous episode, how strongly Joyce is feeling the urgency of developing his themes. Among the oxen these themes have been treated within a series of formal frameworks which suggests a gigantic musical suite. Imagine an opera of Wagnerian dimensions. Two acts have gone by and innumerable musical themes —though some, perhaps, only half a bar long—have been presented. The third act calls for a survey of musical forms from plainchant to post-Webern serialism. The composer would be a fool if he invented new themes, knowing that his audience would not yet have digested the existing ones. And so these latter must appear in new guises, combined in new relationships. Supposing now another act has to follow. The audience can take neither fresh themes nor formal ingenuity. All it will be able to take is a free fantasy, again based on existing themes. This is pretty well the position at this phase of *Ulysses*.

Perhaps sonata-form is a better analogy than opera. In the exposition section of a movement in sonata-form there are usually two main contrasting subjects around which cluster groups of subsidiary themes. In *Ulysses* we have had the equivalent of these in Bloom and Stephen, each with his many satellites of characteristic preoccupations. The exposition will not make sense until it has been followed by a development section in which the subjects combine, lend each other their subsidiary motifs, swirl about each other in an area of dreamlike fantasy, bump into each other drunkenly, melt into each other on the discovery of previously unguessed affinities. After that— in the recapitulation section—they can appear soberly and singly, properly dressed and tidied up, but they cannot be as they were before, in the exposition. They have learned strange things about each other and about themselves, they have had a night out together. That region of dreams has influenced reality.

The technique of this 'Circe' chapter is concerned less with dream than with hallucination. The characters are presented directly to us, in dramatic form, and they meet their fantasies directly. Bloom becomes Lord Mayor of Dublin, gives birth to a number of sons, sees the building of the New Bloomusalem, turns into Ruby, Pride of the Ring, witnesses the end of the world. If he is really seeing these fantasies he is either drunk or drugged. But he is not; he is fully sober. He is exhausted, yes, but not exhausted enough to conjure such visions. The hallucinations, then, are coming from without, are summoned by the author's own magic. Such magic is capable of making an apparition of Stephen's dead mother use a locution from Martha Clifford's letter to Bloom, and Bloom and Stephen see, in a mirror, the same cuckolded travesty of Shakespeare burbling a line of Goldsmith. If the phantasmagorias are subjective, then Bloom and Stephen are the same person. It is easier to conclude that this is a genuine free fantasy in the manner of a sonata's development section, that the *rapprochement* between Stephen and Bloom is something that is made, through magic, to happen extraneously, and that this huge dramatic exercise is not dramatic at all.

Only one real, as opposed to hallucinatory, event is of any significance. This is the striking down of Stephen by a couple of British soldiers at the end of the section. All flee except Bloom, who then assumes responsibility for him. This could have happened as easily outside Burke's in the previous chapter and Joyce, in the interests of fictional economy, could have saved himself a great deal of work. But it is dangerous now to think in such terms. Having come so far with Bloom (and this is Bloom's chapter more than Stephen's), we must go all the way, uncover every conceivable fantasy of which Bloom is capable and see him—like Bottom—in a sort of grisly fairyland. No critic, to my knowledge, has yet invoked *A Midsummer Night's Dream* as a classical source—the uncommon common man set upon by magic. The usual comparison is with the *Walpurgisnacht* scene in Goethe's *Faust* and Flaubert's *Tentation*. But Shakespeare is, first as last, the true patron of *Ulysses*.

Shakespeare's fairies have comic-fantastic names. Joyce's three whores sum up the whole physical world: Zoe stands for animal life, Florry for vegetable life, and Kitty for the mineral kingdom. The presiding sorceress, Circe herself, is Bella Cohen, the brothelmadam, who, in the most masochistic part of the Bloom fantasy, becomes a man and changes her name to Bello. These characters, like the brutal British soldiers, are real enough, but they inhabit the same world as the many dead, fictional, and actual-though-absent persons who flutter or gibber in then off again, and they are subject to the same laws, or lack of them. The vision that merely touched the fringes of Gabriel Conroy's consciousness in 'The Dead' is here not just palpable but larger than life: there is only one world, and it belongs equally to living and dead, to animal, vegetable, mineral and, for that matter, abstract.

The two soldiers, Privates Compton and Carr (their names taken from personal enemies of Joyce in Zürich) appear very early, making 'a volleyed fart' burst from their mouths and calling 'What ho, parson!' when they see black-garbed Stephen. In swirling fog, the companions of Gerty MacDowell, together with the sandcastle-building twins Tommy and Jacky Caffrey, are seen, debased, animalised. Then Bloom makes his entrance, his interior monologue now an audible soliloquy. His father and mother speak to him, Rudolph Virag a comic stage Jew ('They make you kaput, Leopoldleben. You watch them chaps') and Ellen Bloom a pantomime dame. They are hallucinations from the author's brain, not his hero's, but there is nothing vague or shadowy about them. The physical appearance of all the apparitions is most carefully described and their dress detailed scrupulously. Poor suicidal Virag is described as follows: 'A stooped bearded figure appears garbed in the long caftan of an elder in Zion and a smoking cap with magenta tassels. Horned spectacles hang down at the wings of the nose. Yellow poison streaks are on the drawn face.' Ellen Bloom wears a 'stringed mobcap, crinoline and bustle, widow Twankey's blouse with muttonleg sleeves buttoned behind, grey mittens and cameo brooch, her hair plaited in a crispine net'. Under her 'reef of skirt' there is a 'striped blay petticoat' from which fall out 'a phial, an Agnus Dei, a shrivelled potato and a celluloid doll'.

Of course, this detail is characteristic of a certain kind of drugged vision, but Joyce's concern is with the symbolism of clothes in the context of magic. Clothes are what we usually see of a person, but they are so easily changed. They are a kind of secondary body. Magic can change the external form of a creature (Circe turns men into swine) but cannot affect the deeper, God-willed, process of metempsychosis. Bloom is perpetually changing his secondary body – his changes of costume are uncountable – but he remains the same Bloom. Here, encountering his father and mother, he appears in youth's clothes, mud-caked with racing with the harriers: '. . . smart blue Oxford suit with white vestslips, narrowshouldered, in brown Alpine hat, wearing gent's sterling silver waterbury keyless watch and double curb Albert with seal attached, one side of him coated with stiffening mud.'

As for the transformation-into-beasts motif, this is hinted at in animal imagery (Molly Bloom appears in Oriental dress, with camel, 'plump as a pampered pouter pigeon'; a whore, squeaking, 'flaps her bat shawl and runs') and also more boldly expressed in terms of actual enchantment. Thus dead Paddy Dignam appears as a beagle with dachshund coat, worming his way down a coalhole; Tom Rochford, 'robinredbreasted', executes a 'daredevil salmon leap in the air'. The human locomotor apparatus itself is enchanted.

Bloom's bestial imaginings are brought into open court–society women give hair-raising evidence and promise dire punishments: 'Thrash the mongrel within an inch of his life. That cat-o'-nine-tails. Geld him. Vivisect him.' Bloom's masochism shows in joyous tremulous nakedness while a newsboy goes by: '*Messenger of the Sacred Heart* and *Evening Telegraph* with Saint Patrick's Day Supplement. Containing the new addresses of all the cuckolds in Dublin.' But Bloom is not disqualified from being crowned Leopold the First, 'His Most Catholic Majesty'. The mob turns against him, as it turned against Parnell, and, despite his miracles (including giving birth to 'eight male yellow and white children', each with 'his name printed in legible letters on his shirtfront: Nasodoro, Goldfinger, Chrysostomos, Maindorée, Silversmile, Silberselber, Vifargent, Panargyros'), he is burnt alive by the Dublin Fire Brigade. And, while all this, and more, is going on, he is being taken by Zoe to Bella Cohen's brothel.

Stephen and Lynch are there, as well as Zoe's 'two sister whores'. Florry has, appropriately, a stye on her eyelid, and Stephen tells us where we are, tipsily erudite about 'priests haihooping round David's that is Circe's or what am I saying Ceres' altar'. The perversion of the Christian rite in an eventual Black Mass is prefigured here. There are fresh apparitions, including an astonishing one of Bloom's grandfather–a sort of flying weasel that comes down the chimney– before Bella Cohen, massive whoremistress, enters. Almost at once she turns into Bello, all aromatic he-man, and Bloom becomes a shuddering female. But, female or not, he is still taunted for his lack of manhood:

BELLO: . . . Can you do a man's job?
BLOOM: Eccles street . . .
BELLO: (*Sarcastically*) I wouldn't hurt your feelings for the world but there's a man of brawn in possession there. The tables are turned, my gay young fellow! He is something like a fullgrown outdoor man. Well for you, you muff, if you had that weapon with knobs and lumps and warts all over it. He shot his bolt, I can tell you! Foot to foot, knee to knee, belly to belly, bubs to breast! He's no eunuch.

Bloom's humiliation knows no limits, but it is a humiliation he secretly–here, of course, not at all secretly–desires. Soon the practical man reasserts himself, shakes off the hallucinations, and stops Stephen from giving all his money to the whores. But the masochist cannot hide for long. Bloom, dressed as a flunkey, an antlered hatstand on his head, acquiesces in his cuckolding, watching Boylan and Molly in the act, urging them on to the laughter of the whores and the ecstasy of the two Sirens from the Ormond. And then:

> (*Stephen and Bloom gaze in the mirror. The face of William Shakespeare, beardless, appears there, rigid in facial paralysis, crowned by the reflection of the reindeer antlered hatrack in the hall.*)
> SHAKESPEARE: (*In dignified ventriloquy*) 'Tis the loud laugh bespeaks the vacant mind. (*To Bloom*) Thou thoughtest as how thou wastest invisible. Gaze. (*He crows with a black capon's laugh*) Iagogo! How my Oldfellow chokit his Thursdaymomun. Iagogogo!

That vision is not possible, apparently, to either Stephen or Bloom alone – only to both together.

Stephen 'gabbles, with marionette jerks', a broken English prospectus of the delights of Paris night-life: '. . . Enter gentlemen to see in mirrors every positions trapezes all that machine there besides also if desire act awfully bestial butcher's boy pollutes in warm veal liver or omelette on the belly *pièce de Shakespeare.*' All Stephen's dignity is gone, the intellectual imagination has been replaced by a grotesque leer. Both he and Bloom have sunk to the bottom. What is needed now is the horrid consummation of everything in a Dance of Death. The pianola plays 'My Girl's a Yorkshire Girl' and living creatures whirl with dead, the dance ending in the sudden shocking rising from the grave of Stephen's mother 'in leper grey with a wreath of faded orange blossoms and a torn bridal veil, her face worn and noseless, green with grave mould . . . She fixes her bluecircled hollow eyesockets on Stephen and opens her toothless mouth uttering a silent word . . .' A choir of virgins and confessors sings without voice, while Buck Mulligan, in jester's dress on top of a tower, weeps molten butter into a split scone. Grotesquely terrible though it is, this hallucination loses something by coming after so many others: our capacity for being harrowed is somewhat blunted by this time. But Stephen's mother, after using words associated with Bloom – 'More women than men in the world' and 'I pray for you in my other world' – identifies herself with the suffering Christ and, crying 'Beware! God's hand!', makes a 'green crab with malignant red eyes' stick its claws in Stephen's heart. Stephen shrieks his *non serviam*, turns himself into Siegfried so that his ashplant becomes the sword Nothung, and smashes the chandelier of the brothel parlour. In trying to kill the butcher God, Stephen destroys both time and space – the nightmare of history and the noise in the street (back to the 'Nestor' chapter) shatter in glass and toppling masonry.

Stephen dashes into the street to meet a fresh mixture of actuality and fantasy, Bloom following swiftly after. The noise which is God is not there, but the British State, in the shape of Privates Carr and Compton, is waiting. The soldiers are truculent, accusing Stephen of insulting their girl-friend (who happens to be also Gerty Mac-Dowell's). Stephen, like Bloom, preaches pacifism, despite the voices that cry revenge for Ireland's wrongs. The milkwoman of the first chapter of the book appears as 'Old Gummy Granny', but Stephen recognises 'the old sow that eats her farrow'. Edward the Seventh preaches peace more grotesquely and insincerely than Stephen, an *entente cordiale* bucket labelled '*Défense d'uriner*' in his hand, masonic robes over a white jersey stitched with an image of the Sacred Heart. The Citizen confronts Major Tweedy, Molly Bloom's father; the dead of Dublin rise; witches ride the air; Armageddon is sanctified with a Black Mass. Then language cracks into violent obscenity:

PRIVATE CARR: (*With ferocious articulation*) I'll do him in, so help me fucking Christ! I'll wring the bastard fucker's bleeding blasted fucking windpipe!

Bloom the appeaser, the man of good will and calm sense, fails to stop Carr from hitting Stephen in the face. Stephen lies stunned, the crowd clears on the coming of the police, and Bloom assumes responsibility for the dead-out poet. It is the big moment of the book.

Stephen, more drunk than hurt, murmurs words of the song he sang for his dying mother–'Who . . . drive . . . Fergus now. And pierce . . . wood's woven shade? . . .' Bloom does not understand: 'Ferguson, I think I caught. A girl. Some girl.' Then he too murmurs words of magical import: '. . . swear that I will always hail, ever conceal, never reveal, any part or parts, art or arts . . . in the rough sands of the sea . . . a cabletow's length from the shore . . . where the tide ebbs . . . and flows . . .' The imposed magic of the sorceress has dissolved. The stumbling and capering and gibbering of men turned to animals is no more; there is a great nocturnal stillness. Stephen and Bloom must, if they want magic, now make their own. Stephen is a poet, his art is magical. Bloom is a mason, member of an honourable and secret craft. He stands guarding Stephen, 'his fingers at his lips in the attitude of secret master'. At once, as by the conjuration of a white and wholesome sorcery, the final vision of the night takes shape. It is of Rudy, Bloom's dead son as he might have been had he reached eleven years (he would have been just that now), not eleven days. Bloom, wonderstruck, calls his name inaudibly. But Rudy is a fairy boy, 'a changeling, kidnapped'; he reads Hebrew, kissing the page, smiling, unseeing. The forces of life waited on Stephen's dead mother; the trappings of death have been transmuted here to the fanciful dress of resurrection – the glass and bronze of the little coffin have become 'glass shoes and a little bronze helmet'; the white coverlet of lamb's wool that Molly made to keep her son warm in his coffin has turned to a 'white lambkin' peeping out of his waistcoat pocket; the dead delicate mauve face is a live delicate mauve face. In his Eton suit, drawn from his impossibled future, Rudy hovers above recumbent Stephen. Only the hardest-hearted of readers will withhold his tears.

11: Home is the Sailor

'CIRCE' ENDS THE ODYSSEY PROPER; NOW WE MUST HAVE THE *Nostos*, the going home. In a sense, this is less a return than a fresh start, since Bloom will be going home with Stephen and three lives will now be modified for ever. We see now another reason for the massive musical development of themes in the hallucinations of the brothel district: Joyce wanted to 'work them out' in both senses of the term—purge them by magicalising them. The extent to which he has done this is best seen, or heard, in the bit of surrealism which represents the pianola-version of 'My Girl's a Yorkshire Girl' (Stephen's 'Dance of death'). Let us look back a little.

In the 'Wandering Rocks' episode Dilly Dedalus, Stephen's sister, sees and hears 'the lacquey by the door of Dillon's auction-rooms' shake his handbell: 'Barang!' then 'Bang!' then, after a feeble shaking in response to Mr Dedalus's curse, a loud bang again. In the same episode a one-legged sailor swings his way to Eccles Street, singing, receiving an alms from Molly Bloom. Corny Kelleher, at the same time, 'closed his long daybook and glanced with his drooping eye at a pine coffinlid sentried in a corner'. In the 'Æolus' chapter Stephen told the story of the two '*Frauenzimmer*' (this takes us back also to the 'Proteus' scene) climbing to the top of the 'onehandled adulterer's' column and spitting down plum-stones. Bloom, near the beginning of his odyssey, saw the poster of a cycle race showing a 'cyclist doubled up like a cod in a pot'. In the 'Cyclops' episode one of the parodies presents the Provost-Marshal weeping over a beautiful girl to whom a man due for hanging has said farewell: 'Blimey it makes me kind of bleeding cry, straight, it does, when I see her cause I thinks of my old mashtub what's waiting for me down Limehouse way.' Add Father Conmee, the Rev. Love (a minor character of the 'Wandering Rocks'), Stephen's 'Proteus' memory of exiled Kevin Egan's lighting a 'gunpowder' cigarette with 'a blue fuse match', odd beast-themes, drum-beats, and the words of 'My Girl's a Yorkshire Girl', and you end up with the following:

(Bang fresh barang bang of lacquey's bell, horse, nag, steer, piglings, Conmee on Christass lame crutch and leg sailor in cockboat armfolded ropepulling hitching stamp hornpipe through and through, Baraabum! On nags, hogs, bellhorses, Gadarene swine, Corny in coffin. Steel shark stone onehandled Nelson, two trickies Frauenzimmer plumstained from pram falling bawling. Gum, he's a champion. Fuseblue peer from barrel rev. evensong Love on hackney jaunt Blazes blind coddoubled bicyclers Dilly with snowcake no fancy clothes. Then in last wiswitchback lumbering up and down bump mashtub sort of viceroy and reine relish for tublumber bumpshire rose. Barabum!)

A fundamental rule of sonata-form is this: never present a tune or a theme, however lowly or fragmentary, unless you intend to repeat it at a later stage—or, preferably, transform it, develop it, combine it with other thematic material. Joyce has fulfilled that, even to the extent of realising the comic possibilities of a mere name—as when, just before the Black Mass, we re-encounter the librarian of 'Scylla and Charybdis' like this: '*Quakerlyster plasters blisters*'. *Ulysses* differs from other novels in emphasising the importance of musical pattern. If, writing straightforward fiction, I present my hero in the first chapter scratching his nose, that is mere naturalistic detail. To Joyce it would be significant, not in terms of symbolism but in terms of a growing tapestry—a little figure that, worked into one corner of the carpet, must eventually appear in another corner for the sake of formal balance. Music is a sort of tapestry realised in the medium of time. Time changes things; hence the balance achieved by identical repetition of the same motif is out of place; there has to be a transformation, however slight. Another way of looking at this technical peculiarity of *Ulysses* calls on a larger symbolism, that which encloses the whole book. Throughout the whole period of Odysseus's wandering, Penelope has been weaving during the day, unravelling at night. Nighttown is the place for unravelling: the complex fabric of the book, as woven from the *Telemachia* to the 'Oxen of the Sun' episode, is detroyed by magic, and we see familiar elements of the pattern dissolving. Soon there is nothing left. Penelope's trick has been found out. The essence of the *Nostos* is a kind of nakedness—no more clothes, very few tricks, all disguises tentative and easily seen through.

The nakedness of this home-troped trilogy takes a trio of forms. First, Stephen and Bloom go together to a cabman's shelter for a bun and a cup of coffee. They are tired; wit and even understanding go to sleep; they are a couple of men – one near middle age, the other very young – with little of importance or even interest to say to each other: they are stripped to mere paradigm. The prose-style is past playing tricks of virtuosity; it is limp and clumsy though it pretends to brightness; it is fit only for a provincial newspaper or for the waste-paper basket. Our two noctambules (as they are archly called) go to No. 7 Eccles Street for more talk and a temperance nightcap; here the nakedness is of another kind – a bare skeletal catechism in which everything is reduced to factual statistics. The final disrobing is, appropriately, conducted by Molly Bloom – no more civilised disguises, the pretensions of men exploded. All clothes off, we submit to this Eternal Woman who is also Mother Earth. The protean forms that life takes on dissolve utterly. We end with one word only: 'yes'.

In Joyce, though, any direct statement has to be qualified, and metempsychosis teaches us that even nakedness may be a disguise. We strip so much away in the *Nostos*, but we do not discard the sense of a complex pattern. The end looks back to the beginning, and the *Telemachia* and *Nostos* exactly balance each other. The first chapter of the first section was a young man's narrative in which only one character (the milkwoman) was old. The first chapter of the last section is a narrative in which only old and middle-aged men figure, save for one character only – the young Stephen. The middle chapter of the *Telemachia* was a personal catechism; the middle chapter of the *Nostos* is an impersonal one. The final chapter of each section is a long monologue: in the *Telemachia* it was male (Stephen on the beach); in the *Nostos* it is female (Molly in bed). We end with the artist, then, the shaper; even the earth-mother is subject to the divine imagination. Or is she? Penelope is a weaver. Art may be one of the toys that the earth-mother gives to her children to keep them quiet – a sort of parody of reality.

Let us go back to the beginning of the *Nostos*. The Homeric counterpart is the meeting between Odysseus and Telemachus in the hut of the swineherd Eumaeus. The element of deceit, of disguise, is fundamental, since Odysseus must not be recognised by any of the suitors he has come to Ithaca to quell. But, in this atmosphere of near-nakedness, Joyce cannot allow Bloom to be deceitful. Lies, false pretences abound in his 'Eumaeus' chapter, but they are all subjects of thought and conversation, hidden motifs, or else they are practised by characters who get in the way of, rather than assist, this coming together of poet and advertising broker. And the prose-style itself, though it pretends to wide-awakeness, is flat, weary, stale—one-in-the-morning writing:

> Mr Bloom and Stephen entered the cabman's shelter, an unpretentious wooden structure, where, prior to then, he had rarely, if ever, been before; the former having previously whispered to the latter a few hints anent the keeper of it, said to be the once famous Skin-the-Goat Fitzharris, the invincible,[1] though he wouldn't vouch for the actual facts, which quite possibly there was not one vestige of truth in. A few moments later saw our two noctambules safely seated in a discreet corner, only to be greeted by stares from the decidedly miscellaneous collection of waifs and strays and other nondescript specimens of the genus *homo*, already there engaged in eating and drinking, diversified by conversation, for whom they seemingly formed an object of marked curiosity.

There is a horrid and riveting fascination about this: it holds us with its lacklustre eye. The muscularity of imagination is spent, and only the nerves function now (the nerves are the presiding organ of the body). And yet a vigorous art is celebrated quietly here—that of navigation, appropriate to the Homeric theme of the returned wanderer. All day long we have been intermittently aware of a three-masted schooner called the *Rosevean* sailing home from Bridgwater with a cargo of bricks. She is in haven at last, and one of her crew— W. B. Murphy—is in the cabman's shelter to lie about his voyages and shore-adventures (rather like O'Casey's Paycock). He has a monopoly of the vigour which is needed for imagination, and he holds the chapter together. He is a sort of parodic Odysseus.

This ancient mariner holds our attention as any bore or liar will when we are too weary to resist. He says that he knows Stephen's father ('He's Irish . . . All Irish.' Stephen says drily: 'All too Irish') and insists that he saw him once in a circus in Stockholm shooting eggs off bottles over his shoulder—left-handed, too. This left-handedness has its own significance. We keep meeting references to left-handedness throughout the chapter, and Corley (one of the 'Two Gallants' of *Dubliners*) seems to be introduced only because he is alleged to be a bend-sinister scion of a noble family. The left hand is the false hand, literally sinister and metaphorically deceitful. Impostors, pretenders, fit in well with the theme of return from wandering, and they are an important element in the conversation. A man, long believed dead, comes back; how can we know that he is who he says he is? And if (as one of the cabbies believes is all too

---

[1] The 'Invincibles' were concerned with the Phoenix Park murder of Lord Cavendish and Thomas Burke in 1882.

possible) Parnell should return to Ireland, Bloom for one thinks it 'highly inadvisable':

. . . as regards return, you were a lucky dog if they didn't set the terrier at you directly you got back. Then a lot of shillyshally usually followed. Tom for and Dick and Harry against. And then, number one, you came up against the man in possession and had to produce your credentials, like the claimant in the Tichborne case . . .

Moreover, there is disappointment latent in all returns after long absences–places change, oneself changes, Rip van Winkle should have remained sleeping. Bloom, the Dublin Odysseus, does not be-lieve in wandering. Stay home with your wife (he shows Stephen, inevitably, a photograph of his own); be satisfied with the very occasional holiday trip. He remains the 'prudent member'.

But he does not seem to achieve any penetration into the workings of Stephen's more wayward, subtler, mind. Bloom is presented as stupider than he really is (blame weariness, the lateness of the hour). When Stephen, using a schoolman's term, defines the soul as 'a simple substance', Bloom says: 'Simple? I shouldn't think that is the proper word. Of course, I grant you, to concede a point, you do knock against a simple soul once in a blue moon . . .' Stephen says that he is not important because he belongs to Ireland, but that Ireland is important because it belongs to him, Bloom replies: 'What belongs? Excuse me. Unfortunately I didn't catch the latter portion. What was it you . . . ?' Stephen is, of course, an Italian scholar, but Bloom at least showed, earlier in the day, that he knows the words of *Don Giovanni*. Now he is totally inept, with his '*Bella poetria!*' and '*Belladonna voglio*'. Stephen's musical taste is excellent, but Bloom's is not too bad. Still, he is drawn here to praising 'the severe classical school such as Mendelssohn' and Meyerbeer's *Seven Last Words on the Cross*. Stephen talks of the great Elizabethans–Dowland, Tom-kins, John Bull–and Bloom wants to know if the last-named is the 'political celebrity of that ilk'. The near-absurdity of Bloom is pointed by the misspelling of his name in the report of the Dignam funeral in the *Telegraph* (pink edition, extra sporting)–'L. Boom'. But we, the readers, can soften that blow for him. Stephen's name also appears in the list of mourners, though, as we know, he was not there. The mere proximity of 'Stephen Dedalus, B.A.' makes Bloom explode into a (*Boom*) Dutch tree.

The two leave the cabman's shelter at length, Bloom fatherly, Stephen what he is. What Bloom will have Stephen become is a great singer; he listens to his 'phenomenally beautiful tenor voice'

169

discoursing a German ballad about the Sirens as they walk to Eccles Street through the night's quietness. The last line is '*Und alle Schiffe brücken*', which fits in well with the petrifying by the enemy Æolus of Odysseus's own ship on his landing on the shores of Ithaca. The ships are finished, the voyages all over. Arm in arm, Odysseus and Telemachus go to the halls of Penelope, watched by a driver, a navigator of the streets:

The driver never said a word, good, bad or indifferent. He merely watched the two figures, as he sat on his lowbacked car, both black—one full, one lean—walk towards the railway bridge . . . As they walked, they at times stopped and walked again, continuing their *tête-à-tête* (which of course he was utterly out of), about sirens, enemies of man's reason, mingled with a number of other topics of the same category, usurpers, historical cases of the kind . . .

A catalogue of subjects for discussion is here gently adumbrated. By the time we reach the next chapter (the ugly duckling of the whole book and hence Joyce's own favourite) there is no gentleness. The soft flesh is ripped off the skeleton and, like some eternal Gradgrind, the voice of the god of statistics asks cold questions and expects the most comprehensive answers:

Of what did the duumvirate deliberate during their itinerary?
Music, literature, Ireland, Dublin, Paris, friendship, prostitution, diet, the influence of gaslight or the light of arc and glowlamps on the growth of adjoining paraheliotropic trees, exposed corporation emergency dust-buckets, the Roman catholic church, ecclesiastical celibacy, the Irish nation, jesuit education, careers, the study of medicine, the past day, the maleficent influence of the pre-sabbath, Stephen's collapse.

Among the facts that the inhuman catechist wants to find out are, naturally, the 'common factors of similarity between their respective like and unlike reactions to experience'. The facts are, as we expected, not all that enlightening: Bloom and Stephen have not been summoned from opposite ends of the earth to meet in an ecstasy of affinity.

Was there one point on which their views were equal and negative?
The influence of gaslight or electric light on the growth of adjoining paraheliotropic trees.

But the rapprochement is there and, when Bloom, who has forgotten his key, enters his own house by a stratagem (he climbs over the area railings and opens the area door), enabling Stephen to make a more orthodox entrance, we can settle to a long and irrelevant analysis of race, temperament, education, family–exhaustive and exhausting–which runs parallel to the truth. The truth, which has nothing to do with statistics, is that Bloom and Stephen can talk together and get on, that they will meet again and modify each other's lives, that Bloom will gain a suitor-conquering power from his contact with the intellectual imagination, and that Stephen will some day be able to write *Ulysses*.

The comic impertinence of the catechism is best seen when Bloom turns on the kitchen tap for water to make cocoa for his guest:

Did it flow?
Yes. From Roundwood reservoir in county Wicklow of a cubic capacity of 2,400 million gallons, percolating through a subterranean aqueduct of filter mains of single and double pipeage constructed at an initial plant cost of £5 per linear yard by way of the Dargle, Rathdown, Glen of the Downs and Callowhill to the 26 acre reservoir at Stillorgan, a distance of 22 statute miles, and thence, through a system of relieving tanks, by a gradient of 250 feet to the city boundary at Eustace bridge, upper Leeson street, though from prolonged summer drouth and daily supply of 12½ million gallons the water had fallen below the sill of the overflow weir for which reason the borough surveyor and waterworks engineer, Mr Spencer Harty, C.E., on the instructions of the waterworks committee, had prohibited the use of municipal water for purposes other than those of consumption (envisaging the possibility of recourse being had to the impotable water of the Grand and Royal Canals as in 1893) particularly as the South Dublin Guardians, notwithstanding their ration of 15 gallons per day per pauper supplied through a 6 inch meter, had been convicted of a wastage of 20,000 gallons per night by a reading of their meter on the affirmation of the law agent of the corporation, Mr Ignatius Rice, solicitor, thereby acting to the detriment of another section of the public, self-supporting taxpayers, solvent, sound.

All this to get a couple of cups of cocoa.

Yet the statistics do remind us of the unconscious groping towards each other that Bloom and Stephen have, usually off their guard, in the margins of thought, exhibited all day–the 'postexilic eminence' of Moses of Egypt and Moses Maimonides (Stephen has mused briefly on both), to whom Bloom adds Moses Mendelssohn; the Jewish father-and-daughter theme in the National Library, which leads Stephen to sing the anti-semitic ballad of *Hugh of Lincoln*;[1] the parallel between oppressed Jews and oppressed Irish that was rhetorically expounded in the 'Æolus' scene. And yet all this has, when all is said and done, little to do with Bloom and Stephen.

[1] In a setting too low for Stephen's tenor voice. Why?

What at length emerges from the load of abstract facts is something quite strange and unexpected. The duumvirate seem to borrow a kind of abstraction of their own from the skeletal catechism: they lose one kind of substance and gain another. Their reality becomes that of the moon or stars, whose weight and chemical constituents, temperature and canals and mountains may be known, but only remotely. Stephen and Bloom become heavenly bodies, and we note that Joyce has made *Comets* the special symbol for this chapter. It is not excess of factual matter that has wrought the metamorphosis; it is the lack of human reference, the sucking out of blood from the human. Stephen and Bloom soar above the world of sense and take their places among the constellations, 'the heaventree of stars hung with humid nightblue fruit'.

Bloom invites Stephen to spend the night in his house, but Stephen declines. This is far from goodbye, though: the two will meet again for further talks; there is also the question of Stephen's voice and Stephen's Italian and Molly Bloom. They propose 'to inaugurate a prearranged course of Italian instruction, place the residence of the instructed' (that will put Molly's '*voglio*' right: Bloom has never been too happy about her pronunciation of it); 'to inaugurate a course of vocal instruction, place the residence of the instructress'. And so Stephen leaves, going we know not where under 'the infinite lattiginous scintillating uncondensed milky way' and 'Orion with belt and sextuple sun theta and nebula in which 100 of our solar systems could be contained'. Bloom is left alone among the rearranged furniture of the sitting-room (wifely whim) and quiet meditations which may induce peaceful sleep. We are face-to-face with him for the last time, and so we must have our catechistic fill of his residual thoughts, dreams, hopes for the future. Nor is his house (after all, this is Ithaca) neglected: contents of drawers and bookshelves are fully listed, and there is an inventory of the thoughts and sensations called up by such items as an 'indistinct daguerreotype of Rudolph Bloom (born Virag)' and the letter from Martha Clifford which he adds to his secret hoard. But Bloom tires as we do. Undressed, he goes to the bedroom, where Molly lies awake. He views the adulterated bed with equanimity; he answers Molly's questions about the long day with fair frankness, though omitting certain items which she might neither understand nor appreciate. But she catches at the mention of Stephen Dedalus, 'professor and author'–son, lover, messiah–and will soon weave him into her before-sleep meditations. Bloom, more self-assertive than he has been for years, asks for his breakfast in bed. There is no doubt he will get it.

He lies as Joyce himself used to lie – with his feet towards the head of the bed, 'laterally, left, with right and left legs flexed, the index-finger and thumb of the right hand resting on the bridge of the nose . . . the childman weary, the manchild in the womb'. The questioner will not give up even now:

Womb? Weary?
He rests. He has travelled.
With?
Sinbad the Sailor and Tinbad the Tailor and Jinbad the Jailer and Whinbad the Whaler and Ninbad the Nailer and Finbad the Failer and Binbad the Bailer and Pinbad the Pailer and Minbad the Mailer and Hinbad the Hailer and Rinbad the Railer and Dinbad the Kailer and Vinbad the Quailer and Linbad the Yailer and Xinbad the Phthailer.

The rhythms of these names are the rhythms of steady breathing. If the questioner wants another answer he must expect a nonsensical one. Finally he will get no answer at all.

When?
Going to dark bed there was a square round Sinbad the Sailor roc's auk's egg in the night of the bed of all the auks of the rocs of Darkinbad the Brightdayler.
Where?

Bloom is asleep.

Molly Bloom is not, however, not yet. Penelope has to be revealed as, despite everything, fundamentally faithful, and Bloom's conquest of the suitors – again despite everything – must be celebrated in grudging, though never spoken, admiration. More than that, we have lived for hundreds of pages in a man's city, and woman has had very little to say. Underneath man's artefacts lies eternal, unchanging woman, giver of life, repository of the true creative urge. Woman is the earth; Molly lies 'in the attitude of Gea-Tellus, fulfilled, recumbent, big with seed'. She has her own laws, which are not man's; the rhythms of her meditation despise man's dams and fences:

Yes because he never did a thing like that before as ask to get his breakfast in bed with a couple of eggs since the *City Arms* hotel when he used to be pretending to be laid up with a sick voice doing his highness to make himself interesting to that old faggot Mrs Riordan that he thought he had a great leg of and she never left us a farthing all for masses for herself and her soul greatest miser ever was actually afraid to lay out 4d for her methylated spirit telling me all her ailments she had too much old chat in her about politics and earthquakes and the end of the world let us have a bit of fun first God help the world if all the women were her sort down on bathingsuits and lownecks of course nobody wanted her to wear I suppose she was pious because no man would look at her twice . . .

And so on and so on and so on: twenty-five thousand words (a third of an average-length novel) without any punctuation at all. The nakedness is total, and in the French version of *Ulysses* Molly even takes out her accents, like so many hair-pins. It is the final, and in many ways the most astonishing *tour de force* of the book.

And yet it is less a display of art than a revelation of insight. Joyce has dared to think his way into a woman's mind: it would be dangerous to shape, use the artist's cunning: it is safer to leave the floodgates open and let the dark turgid flow have its will; otherwise the spell might be broken. And so we listen to an incredible torrent of reminiscence, a great deal of it erotic, out of which we must pick out a wife's portrait of Leopold Bloom. His faults are many—arguing, familiarity with servants, saying that Our Lord was a carpenter and the first socialist, pretending that he is dying when he has cut his toe with a razor, being a nuisance about the house, bringing her, his wife, to the sin of adultery through his own neglect, and so on. He is so unsatisfactory that she is glad to think that she may soon be able to replace him with Stephen, artist-son-lover. But, when she compares him with Boylan and other Dublin drinker-lechers, she is prepared to concede good points. He can be gentle, his manners are good, he is not led astray by male cronies, there is something of the artist in him, he understands a woman and knows how to give her pleasure. There was a time when he demonstrated that he had more spunk than the others, shot a stronger arrow. At the least, he is to be tolerated, even protected. Boylan, who laid a lionlimb by her that afternoon, is coarse by comparison: his thrusting yard is not the whole of manhood. Ultimately Molly feels that she encloses all the men she has ever known, a tolerant mother. But with her husband there remain certain imponderables; she cannot be too sure of him; he is always capable of doing the unexpected. Boylan may have brought wine and peaches and a great readiness to be at it, but Leopold, Poldy, Don Poldo de la Flora, has brought a fatherless and motherless poet, asking only in return his breakfast in bed (two eggs—the return of his manhood). Bloom will do very well; in his passive way (but is not passivity a kind of cunning?) he has killed all the suitors.

There, then, is Penelope. But she is also Gea-Tellus, Cybele, our great earth-mother. That she herself should have had a mother seems ridiculous; we cannot take Lunita Laredo–Spanish–Jewish bride of Major Brian Cooper Tweedy–all that seriously: after all 'Lunita' means 'little moon', and little moons do not produce their own planets. Molly is eternal earth, rolling round unsleeping on her creaking bed. Dirt is of her essence: she likes smutty books; she is not embarrassed by corner-boys' talk of what is 'only natural'. She is uncertain of her age, but she recalls epochs in her long geological history–the fire inside her gushes out; there was a terribly cold ice-age winter when she played with little dolls, primordial men; she loves the mornings when the world is deserted save for flowers and vegetables all dewy on the market-stalls. She is passionate for flowers, would like to have the whole house full of them; for her there is nothing like nature.

But she is endearing as well as formidable. Her womanly common sense makes her husband's seem like higher mathematics. She is all for life, detests wars and the men who make them, is angry at the ravaging of fine bodies on the battlefield to serve some factitious ideal. She loves love. She loves God, but her God is not the comic-cruel butcher of Stephen's tortured broodings:

. . . God of heaven theres nothing like nature the wild mountains then the sea and the waves rushing then the beautiful country with fields of oats and wheat and all kinds of things and all the fine cattle going about that would do your heart good to see rivers and lakes and flowers all sorts of shapes and smells and colours springing up even out of the ditches primroses and violets nature it is as for them saying theres no God I wouldnt give a snap of my two fingers for all their learning why dont they go and create something I often asked him atheists or whatever they call themselves go and wash the cobbles off themselves first . . .

Her God is the creator; the God of Stephen's mother is the destroyer. In her the whole complex of remorse, 'agenbite of inwit', the sense of blasphemy against *amor matris* (which may, after all, be the most important thing in life) is cleansed and purged away in a concept of motherhood which is not mean and nagging and tearful and self-pitying but humorous, drenched in light, born of the sun.

Before sleep Molly makes her affirmation, says 'yes' to life, in a glorious fantasy that combines God, Bloom's kisses and promise– 'tomorrow the sun shines for you'–on Howth Head, and her girl-hood and first love in Gibraltar, when she was 'a flower of the mountain'. Gibraltar is right for her–the gateway to the middle sea of sun and wine, the eternal flower-covered rock. Her final reminiscence is, after the long years of sour banning, at last in the anthologies, learnt by heart, a classic quotation, but incapable of being wearied or staled by repetition:

> . . . yes when I put the rose in my hair like the Andalusian girls or shall I wear a red yes and how he kissed me under the Moorish wall and I thought well as well him as another and then I asked him with my eyes to ask again yes and then he asked me would I yes to say yes my mountain flower and first I put my arms around him yes and drew him down to me so he could feel my breasts all perfume yes and his heart was going like mad and yes I said yes I will Yes.

There is nothing in all literature more joyous. The book is ended, and yet we are called back, after its final period, to the memory of a weary odyssey that contains this of Bloom's, the artist's exile and wanderings, the long years of toil and disregard:

Trieste–Zürich–Paris, 1914–1921.

There are twenty more years of travel to come–seeking, striving, refusing to yield. One may sleep in Ithaca, but one does not die there.

12: The Bedside Labyrinth

Ulysses IS A BOOK TO OWN, A BOOK TO LIVE WITH. TO BORROW it is probably worse than useless, for the sense of urgency imposed by a time-limit for reading it fights against the book's slow pace, a leisurely music that requires an unhurried ear and yields little to the cursory, newspaper-nurtured eye. Most of our reading is, in fact, eye-reading – the swallowing whole of the cliché, the skipping of what seems insignificant, the tearing out of the sense from the form. *Ulysses* is, like *Paradise Lost*, an auditory work, and the sounds carry the sense. Similarly, the form carries the content, and if we try to ignore the word-play, the parodies and pastiches, in order to find out what happens next, we are dooming ourselves to disappointment. *Ulysses* is not an action-crammed thriller. It will, however, yield to a reading-plan that combines the approach of the ordinary novel-reader and the more rarefied poetry-taster. When I first read *Ulysses*, at the age of sixteen, I tried to gobble it and failed, but I still contrived to make a comparatively swift meal of it – four full days of a school vacation. Did I read every word, then, or did I skip? I skipped a little, chiefly in the 'Oxen of the Sun' episode and in Molly Bloom's final monologue. I was impatient with some of Bloom's interior musings and faintly irritated with the 'Sirens' scene. But, at the end of my four days, I knew what the book was about. In the thirty-odd years since that first reading – an experience that made my examination set-books look a little pallid – I have only twice re-read the book continuously through, from stately plump Buck Mulligan to the final 'yes'. I have preferred to take it in chapters, choosing any one I fancied at any particular time, recognising favourites – usually the episodes I liked least when I first met *Ulysses* – and, inside those favourites, turning to certain passages again and again.

Ulysses (and, even more so, as we shall see, *Finnegans Wake*) invites this approach, rather as the Bible does. It is, in many ways, a precursor of the new wave in the novel, which is quite capable of asking us to treat a work of fiction as if it were a dictionary or an encyclopaedia–something to be stepped into at any point we please, begun at the end and finished at the beginning, partly read or wholly read, a plot of space for free wandering rather than a temporal escalator. The 'Wandering Rocks' episode of *Ulysses* is a reminder that the whole book has a spatial scheme in which time has been divested of its bullying hurry-along authority, and this is reinforced by our knowledge that the final image is of a human body, presented piecemeal in its various organs. Time is the great enemy, and books like *Ulysses* and *Finnegans Wake* triumphantly trounce it. Time has to be put in its place.

Ulysses, then, is a labyrinth which we can enter at any point, once we have satisfied ourselves as to its general plan and purpose. It is one of the very few books in existence that can be picked up at any time, enrichening any odd moment and–rather than a tome we have to engage strenuously at a library table–it is a book for the bedside. To say that one has to live with it is not to utter a prejudiced, partisan claim but to state quite objectively that there is enough meat in it to last a lifetime. Its scope is deliberately encyclopaedic and its subtleties and puzzles require a sort of retired leisure for their working-out. One can never thoroughly understand *any* book (not even one's own), mainly because words are autonomous and have an endless range of possible meaning and because time itself, the flux that the author tries to trap, has a habit of opening up new significations in a book, shifting stresses, achieving new topicalities, suggesting fresh patterns of relationship with the rest of emergent literature. The paradox about *Ulysses* is that it remains, at any given time, more immediately intelligible than books that essay a greater lucidity: it does not wrest its meanings from here-and-now, it clamps down on time instead of riding with it. At the same time it invites further exploration and discovery, not of the answers to conundrums but of a greater richness of understanding of what is already well enough understood.

Let it join the bedside library, then, along with Joyce's other big book, Shakespeare, the Bible, Boswell, *The Anatomy of Melancholy*, Rabelais, Nabokov's *Pale Fire*, *Tristram Shandy*, and other works which are more concerned with solid objects in space than with the illusory current of mere time. And now let me attempt to sum up its qualities. I am wretchedly and impotently aware of my failure to celebrate these in the brief survey I have just completed. There is the awful danger of solemnity, which turns readers as well as writers into bloody owls. Joyce wrote *Ulysses* to entertain, to enhance life, to give joy. It is all too easy to destroy the winged life, not by binding so much as by brooding.

First, then, *Ulysses* is a great comic novel. It is one of the very few books that can make one laugh aloud. Its humour is of an immense variety, ranging from stage Irish knockabout to the most rarefied wit. The humorous tradition in English literature has—since the Puritans slammed shut the doors of the playhouses in 1642—been somewhat limited, and the typical comic English book in the period on which Joyce supervened gained its effects by making sandwiches of farce and sentimentality. Jerome K. Jerome is more typical than Lewis Carroll, and the humour resident in the English language itself—a language with two warring elements—has never been much exploited. Joyce is remarkable in that the *vis comica* operates consistently in his work, and that even the shocking and pathetic is presented in terms of comic bathos: the two apparitions of the 'Circe' episode, the ghosts of Stephen's mother and Bloom's son, owe all their effectiveness to the deployment of a technique traditionally associated with laughter. Earnestness is always forbidden, and even the raptures of sex (which Lawrence taught us to take too seriously) are deflated to the near-grotesque. The laughter of Jonathan Swift turns all too easily into a snarl or a howl, but the *saeva indignatio* has no place in *Ulysses*, any more than that horrified fascination with the lowlier bodily functions that attests Swift's dementia. Joyce, like all Ireland, was washed by the Gulf Stream; Swift cleansed himself with (Dr Johnson's words) 'Oriental scrupulosity'. It is healthier to accept a bit of dirt—some would say there is more than a bit in *Ulysses*—than to go through the vain motions of washing out original sin. And so some of the satisfaction we obtain from the coarser jokes of *Ulysses* is not an aspect of the 'cloacal obsession' that Professor MacHugh attributes to the English: it is part of a total, cosmic, laughter that takes in drains, love, politics, and the deathless gods, and feels guilty about nothing.

One of Joyce's deathless gods is language, and it is proper that he should find inherent comedy there. English is peculiar among the tongues of the world in that its two basic elements—Latin and Anglo-Saxon—are, though both derived from Indo-Germanic, different in genius, tugging opposite ways. The Anglo-Saxon favours the short word and the earthy denotation; Latin is more dignified, an intellectual language, happiest with orotundity and abstraction.

179

Joyce does not attempt to make an easy digestible cocktail out of them; he tends rather to push each to its limits. Gerard Manley Hopkins overstressed the Anglo-Saxon in English, John Milton the Latin, and the aim of each was highly serious. Joyce does what both did but knows that both processes best serve a comic purpose. And so Stephen's remorse over his dead mother and decaying family is lifted to a comic-ironic region by being expressed as 'agenbite of inwit', and 'ineluctable modality of the visible'–especially as it comes immediately after 'through the checkerwork of leaves the sun flung spangles, dancing coins'–will warn us not to take the earnest young Stephen too seriously. When parodies appear they are usually parodies of silly-pompous Latinate prose, but Anglo-Saxon can be pushed far enough to take the edge of earnestness off even the most blood-chilling description: 'Hauled stark over the gunwale he breathes upward the stench of his green grave, his leprous nosehole snoring to the sun.'

After humour, and cognate with it, humanity. *Ulysses* is one of the most humane novels ever written. There is no cruelty to any animal (not even to dogs, which Joyce feared), and there are no notable acts of violence. The Citizen hurls a biscuit-tin after Bloom but misses him: even if he had hit him no great damage would have been done. A more sensational writer would have been glad to send Bloom off to lick genuine wounds. But the violence is symbolic here, as it is in the 'Circe' episode when the soldiers knock down Stephen. Stephen is more drunk than hurt, and even the expressed intention of violence brings on the Black Mass and Armageddon, as though the normal order of things can barely sustain it. The Croppy Boy is hanged in song and hallucination, and the technique of hanging in general is discussed, but it is all cleansed to comedy. *Ulysses* may do violence to language, but never to people.

There is plenty of hate in the book, as there are plenty of the hateful, but Joyce's doctrine of stasis insists on the artful purgation of strong feeling. The Sinn Fein attitude to the English oppressor is a convention, like the legend of poor suffering Ireland, Deirdre of the Sorrows, Kathleen na-Houlihan, the Shan van Vocht. It is blown up, especially in the 'Cyclops' chapter, to a pitch of absurdity, so that the oppressive English reader may even enjoy the hate. As for the hateful, these are, by definition almost, those characters who are inimical to Stephen and Bloom, and their author's only revenge on them is to make them gently ridiculous. It seems that Joyce's intention was that the reader should find Buck Mulligan more and more detestable on each appearance, but this never happens: he is always welcome because of his wit. As for the other Antinous, Blazes Boylan, he is doomed to be ridiculous from the very start of his adulterous journey to Eccles Street, and we end with pity rather than hate. If we are really anxious to find someone to dislike in *Ulysses*, we should look rather in the direction of its secondary hero, Stephen Dedalus–insolvent, bumptious, full of intellectual pride and irreligious bigotry, drunk, would-be lecher, *poseur*. But, of course, we need his weaknesses as we need Bloom's strength, and without an imperfect Stephen the book could have neither plot nor pattern. We end up, to our surprise, by looking for the good in everyone and discounting faults (there is nothing that can be called evil) as so many shadows.

Joyce is no Wellsian optimist–he does not believe in the perfectability of man–but he accepts the world as it is and relishes man's creations (why, otherwise, glorify an art or science in every chapter except the last ?). The greatest of man's achievements, after language, is the community, and Joyce's Dublin stands for every city-state that ever was. The impersonal conurbation, what Auden calls the 'abstract civic space imposed upon the fields', has no place in this concept. To Joyce, a community is men meeting, drinking, arguing, recognising each other in the streets, and one of his peculiar miracles is to make a real historical Dublin (the Dublin that flourished in summer, 1904) an eternal pattern of human society. All men gain strength and even a certain nobility from belonging to it, and Bloom and Stephen are equally citizens of a blessed imperfect city, despite their intermittent sense of inner exile. They are Dubliners first and all else after.

But, beyond the city, lies the whole of Western civilisation, and Bloom's strength can be properly exhibited only in relation to that. It strides through the book in many of its aspects–economics, politics, literature, architecture, music and the rest–trying to dwarf Bloom, shout him down, overawe him. But he comes through it all unscathed, the common man undiminished by the acts of uncommon men. More than that, the 'Laestrygonians' episode shows him (as the 'Nestor' episode shows Stephen) as aware of the true nature of the time-process all men must suffer that civilisation (which is *not* the same as history) may be achieved. History is a mess, an imposition of the dead on the living, a nightmare from which one is always trying to awaken (*Finnegans Wake* is to demonstrate that history is a sham); art and science and the wonder of the human community are, nevertheless, distilled out of history. It is the old business of the opposition of time and space. In *Ulysses* civilisation, like civic statues and an opera-house, fills up a spacious city; time is cut down to its minimum–nine-hundred-odd pages and far less than twenty-four hours. The next task (reserved for *Finnegans Wake*) will be to get rid of time altogether.

The spatial representation of the whole of Western culture–an heroic background for an advertising canvasser who is also a cuckold –calls for vast linguistic resources and justifies the stretching to the limit of the English language, the creation of new words and the resurrection of old ones. The need to tell the truth about man's daily mind necessitates the fracture of syntax, the fusion and truncation of words, the phonetic transcription of vocables which are not properly words at all. No reader will find this linguistic display purely wanton, knowing Joyce's deeper aim. But he will be justified in being apprehensive about Joyce's next book. After the exploitation of the pre-verbal conscious mind, and even the odd trip to the borders of sleep, what can Joyce do next? He can only plunge straight into the unconscious mind and, for the purpose of describing it, create something like a new language. We must take a deep breath before plunging with him. But, wherever we go and whatever we hear, we shall still be in Dublin listening to the speech of Dubliners, glorifying the family and the civic community, and tracing the adventures of a father, an exile, an unheroic hero.

PART THREE

THE MAN-MADE MOUNTAIN

1: Big Night Music

STONES WERE THROWN AT STEPHEN, THE PROTOMARTYR. BY A miracle, he escaped hurt, kept the stones, and used them for building a labyrinth. Then, dissatisfied Daedalus, he broke up that all too merely superhuman structure and fused the stones into the first-ever fabricated mountain. The artist had been a metaphorical God-the-Father only; the time had come for him literally to rival the primal Creator by making something whose majesty and terror all men would perceive but which they would spend their lives trying to interpret. *Finnegans Wake* is as close to a work of nature as any artist ever got—massive, baffling, serving nothing but itself, suggesting a meaning but never quite yielding anything but a fraction of it, and yet (like a tree) desperately simple. Poems are made by fools like Blake, but only Joyce can make a *Wake*.

It took seventeen years to synthetise, starting after the launching of *Ulysses* and reaching completion just before the outbreak of the second World War. It looked like a warning of the chaos to come; actually, so the interpreters found, it was all the bitterness of past time healed, Humpty Dumpty put together again, a secret guide to reconstituting any given chaos into a cosmos. None of this was clear during the long period of gestation: those who had given Joyce most support during the making of *Ulysses* were inclined to desert him as a man who was going further than was either sane or decent. But the fragments that appeared in the journal *transition* and the little pamphlets that came from Faber during the thirties—*Anna Livia Plurabelle, Haveth Childers Everywhere, Tales Told of Shem and Shaun*—seemed to us sixth-form boys merely charming:

O tell me all about Anna Livia! I want to hear all about Anna Livia. Well, you know Anna Livia? Yes, of course, we all know Anna Livia. Tell me all. Tell me now. You'll die when you hear. Well, you know, when the old cheb went futt and did what you know. Yes, I know, go on. Wash quit and don't be dabbling. Tuck up your sleeves and loosen your talktapes. And don't butt me–hike!–when you bend. Or whatever it was they threed to make out he thried to two in the Fiendish park . . .

Everybody knew that these were substantial trailers of a big emergent book called, because the mystery-loving author would not divulge his ultimate title, *Work in Progress*. Something of the whole ambitious plan was revealed in a volume of essays called *Our Exagmination round His Factification for Incamination of Work in Progress*, but it seemed possible to take the verbal fun of *Anna Livia* not too seriously, especially as Joyce himself had advertised it like this:

> Buy a book in brown paper
> From Faber & Faber
> To see Annie Liffey trip, tumble and caper.
> Sevensinns in her singthings,
> Plurabelle on her prose,
> Seashell ebb music wayriver she flows.

What was it all but a more sophisticated 'Jabberwocky'? The derivation from *Alice* was pointed by the identification of the hero of *Haveth Childers Everywhere* with, though without his talent for semantic exegesis, Humpty Dumpty himself:

> Humptydump Dublin squeaks through his norse,
> Humptydump Dublin hath a horrible vorse
> And with all his kinks english
> Plus his irismanx brogues
> Humptydump Dublin's grandada of all rogues.

It was in an honoured English tradition–puns, portmanteau-words, teasing mystifications–but there were times when it seemed to go too far. How about all those names of rivers flashing like fish through the prose of babbling, bubbling, deloothering, giddygaddy, grannyma, gossipaceous Anna Livia, water and woman?

Tell me the trent of it while I'm lathering hail out of Denis Florence MacCarthy's combies.

Is there irwell a lord of the manor or a knight of the shire at strike . . .?

. . . tapting a flank and tipting a jutty and palling in and pietaring out and clyding by on her eastway.

Not where the Finn fits into the Mourne, not where the Nore takes lieve of Bloem, not where the Braye divarts the Farer, not where the Moy changez her minds twixt Cullin and Conn tween Cunn and Collin?

Moreover, the portmanteau-words of 'Jabberwocky' play fair. Forms like 'brillig' and 'slithy' resolve themselves into simple

186

English, but Joyce knows more languages than Alice (whose dream-poem, after all, 'Jabberwocky' really is) and his puns and portmanteaux seem to be the thin end of a wedge that, driven into English, will cause it to crack, collapse, and be capable of being put together again only under the auspices of UNO. Joyce's language is a weird sort of pan-European, Eurish (I thank Michael Frayn for that term) with Asiatic loan-words added. Pun-European, rather. If one knows many foreign languages well, it is difficult to keep them out of the pun-mixer. Not that any average reader would cavil at 'silvamoonlake', where 'silva' is not only 'silver' but a Roman wood. But one needs a sliver of Slav to cope with Anna Livia's soothing words to her crying son (almost at the end of *Finnegans Wake*): 'Muy malinchily malchick!' This is evidently a sleepy deformation of 'My cold and melancholy male chick' but it is also the Russian '*Moiy malyenki malchik*' – 'my little boy'.

How far can word-play legitimately go? The foreign language I know best is Malay, and were I writing a new *Finnegans Wake*, I might be tempted to produce a sentence like 'Lanky Suky! Seidlitz! Bear ma stout in!' One has a dream-sensation of a headachy Negro or Scot calling his wife or servant for a seidlitz powder followed by a bottle of stout, but at the same time the caller is stating that he is now thoroughly settled in Malaya (*Langkasuka*–the old Indian name for the country; 'seidlitz' pronounced 'settlers'; *bermastautin*–Malay for a settler). Would Joyce be pleased with that? Probably not with the clumsiness, but he would approve the attempt at widening the linguistic resources available for the punning technique. His aim, as we shall see, is the creation of a universal myth, to which all cultures and languages are relevant (Chinese would have to be soft-pedalled, though, since it is a tongue incapable of admitting puns). If we do not catch all the references, even on a twentieth reading, that does not matter: the references are there, waiting for when we shall understand them. *Finnegans Wake*, like Eliot's *The Waste Land*, is a terminus for the author–all the trains of his learning end up there–but it is also a starting-point for the reader: catch this slow train for Upanishad country; this express goes to German metaphysics; here is the special for the *Book of Kells*. We must not attempt to understand everything at once: that way madness lies. But *Finnegans Wake* hides in its word-play a very great amount of world culture, as well as Dublin street-cries, music-hall songs, cowheel, tripe, and best-sellers, and it waits on our becoming as erudite as Joyce himself.

I must not, anywhere in this part of my book, give the impression that *Finnegans Wake* is a humourless monster crammed with learning and merely seasoned with a few puns. It is always funny where it is not touching and inspiring, and it is provocative of loud laughter, just as is *Ulysses* (Nora Joyce heard that laughter constantly coming out of her near-blind hard-working husband's work-in-progress-room). The book has already revivified language for us, so that we all accept 'clapplause', the 'abnihilisation of the etym' (which means, optimistically, the re-creation of meaning out of nothing), 'In the name of the former and of the latter and of their holocaust. Allmen' and a host of other felicities. The play extends beyond mere words and embraces music: A.D. and B.C.–the whole of history–are reduced to a tinkling tune; Shaun, one of Anna Livia's sons, has a GBD pipe in his face or FACE, thus turning himself into a treble stave. A ghastly sequence of world-history ends with a marginal drawing of dry bones and a nose with fingers put to it. The initial of the hero, Earwicker, falls on its back or claws the ground with its three feet. Anna Livia Plurabelle is turned into an ALP. Fancy knows no limits.

A giant disports itself with all learning and all language, a terribly irreverent giant. But no man writes a book of six hundred and twenty-eight pages (especially a man with Joyce's lack of sight, wealth and encouragement) for the sake of pure play and sheer irreverence. The technique is in the service of something important, and we must now consider what that something important is. *Alice* again gives us our first clue. Her two books were all about dreams, and so is *Finnegans Wake*–or rather it depicts one great dream, the dream which is life ('Ever drifting down the stream–Lingering in the golden gleam–Life, what is it but a dream?': Lewis Carroll's epilogue is also an epigraph). In dreams we are released from the limitations of the spatio-temporal world. That world insists on one event following another and on keeping identities distinct, so that A cannot occupy the same bit of time-space as B; nor can A ever become B. But a dream permits Jonathan Swift to be also the Tristram that fell in love with Iseult and, at one and the same time, Parnell. A dream permits one's wife to become confused with one's daughter. In a dream Napoleon can defeat Wellington, and in the year A.D. 1132 at that. Dreams represent, however feebly, the world we all yearn for, a world of infinite plasticity.

To represent a dream convincingly, one needs a plastic language, a language in which two objects or persons can subsist in one and the same word. More than that, one requires a technique for killing the time-element that resides in all language. I say, in waking language, 'My corpse will eventually fertilise the earth and help the crops to grow', and that spatial process loses its quality of miracle (from death comes life) because of the dilution caused by the time-bound verb and adverb. Joyce throws the whole structure overboard, uses simple metathesis: 'corpse' becomes 'cropse'. Could anything be more beautiful or legitimate? At the same time, a dream is not to be regarded as primarily a revealer of identities which the space-time world (that world of phenomenon, not ultimate truth) seeks to hide from us. We live primarily in a waking world, and we cannot be expected to understand everything that takes place in the world of dream. Hence dream-language must often deliberately conceal things from us: it must appear to us as strange, almost gibberish—a non-stop babble which throws up images of the non-time-space-world only intermittently. In reading *Finnegans Wake*, we are sometimes shocked by a sudden appearance of what looks like waking sense, as in some of the footnotes to the long chapter that seems to satirise scholarly learning: 'All the world loves a big gleaming jelly'—a fair enough television commercial slogan; 'Real life behind the flood-lights as shown by the best exponents of a royal divorce.' It is a relief to find that dream-logic kills the waking sense: we refer to the words of the text which these footnotes seem to gloss and find nothing but nonsense. The word 'brandnewburgher' in the text is defined in the footnotes as 'A viking vernacular expression still used in the Summerhill district for a jerryhatted man of forty who puts two fingers into his boiling soupplate and licks them in turn to find out if there is enough mushroom catsup in the mutton broth.' We would like more word-play there, more of the look of nonsense. We become used to the mad idiom as we become used to the dark—either in sleep or at the cinema—and to blink one's eyes in the light of a sentence capable of orthodox grammatical analysis (even if the total sense has little to do with the real world) is somewhat painful. Let us have more of 'Tomley. The grown man. A butcher szewched him the bloughs and braches. I'm chory to see P. Shuter.'

Joyce, however, in planning his work, did much of it in the light. It is shocking to see how much of the early drafts of *Work in Progress* makes pedestrian sense. Here is the first version of part of the *Anna Livia Plurabelle* chapter, as published in *Navire d'Argent*, 1925:

Tell me, tell me, how could she cam through all her fellows, the dare-devil? Linking one and knocking the next and polling in and petering out and clyding by in the eastway. Who was the first that ever burst?

Someone it was, whoever you are. Tinker, tailor, soldier, sailor, Paul Pry or polishman. That's the thing I always want to know.

Two years later, in *transition*, it had become

Tell me, tell me, how could she cam through all her fellows, the neckar she was, the diveline? Linking one and knocking the next, tapping a flank and tipping a jutty and palling in and petering out and clyding by on her eastway. Wai-whou was the first that ever burst? Someone he was, whoever they were, in a tactic attack or in single combat. Tinker, tailor, soldier, sailor, Paul Pry or polishman. That's the thing I always want to know.

The following year it had thickened to

Tell me, tell me, how cam she camlin through all her fellows, the neckar she was the diveline? Linking one and knocking the next, tapting a flank and tipting a jutty and palling in and pietaring out and clyding by on her eastway. Waiwhou was the first thurever burst? Someone he was, whuebra they were, in a tactic attack or in single combat. Tinker, tilar, souldrer, salor, Pieman Peace or Polistaman. That's the thing I always want to know.

In the final version the thickening has gone further and, since Joyce never lived to prepare a revised edition, furthest:

Tell me, tell me, how cam she camlin through all her fellows, the neckar she was, the diveline? Casting her perils before our swains from Fonte-in-Monte to Tidingtown and from Tidingtown tilhavet. Linking one and knocking the next, tapting a flank and tipting a jutty and palling in and pietaring out and clyding by on her eastway. Waiwhou was the first thurever burst? Someone he was, whuebra they were, in a tactic attack or in single combat. Tinker, tilar, souldrer, salor, Pieman Peace or Polistaman. That's the thing I'm elwys on edge to esk.

That final sentence, you will agree, is a great improvement on the first draft (retained, you will notice, in the next two versions), but I cannot help feeling that Joyce might have been happier if he had been able to revise 'in a tactic attack or in single combat' – painfully nakèd! – to something like 'in a tackstick tattack or in sinful wombat'.

We accept the language of dream, then, and the author's laying on of thicker and thicker blankets of dark (with holes in to let in a little light), but now we must ask what the dream is about. Life, yes, but whose life? The answer is: the life of the whole human race – in a word, history. Stephen Dedalus, like Bloom, was oppressed by that nightmare from which he was trying to awake: is he now submitting to the nightmare, settling down to a long sleep the better to be frightened by it? No, because he has rejected Mr Deasy's vision of history as a long line of events leading to the emergence of God.

Time remains the enemy; history must be spatialised. How? By seeing it as a circle, a wheel perpetually turning, the same events recurring again and again. In that 'Nestor' episode of *Ulysses* there is a reference to Vico Road, Dalkey, and it is the Italian historiographer, Giovanni Battista Vico (1668-1744), who shows the way to the wheel.

Joyce took to the 'roundheaded Neapolitan', and was particularly interested in the fact that he seemed to have feared thunderstorms, just like himself. 'It is almost unknown to the male Italians I have met', he said. Thunder plays a big part in the scheme of history presented in the *Scienza Nuova*: it starts off, a terrible voice of God, each of the four segments into which Vico divides his circle–the theocratic age, the aristocratic age, the democratic age, the *ricorso* or return to the beginning again. It is the thunder which drives men to change their social organisations (they run into shelters, which foster the building of communities, to escape from it). Language is an attempt to present in human vocables the noise which the thunder makes. Thunder–which is only heard, like God, as a noise from the street in *Ulysses*–becomes part of the very fabric of the sound-stream that is *Finnegans Wake*.

Joyce did not borrow from Vico's theory consistently. It fired his imagination; he especially liked Vico's insistence on the importance of mythology and etymology in the interpretation of history and his granting to mere events a secondary role. But he did not take the cyclical theory as chronologically true: it was rather in the field of the human psyche that the awareness of repetition and return could be best exploited. Joyce's pseudo-Viconian pattern starts off with the cult of the giant, the colossal hero who is too big to be true. When he dies, he can all too easily wake again, but he must be kept asleep so that the truly human ruler can come along–the father-figure who has a wife and begets sons and daughters. A son will debase the doctrines of the father, leading a so-called people's state which has the elements of decay in it because the ancient laws which make for stability have been ill-remembered or falsely interpreted. There has to be a *ricorso*–a return to the rule of the gigantic hero, and the cycle starts all over again, for ever and ever, allmen. In Joyce, the thunder is not so much the voice of God as the noise of a fall–the fall of the primal hero, the fall of man–and its dynamic charges the wheel and makes it turn. All history (at least, as it appears in a dream) is the story of falling and–through the force of that fall which makes the wheel go round–returning. Time as we

191

know it from the calendars and the history-books has no place here. If we want a perpetual patient current, underlying all the thumping falls and painful resurrections of man, we had best look for it in woman, who carries sin (Eve) but does not herself sin (the Virgin Mary), who is spatial and solid but also fluid, renewed as a river is renewed, and not through the thunderous dynamism of a fall. As for dates in our dream-history, let these have very little chrono-logical significance. The big year of *Finnegans Wake* is 1132. Falling bodies (we are back with Leopold Bloom) drop at the speed of 32 feet per second per second; 11 is the figure of return – we have finished counting on our ten fingers and must start all over again. 32 is for Adam and Parnell and Humpty Dumpty. 11 is for doing what the king's horses and men could not do, what the Irish people did not wish to do, and what Christ alone was able to do. But, in a dream where Christ joins the other dead and resurrected gods, it is left to woman to gather the broken fragments of the egg and, 'sunny side up with care', transmit them to the next generation, enabling old Parhumptyadam – my portmanteau-name, not Joyce's – to live on, through met him pike hoses, in the flesh and spirit of others.

Soon we must plunge into this dream of history with great tea-or-whiskey-or-Guinness-fortified courage. But a very pertinent question now is: who, in *Finnegans Wake*, dreams the dream? The obvious answer is: Joyce himself, since only Joyce knows all that Joyce knows. Similarly, those briefer summer and winter dreams are dreamed by Lewis Carroll. But Carroll has Alice as his dreamer-within-the-dream, while he dreams on the outside. Joyce must have his dreamer, too. Now *Finnegans Wake* is ceasing to be merely history ridden on a cycle down a road of portmanteau-word cobbles; it is becoming a novel.

Joyce's hero is a common man, like Bloom. He is a publican in Chapelizod, a suburb of Dublin, and his name is Humphrey Chimp-den Earwicker. This is no very Irish name, and we learn, through the devious mists of dream-language, that Earwicker is in fact a foreigner, just like Bloom. But he is not a Jew: his race is Scandi-navian and his religion Protestant Christian. He thus belongs to the stock of the conquering Teutons – Danes, English – who took over Dublin and whom Dublin is likely to resent. Because he is a foreigner he is turned – by a malevolent xenophobic citizenry – into all foreign-ers; host of an inn, he is the uneasy guest of a city. He has a wife, Anna, and three children – Isabel (or Issy, or Izzy) and boy-twins whose real names are never made clear (they appear at the end of the book as Kevin and Jerry, but they sustain major roles throughout the dream mainly as Shem and Shaun).

The dreamer Joyce dreams of a Saturday night in which–between rumbustious carousal and Sabbath peace–Earwicker is dreaming in bed, his wife beside him. The five of the family have to act the whole of human history in dream, and this is a difficult task, necessitating a great deal of doubling, trebling and so on to the figure *n*. But support is obtainable from the bar-help and the cleaning-woman, and even a picture on the wall–the Archangel Michael quelling Satan–will assist with the mythology. The four corners of the bed can be Matthew, Mark, Luke and John (fused into Mamalujo), and a calendar could originate the seven rainbow girls, the twenty-eight girls who follow Issy, and the ponderous twelve who (like the twelve contributors to *Our Exagmination round His Factification for In-camination of Work in Progress*) give judgement in -ation-ending polysyllables. And, of course, these characters can have their origin in some of the pub-customers. Human history, this bed thy centre is, these walls thy sphere.

Alice is the centre of her dreams, but she originates none of the action: she is the driven, not the driver. Earwicker has to have a deep unconscious motive for re-enacting man's perpetual fall and resur-rection–an in-built guilt which starts history off and keeps the wheel turning. This guilt is never far to seek in a man who, himself ageing, has an ageing wife and a nubile daughter. He seeks his youth again, he looks for the wife he once courted. An incestuous longing for his daughter is a pathetic attempt to remain loyal to his wife while indulging the last spurt of desire for a body comely and sweet as cinnamon. This longing is too terrible to be revealed nakedly in dreams: it becomes a sin as vague as Adam's–something that was done in a park, the guilt of it making HCE (the initials are more important than the name) indulge in Freudian self-defence, usually with a stutter. It identifies him with all guilty lovers, from Tristram to Parnell, and even with the great god-giant Finnegan, whose pre-historic fall still has the whole world (Dublin, that is) rumbling. It is time for us to meet Finnegan. After all, this is his wake.

2: Bygmester Finnegan

A LARGE NUMBER OF THE LITERATE, INCLUDING CRITICS AND literary historians, insist on punctuating Joyce's title for him, believing that–through inadvertency or ignorance–he left out an apostrophe in *Finnegans*. Their pedantry destroys a pregnant ambiguity. *Finnegans Wake* fuses two opposed notions–the wake, or funeral feast, of Finnegan; the waking up of all Finnegans. In the very name Finnegan the whole of Vico's *ricorso* is summed up: we finish (*fin, fine,* finn) and we start egan or again.

There is, however, a piece of folk-literature called 'Finnegan's Wake', complete with apostrophe–an Irish-American comic song that goes like this:

> Tim Finnegan lived in Walker Street,
>   An Irish gintleman, mighty odd.
> He'd a bit of a brogue, so neat and sweet,
>   And to rise in the world, Tim carried a hod.
> But Tim had a sort of tippling way:
>   With a love of liquor Tim was born,
> And to help him through his work each day,
>   Took a drop of the creature every morn.
>
> *Chorus:*
>   Whack! Hurroo!–now dance to your partner!
>   Welt the flure, your trotters shake;
>   Isn't it the truth I've told ye,
>   Lots of fun at Finnegan's wake?
>
> One morning Tim was rather full,
>   His head felt heavy and it made him shake.
> He fell from the ladder and broke his skull,
>   So they carried him home, his corpse to wake.
> They tied him up in a nice clean sheet,
>   And laid him out upon the bed,
> Wid a gallon of whiskey at his feet,
>   And a barrel of porter at his head.

His friends assembled at his wake.
 Missus Finnegan called out for lunch:
And first they laid in tay and cake,
 Then pipes and tobaccy and whiskey punch.
Miss Biddy Moriarty began to cry:
 'Such a purty corpse did yez ever see?
Arrah, Tim mavourneen, an' why did ye die?'
 'Hold yer gob,' sez Judy Magee.

Then Peggy O'Connor took up the job.
 'Arrah, Biddy,' sez she, 'yer wrong, I'm sure.'
But Biddy gave her a belt in the gob
 And laid her sprawling on the flure.
Each side in war did soon engage;
 'Twas woman to woman and man to man;
Shillelah law was all the rage
 And a bloody ruction soon began.

Mickey Maloney raised his head,
 When a gallon of whiskey flew at him;
It missed and, falling on the bed,
 The liquor scattered over Tim.
'Och, he revives! See how he raises!'
 And Timothy, jumping up from bed,
Sez, 'Whirl your liquor around like blazes—
 Souls to the devil! D'ye think I'm dead?'

Chorus:
 Whack! Hurroo!—now dance to your partner!
  Welt the flure, your trotters shake;
 Isn't it the truth I've told ye,
  Lots of fun at Finnegan's wake?

Joyce, writing one of the most difficult books of all time, at least bases it on very lowly material. He takes his theme of death and resurrection from a vaudeville song and, working out his theme, makes more references to popular art than to the best that has ever been thought and said. This is in conformity with the dream-maker's technique of building his elaborate structures out of shreds and patches (who ever dreamt through even a page of *The Critique of Pure Reason?*), but it is also the consummation of that fateful cocoa-session in No. 7 Eccles Street. Joyce has committed himself to the exaltation of the common man, whose timeless saga *Finnegans Wake* is. Deathless heroes and resurrected gods float through the book to the tunes of street-songs, fourth-form parodies of prayers, bits of scandal out of the Sunday papers. Whatever *Finnegans Wake* may be, it is not a highbrow book. Or rather its highbrow elements float on the top like tea-leaves: the brew is all.

The very term 'wake' is a suggestive one to a word-loving artist, containing as it does the opposed theses of death and life. In essence, *Finnegans Wake* is all about what happens while Finnegan lies, life suspended, on the bed, the twelve mourners all about him. In the great dream he is, inevitably, transmuted from a mere drunken bricklayer to an archetypal builder of ancient civilisations, whose fall is so loud that it becomes Vico's thunderclap (always easily recognisable as a word of exactly one hundred letters), who is identifiable with Ibsen's Masterbuilder (*Bygmester* in Dano-Norwegian), with the legendary Irish giant Finn MacCool, who was fifteen cubits high, and with Joyce's own mythical hero, HCE. This last identification may seem confusing: after all, Earwicker is supposed to replace Finnegan as a new heroic type–the family man as opposed to the fabulous giant. But we must constantly remember how small our cast is, and Earwicker, as father of the acting troupe, must take all the heavy parts.

Finnegan's fall, acted by HCE, opens the book, but only after Joyce has swiftly presented the story's main themes and symbols (as he presented all the musical subjects of the 'Sirens' episode in *Ulysses* before actually striking up his fugue). Let us gulp back all our apprehensions and wade into this opening:

riverrun, past Eve and Adam's, from swerve of shore to bend of bay, brings us by a commodius vicus of recirculation back to Howth Castle and Environs.
   Sir Tristram, violer d'amores, fr'over the short sea, had passencore rearrived from North Armorica on this side the scraggy isthmus of Europe Minor to wielderfight his penisolate war: nor had topsawyer's rocks by the stream Oconee exaggerated themselse to Laurens County's gorgios while they went doublin their mumper all the time: nor avoice from afire bellowsed mishe mishe to tauftauf thuartpeatrick: nor yet, though venissoon after, had a kidscad buttended a bland old isaac: not yet, though all's fair in vanessy, were sosie sesthers wroth with twone nathandjoe. Rot a peck of pa's malt had Jhem or Shen brewed by arclight and rory end to the regginbrow was to be seen ringsome on the aquaface.

Difficult? Oh yes, difficult. But a certain difficulty is the small price we must pay for excitement, richness, originality. And we must learn to smile rather than frown: this is the world of 'Jabberwocky'. But the dream is not Alice's. We are dreaming a mature dream, remembering the past of mankind and the primal guilt that history hides but reveals. Yet the dream is a joke, as life itself may be.

That first sentence is the only one of the whole book that begins without a capital letter. Joyce tells us why in the word 'vicus' (Latin for Vico) and also in 'recirculation'. We are not beginning; we are resuming. History is a circle, as Vico taught, and we have entered it in the middle of a sentence. If we want the start of that sentence, we have to look at the last line of the book, where we find 'A way a lone a last a loved a long the'–no full stop. Ideally, then, having finished the book we have to turn back again to the first page and ride with the cycle once more. Time may have a stop but history's wheel is in perpetual motion.

Joyce sets his book in Dublin. 'Eve and Adam's' refers primarily to Adam and Eve's Church, but it also implies the mythical beginning of human life: we are in the giant age of fable. The running river is the Liffey–Anna Livia–but also, as we shall learn, eternal woman. 'Howth Castle and Environs' is the first sounding of the HCE chord, one which, in many transformations, will hold us down to our hero throughout the book. The castle on Howth Head was built by a Sir Almeric Tristram (not the Tristram of the Arthurian legend, though we must accept a dream-identification of the two): it stands, as Finn MacCool stood, on the headland, vainly resisting invasion. HCE is both fortification and invader (as the true Dubliner is both Celt and Teuton).

Then we meet our double Tristram, though here in the aspect of guilty love. 'Violer d'amores' means both the musical instrument called the viola d'amore (suggesting minstrelsy and ideal love) and the violation of love and trust: Tristram came to Ireland to take Iseult to Cornwall, a bride for his uncle King Mark, but fell in love with her himself: we have been given two guilt-myths already in four lines–Adam and Tristram, both of whom fell through sin. 'Fr'over' is an archaic form of 'from over', but it suggests 'rover'. 'Passencore' starts off like 'passenger', though its main meaning (the French *pas encore*) is 'not yet'. 'Rearrived' means what it says: these events, like all the events of history, recur perpetually. 'Armorica' is Brittany but also America: the old world and the new subsist side by side in Joyce's mythology, and, by the stream Oconee in Laurens County, Georgia, there stands (check this with any gazetteer) another city of Dublin. As the Viconian cycle turns and turns, showing the essential impulses of history to be always the same, so any new world must re-enact the history of the old. Indeed, the new world *is* the old, Lawrence's County being the old Dublin by virtue of the name of its bishop–Lawrence O'Toole–at the time of the English invasion of Henry II, as also the name-change to Lawrence that Tristram (castle-builder, not lover of Iseult) effected when he settled in Dublin. 'Topsawyer' refers us to Mark Twain–a second King Mark, famous in the new world, as well as to Tom Sawyer and Huckleberry Finn (a brotherly pair). Note Joyce's spelling of 'Georgia' as 'gorgios'–'gorges', yes, as also the gipsy word for 'young' (a young Dublin built across the seas), but also the author's own son Giorgio (though now he calls himself George). Joyce can never keep his family out, and why should he? World history is family history, dreamt in a bedroom. Did he not first meet Nora Barnacle when she was a chambermaid in Finn's Hotel? Is not HCE a sort of John Joyce, roaring father? Are not Shem and Shaun (James and John) really the two antithetical brothers James ('Sunny Jim') and Stanislaus ('Brother John') Joyce?

Anyway, in 'doublin their mumper all the time' we recognise the spirit of growth, the perpetual building of new Dublins. 'Wielder-fight' is wielding a weapon in battle but also fighting again and again (German *wieder* as in *Auf Wiedersehn*). What kind of fighting? The 'penisolate' war can be one fought with the penis (the vigorously randy Shaun-type brother) or with the pen in isolation (that will do for Shem, the solitary artist); also it can refer to the Peninsular War and the opposition of Wellington (Irish general) to Napoleon (foreigner, would-be invader, a kind of HCE). But let us not forget that we are dealing with early history: 'avoice from afire bellowsed mishe mishe to tauftauf thuartpeatrick'. That voice is God's saying 'I am' twice in old Erse–it is also St Bridget's saying 'I am a Christian'; St Patrick is Ireland herself, the peat-rick; St Germanicus, St Patrick's tutor, appropriately says 'Baptise baptise' ('tauftauf') in German. Soon we are led to the Bible. 'A kidscad buttended a bland old isaac.' We should now be learning the trick of expanding such dream-compression into straight narrative. Jacob (whose name suggests James, or Shem) showed artist's cunning in disguising himself, the cadet but also cad, as his elder brother Esau by means of a kidskin, thus duping his bland-blind old father Isaac into giving him his blessing. (Here too, if we want him, we can find Isaac Butt, whom Parnell trickily ousted from the Irish leadership.) 'Sosie sesthers wroth' near-disguises Susannah, Esther and Ruth–all loved by older men, as HCE loves Issy–but also brings in a reference to Swift's love for Stella and Vanessa (heralded by 'venissoon', developed further in 'all's fair in vanessy'). HCE is Swift, father-type desiring daughter-type, earning 'wroth'. Swift himself is 'twone nathandjoe'–Nathan and Joseph (unyielding to sexual importunities of an unlawful kind) in one, anagrammatised Jonathan. We end with

Shem and Shaun, the eternal brothers whom we shall meet *in extenso* later, now become a trio–Jhem and Shen: Shem, Ham and Japhet–superseding their father Noah, brewing under God's covenant–the 'regginbrow' or rainbow. The Teutonic motif, appropriate to the Scandinavian invader HCE, is there–*Regenbogen*–as also in 'ringsome'–circlewise, the cycle of God's promise, matching the cycle of his thunder.

The compression is extreme in these opening paragraphs, but we would be wrong to unravel everything at once. The deeper references are there if we want them, but the general theme of the book floats, in something like sunlight, on the surface of the 'aquaface'. We are concerned with the cycle of history–the things that have both happened and not yet happened–and with a Dublin that is everyplace. In this Dublin, the one in America as the one in Ireland, there is a father who is eternal rock with a castle on it, driven to a guilty fall by unlawful love of a younger woman, a girl, a daughter. In him there are two opposing elements, his sons. As the duality of God the Father and God the Son calls into being a third element to make a trinity, so these two sons can appear as a trio. Woman appears in two aspects–mother Eve and daughter Iseult or Stella or Vanessa or Ruth or Susannah or Esther (Stella's real name was Esther Johnson; Vanessa's real name was Esther Vanhomrigh–watch out for this latter surname, too). The two aspects are fused in the image of a river which, old with the accumulations of the life of a city, dies by mingling itself with the sea; clouds from the sea move in to the river's source, so that death is a kind of renewal of life: the fall of the rain is woman's fall, life-giving. As for man's fall, Finnegan's fall, that thunder brings no rain.

As time means nothing in Joyce's universal Dublin-centred chronicle, we must not be puzzled if, in the account of Finnegan's fall that now follows, we anticipate a great deal of the story of HCE. The fall itself is all falls, and its thunder sounds in many languages. It is mythical (Finnegan has a 'humptyhillhead') and it is yesterday ('wallstrait' echoes a financial crash in the thirties). What caused the fall we cannot exactly say, but drink brought Tim Finnegan low in the song, and Joyce's Finnegan is a sort of wine-god: 'Comeday morm and, O, you're vine! Sendday's eve and, ah, you're vinegar!' A sexual sin is imposed on him by HCE himself ('Haroun Childeric Eggeberth') and he has HCE's own guilty stutter ('Bygmester Finnegan, of the Stuttering Hand' . . . 'oftwhile balbulous'–and it was Balbus, whose name means 'Stutterer', who was always building a wall). The fall takes place prehistorically, but also at the time when the Pope, the Englishman Nicholas Breakspear, granted the rule of Ireland to Henry II. Hence Finnegan's building has 'larrons o'toolers clittering up and tombles a'buckets clottering down'– Lawrence O'Toole, a rising prelate; Thomas à Becket, a falling one.

Dead Finnegan, really sleeping Finnegan, is mourned by twelve citizens, but the feast is to be no mere matter of fish and ale and bread, though these are spread on the table: it is the flesh of the god himself that is to be sacramentally devoured. But, before this can happen, we are made to see the body of Finnegan as part of the Irish landscape. He is the giant Finn MacCool asleep. His head is the Hill of Howth, his feet are near Earwicker's pub at Chapelizod (or Iseult's chapel). His fall, we hear, has taken place in Dublin's Phoenix Park–a sort of Eden where a notorious political murder was to herald Ireland's phoenix-resurrection. But this same park saw the fall of HCE, whose vague sin involved two girls (his wife and daughter in disguise) and was witnessed by three soldiers (his two sons as a Ham-Shem-Japhet trio). But the mention of soldiers brings us to the theme of conflict. The bloody ructions that were to wake Tim Finnegan are swollen into a panorama of war in general. We go to the Wellington Memorial in Phoenix Park and are shown round it by an old woman (the eternal ageing wife who preserves fragments from the past as she gathers the smashed bits of the body of her dead lord, Humpty Dumpty, for transmission to the future). The Irishman 'Willingdone', the battle of Waterloo, a couple of cavalry mares who turn into female camp-followers and the two girls in the park– these symbolise the conflict in HCE's sinning soul, but they also suggest how wars are merely a vast projection of family conflict. The father, aware of his failing sexual powers, will want to kill younger men; the younger men quarrel between themselves. We are brought back to HCE's bedroom with the sound 'Tip'–a branch tapping on the window. History is here and now.

We leave the museum and, in the open air again, see how the old woman, eternal widow, has been transformed into a bird, pecking up fragments of the past (and particularly of the smashed body of the dead hero) to feed us in the future:

How bootifull and how truetowife of her, when strengly forebidden, to steal our historic presents from the past postpropheticals so as to will make us all lordy heirs and ladymaidesses of a pretty nice kettle of fruit.

But we are concerned with Dublin – 'Dyoublong?' (Yes, we do. This is everybody's eternal city.) 'Hush! Caution! Echoland!' (There he is again – HCE.) What we need is a guidebook, and we find one written by 'Mammon Lujius' – Mamalujo – Matthew, Mark, Luke and John, chroniclers of the past, four bedposts who look inward to the sleep of history, not outward to the emergent future. 'Four things . . . ne'er sall fail', they say, 'til heathersmoke and cloudweed Eire's ile sall pall.' These four things are a humped old man (Humphrey Chimpden Earwicker), 'a shoe on a puir old wobban' (Anna Livia Plurabelle, ALP, river, ageing wife), 'an auburn mayde, o'brine a'bride, to be desarted' (their daughter) and 'a penn no weightier nor a polepost' (the two sons – Shem with his pen and Shaun, who can write no word of truth but can at least, like a postman, deliver it). These four eternals (Shem and Shaun are one, twin yolks of the father-egg) are then seen emerging at various phases of mock-history: A.D. 1132 produced the father; A.D. 566 the mother (a woman is half a man). There is a pause, and then history goes round, only backwards (history is only a wheel): A.D. 566 brought the daughter and A.D. 1132 the two sons Primas and Caddy – the man of action ('Primas was a santryman and drilled all decent people') and the poet ('Caddy went to Winehouse and wrote o peace a farce').

We look up from the book at the land again, and here is prehistoric Dublin. The two brothers seem to merge into a pair of comic primitive men, one the native Celt Mutt and the other the Scandinavian invader Jute. It is evident that there is a good deal of stuttering HCE in the latter: 'What a hauhauhauhaudibble thing, to be cause!' But some play is made with the word 'hesitancy', and we recognise a reference to those forged letters with which Piggot tried to incriminate Parnell (Piggot spelled the above word as 'hesitency' and thus trapped himself). 'Hasatency?' says Mutt and also, to remind us of one of Parnell's reincarnations, 'hence, cool at ebb' (HCE). Jute, though, says 'Hasitancy'. Even in Ireland's prehistory the seeds of Ireland's later sorrows (the invader, the betrayal of the redeemer) are being sown.

But there is another theme of treachery to be stated and developed. Joyce takes the historical character of Grace O'Malley who called at Howth Castle for a night's lodging and, because the family was at dinner, was refused entrance. In revenge she kidnapped the son of the Earl of Howth and kept him until the Earl promised never again to close the doors of the castle at mealtimes. Joyce makes the Earl into a Scandinavian–'Jarl van Hoother', a sort of HCE–and gives him two sons, Tristopher and Hilary, who are shown 'kickaheeling their dummy on the oil cloth flure of his homerigh, castle and earthenhouse' (HCE, also the father of Swift's Vanessa). The dummy seems to be their sister, forbidden fruit the dream keeps shapeless and anonymous, especially as ('Dare! O dare!') we see 'the jiminy Toughertrees and the dummy . . . belove on the watercloth, kissing and spitting, and roguing and poghuing, like knavepaltry and naivebride and in their second infancy'. Grace O'Malley, who is called 'the prankquean', is twice refused 'a poss of porterpease' and, in revenge, kidnaps each son in turn, turning the 'jiminy' or twin Tristopher into a blackguard and Hilary into a Cromwellian. The third time she comes, the door is shut in her face with a thunderclap hundred-letter word. It is an allegory of HCE's inability to control the destinies of his children, his impotence in the face of a desired but forbidden relationship. The thunder is the noise of guilt.

But, says Joyce, 'O foenix culprit!', parodying St Augustine's *'O felix culpa'*–happy that sin of Adam which was to bring us a redcemer. The vague crime in Phoenix Park takes us back to the body of the giant Finnegan. A voice cries: *'Usqueadbaugham!'* which, among other things, means 'whiskey', and the great god awakens with 'Did ye drink me doornail?' But he is told to lie down again–'Now be aisy, good Mr Finnimore, sir. And take your laysure like a god on pension and don't be walking abroad.' Life is going on well enough without Finnegan. Besides, 'there's already a big rody ram lad at random on the premises of his haunt of the hungred bordles, as it is told me':

. . . humphing his share of the showthers is senken on him he's such a grandfallar, with a pocked wife in pickle that's a flyfire and three lice nittle clinkers, two twilling bugs and one midget pucelle . . . Humme the Cheapner, Esc, overseen as we thought him, yet a worthy of the naym, came at this timecoloured place where we live in our paroquial fermament one tide on another, with a bumrush in a hull of a wherry . . .

The Scandinavian successor to homegrown Finnegan has arrived by water, and henceforth the tale is all his. 'Humile, commune and ensectuous from his nature', it is he 'who will be ultimendly respunchable for the hubbub caused in Edenborough'. In its sly way, that word 'ensectuous' tells us a great deal. When is a man an Earwicker or earwig? When he's an insect. When is he an insect? When his dream refuses to pronounce the word 'incest'.

3: Here Comes Everybody

<small>LET US NOT BE TOO MUCH TEMPTED TO DRAG THE BIG DREAM UP</small>
towards the light: shadowiness, confusion, the melting of one personage into another, of youth into age, friend into enemy–these are of the essence of the dream. Thus, when we meet Humphrey Chimpden Earwicker, we cannot be sure whether we are looking at a real historical figure (one who kept a pub in Chapelizod) or at a sort of paradigm of humanity. Nor can we be sure whether we meet him first as a child or as Adam, fully grown gardener. His name may be Humphrey or it may be Harold; it may even be best to call him Haromphreyld. Where did he get his surname? The anecdote about the sailor king talking to our 'lobstertrapping honest blunt' hero on a 'sultry sabbath afternoon' has the portentous emptiness of all dream-stories. We can imagine ourselves laughing heartily at HCE's 'aw war jist a cotchin on thon bluggy earwuggers' and then, on waking, feeling foolish about it. Anyway, there soon emerges a vague big Nordic father-figure–a 'folksforefather all of the time . . . having the entirety of his house about him, with the invariable broadstretched kerchief cooling his whole neck, nape and shoulder-blades' and then, with a sort of urgency, we have to consider the nature of his primal Adam-sin. Everything is hearsay, a matter of tales and rumours, like the whole of early history; indeed, the narrator of this part of the dream doubts whether there was a sin at all:

. . . To anyone who knew and loved the christlikeness of the big clean-minded giant H. C. Earwicker throughout his excellency long vicefreegal existence the mere suggestion of him as a lustsleuth nosing for trouble in a boobytrap rings particularly preposterous.

Nevertheless, the story has it that Earwicker 'behaved with on-gentilmensky immodus opposite a pair of dainty maidservants in the swoolth of the rushy hollow whither . . . dame nature in all innocency had spontaneously and about the same hour of the eventide sent them both'. Whatever the 'ongentilmensky immodus' was, three soldiers saw it.

The trouble starts when, 'ages and ages after the alleged misdemeanour', Earwicker meets a 'cad with a pipe' in the park. The word 'pipe' seems to suggest musical connotations: CAD is a musical phrase; later, Shaun is to have a GBD in his FACE. The cad asks Earwicker the time. Earwicker, quite unnecessarily, launches into a stuttering refutation of the alleged accusations against him: '. . . there is not one tittle of truth, allow me to tell you, in that purest of fibfib fabrications'. The cad goes home, brooding on this, tells his wife about it, and 'our cad's bit of strife . . . with a quick ear for spittoons' tells a priest–'her particular reverend'–that there is something fishy about HCE. And so the poison starts to spread, despite the priest's promise that 'the gossiple so delivered in his epistolear . . . would go no further than his jesuit's cloth'.

It is at this point that Joyce introduces the names of the Dublin publishers Browne and Nolan. They are useful names, for 'Browne' can be Italianised to 'Bruno', and the philosopher Bruno came from Nola (very early in his writing career Joyce called him 'the Nolan'). Bruno taught that, in a God-run universe, all opposites must eventually merge. He thus provides Joyce with a metaphysical justification for uniting opposing characters in a single personage, as Shem and Shaun, warring brothers, are reconciled in the father HCE. Similarly, HCE's accusers can take on the qualities of HCE himself. The tale-telling priest is called 'Mr Browne'; 'in his secondary personality as a Nolan', he soon has slanders about our hero circulating among the Dublin layabouts, particularly Peter Cloran, Hosty ('an illstarred beachbusker' or penniless maker of scurrilous ballads), and O'Mara, 'an exprivate secretary of no fixed abode (locally known as Mildew Lisa)'. Take note of that parenthetical 'Mildew Lisa', since it hides the true nature of HCE's guilt. It is a deformation of the German '*Mild und leise*', the opening words of the love-death aria that Isolde (Iseult) sings over dead Tristan (Tristram) in Wagner's opera.

The scandal culminates in 'The Ballad of Persse O'Reilly', which–after a guilt-and-fall-symbolising thundred-letter word–Hosty sings to a tune that Joyce kindly gives us–literate, undistorted, in the key of A major. 'Persse O'Reilly' is a folk version of the French *perce-oreille*, which means an earwig. Like Bloom, HCE is a foreigner–

any foreigner, all foreigners – with the vices of a foreigner. The song is delightful:

> He was one time our King of the Castle
> Now he's kicked about like a rotten old parsnip.
> And from Green street he'll be sent by order of His Worship
> To the penal jail of Mountjoy
> (Chorus) To the jail of Mountjoy!
> Jail him and joy.

In it, HCE is identified with the falling Humpty Dumpty, likened to 'Lord Olofa Crumple', accused of a number of bizarre crimes, cursed as a black and tan and a 'brave son of Scandiknavery', and threatened with execution and burial:

> And not all the king's men nor his horses
> Will resurrect his corpus
> For there's no true spell in Connacht or hell
> That's able to raise a Cain.

And so we come to the third and fourth chapters and the fulfilment of the threat. First, though, we have to go through the form of a trial. The trio Hosty, O'Hara or O'Mara, and Cloran-Horan-Moran (how the names melt and shift, dreamlike) are no more, and, as far as the collecting of evidence is concerned, we have chiefly to rely on the priest Father San Browne or Padre Don Bruno. But opposites (Browne and Nolan) fuse into each other, nothing is certain, vast eras of time have confounded the issue: all that emerges from the murmurs and shouts is the fact of HCE's guilt. Still, he has his defenders:

. . . three tommix, soldiers free, cockaleak and cappapee, of the Coldstream Guards were walking in Montgomery Street . . . It was the first woman, they said, souped him, that fatal wellesday, Lili Coninghams, by suggesting him they go in a field. Wroth mod eldfar, ruth redd stilstand, wrath wrackt wroth, confessed private Pat Marchison *retro*.

The real facts of HCE's sexual guilt strive to reach the surface, but the girl he longs for is herself a temptress, a sort of prankquean. So Adam blamed Eve. But before Eve there was Lilith: the seducible maiden is turned into the seducing older woman.

Many voices, as in a series of television interviews, give opinions and make judgements. It is we ourselves, we begin to recognise, who will soon be on trial: HCE means 'Here Comes Everybody'. Solidities emerge – a letter written by HCE's own wife (at least, it is signed 'A Laughable Party' – ALP – Anna Livia Plurabelle), and a

coffin. This coffin has 'been removed from the hardware premises of
Oetzmann and Nephew, a noted house of the gonemost west, which
in the natural course of all things continues to supply funeral
requisites of every needed description'. It is destined for HCE: he
must be buried deep down, unable to rise again. Finnegan was an
amoral giant, but Earwicker is a man, and man must be cast into the
bottomless depths for his primal sin. There is, as yet, no redeemer.

And so to the trial. Long Lally Tobkids, 'the special', gives evidence in which HCE appears as a sort of drunken butcher (he delivers 'mattonchepps and meatjutes'–we are back with Mutt and
Jute, foreigner-hating native and invading Teuton). But a certain
MackPartland defends HCE: 'these camelback excesses are thought
to have been instigated by one or either of the causing causes of all,
those rushy hollow heroines in their skirtsleeves'. And, he adds, 'has
not levy of black mail from the times the fairies were in it, and fain
for wilde erthe blothoms followed an impressive private reputation
for whispered sins?' HCE, like Parnell, is suffering for his greatness.
As for the accused himself, he has shut himself away from it all with
his Swiftian guilt: 'And let oggs be good old gaggles and Isther
Estarr play Yesther Asterr'–there is Esther; there is ('Estarr') Stella.
But he has an unsolicited visitor–'Davy or Titus, on a burgley's clan
march from the middle west, a hikely excellent crude man about
road who knew his Bullfoost Mountains like a starling bierd.' The
new world of America has to have its say–

. . . weathering against him in mooxed metaphores from eleven thirty to
two in the afternoon without even a luncheonette interval for House, son
of Clod, to come out, you jewbeggar, to be executed Amen.

(Note the significant period of time–11.30 to 2.0, which can be
telescoped into the only real date in the whole book: 1132.)

Poor Earwicker has compiled a long list of 'all abusive names he
was called'. Some are dream-nonsense; others make all too much
sense–*Unworthy of the Homely Protestant Religion, I Divorce Thee
Husband, Cumberer of Lord's Holy Ground, Dirt, Miching Daddy,
Guilteypig's Bastard,* and so on. The people are against him, even
though the trial went in his favour. And so, 'playing on the least
change of his manjester's voice, the first heroic couplet from the
fuguall tropicall, Opus Elf, Thortytoe: *My schemes into obeyance for
This time has had to fall*' (1132 again), he goes off to 'the duff and
demb institutions' and we bid him 'Adyoe!' He is not yet to die, but
he is to shut himself away from all communication with men:

'Humph is in his doge. Words weigh no no more to him than rain-drips to Rethfernhim.' His death and resurrection are reserved to Joyce's next chapter.

This man *'Devoyd of the Commoner Characteristics of an Irish Nature'* remembers, in his incarceration (like 'the lion in our tear-garden' remembering 'the nenuphars of his Nile'), those two 'lililiths' who undid him, combining as they do in 'corngold Ysit', desired daughter. But the time has come for an indignant people to shove him, guilt and all, in that stolen teak coffin and then bury him deep under Lough Neagh. The making of 'this wastohavebeen under-ground heaven, or mole's paradise which was probably also an inver-sion of a phallopharos, intended to foster wheat crops and to ginger up tourist trade' is a big civilised job, involving blasting with T.N.T., but HCE remains a primitive hero, whose buried corpse is–despite the lack of a redeemer–a potential source of new life: 'abide Zeit's sumonserving, rise afterfall'. Even in the ground (or, rather, in his watery grave) HCE seems to send out shoots of chaotic energy–lightning and flood abound. He becomes as legendary as sleeping Finncgan, 'all this time of totality secretly and by suckage feeing on his own misplaced fat'. And the times, too, we see, are legendary–'pagan ironed times of the first city (called after the ugliest Dana-dune)'.

Lest we should think all this some remote fairy tale, however, we are dragged back to the Earwicker bedroom to hear the tapping of the dead branch on the window-pane: 'Tip! Tiptip! Tiptiptip!' The sleeping mind picks on Kate, the Earwickers' cleaning-woman, to take on the role of eternal widow, gatherer of the scattered fragments of her dead lord, to paint a picture for us, 'in a dreariodreama setting, glowing and very vidual, of old dumplan as she nosed it'. We see that she is a very old aspect of ALP, as Issy or Iseult is a very young one. She recalls the mythical past, ending up, as we must always end up, in the park with HCE's fall. We ought really to reconsider that sin, the trial, the incarceration and burial, but the sinner-victim is long dead. All we can do is to call on his two sons, Shem and Shaun, to re-enact the whole affair. Shaun plays a character called Festy King–'of a family long and honourably associated with the tar and feather industries'. But, though it is he who is arraigned on various charges, there is a great deal of confusion caused by the fact that the chief witness for the prosecution is his twin brother, Shem. The verdict of the four judges (Mamalujo, the four old men who praise the past, the four bedposts) is 'Nolans Brumans'. This (Bruno the

Nolan, with his doctrine of the identity of opposites, is hidden in the mock-Latin) encapsulates the defence of Shaun ('Show'm the Posed'). The twins are –

. . . equals of opposites, evolved by a onesame power of nature or of spirit, *iste*, as the sole condition and means of its himundher manifestation and polarised for reunion by the symphysis of their antipathies. Distinctly different were their duasdestinies.

Shaun is a mere shadow of his father HCE. He is incapable of guilt, and he revels in the admiration of 'the maidies of the bar', the twenty-eight girls who flutter and flatter around him. There is a twenty-ninth girl, for Leap-year ('a lovelooking leapgirl'), who is evidently a manifestation of Issy: she too adores him. He is made for sexual success, the unworthy demagogic successor of his father, though his time is not yet. As for Shem ('Shun the Punman!'), he is recognised as the enemy, the real betrayer of the father who, presumed dead and made mythical, is no longer a sinner but a saint. Hard words are spoken to Shem: 'You and your gift of your gaft of your garbage abaht our Farvver! and gaingridando: Hon! Verg! Nau! Putor! Skam! Schams! Shames!' The artist, truth-seeker, is always reviled.

The four old men, judges, bedposts, gospellers, provinces of Ireland, drone on among themselves about the glorious past. But the truth is surely not to be found in old men's drivellings but in that letter from ALP we all heard about before. Anyway, what happened to HCE? Previously he was presented to us (among so many things) as John Peel, the hunter, complete with horn in the morning, but now it seems that he is running up and down like a fox, a quarry like poor Parnell ('But the spoil of hesitants, the spell of hesitency'). Or else 'he had laid violent hands on himself . . . lain down, all in, fagged out, with equally melancholy death'. It is best to assume that he is gone, his successor elected, a new pope ('the prisoner of that sacred edifice'). We must turn now to his widow, ALP, the brave little woman, cleanser of the reputation of her dead lord, always ready 'to crush the slander's head'. She is the river by which we mourn his death, the water which will purify him into sainthood:

. . . For we, we have taken our sheet upon her stones where we have hanged our hearts in her tress; and we list, as she bibs us, by the waters of babalong.

The next few chapters of *Finnegans Wake* will be all about Anna Livia.

4: ALP and her Letter

I SHALL TRY NOW TO SAY SOMETHING USEFUL ABOUT THE NEXT four chapters of *Finnegans Wake*. We are still on the first great section of the book, which deals mainly with the coming of the archetypal family man after the fall of the primitive god-giant, and this section divides itself about equally into an account of Earwicker's fall, trial, death and burial (though his substance is spread, like a great spilt egg, all about the world) and his wife Anna's life and letter—that hidden letter which tells the truth about HCE and thus, in a cryptic way, explains the universe. There are eight chapters in all—four chapters for the man-hill, four chapters for the woman-river. Now, then, we come to Anna Livia Plurabelle—the river Anna Liffey, a plurality of femininity and beauty. She is hymned at the outset, however, as if she were God the Father:

In the name of Annah the Allmaziful, the Everliving, the bringer of Plurabilities, haloed be her eve, her singtime sung, her rill be run, un-hemmed as it is uneven!

But, of course, she reflects the eternal father, she bore his sons, she is the custodian of the truth about him. She deserves divine honours. First, though, we are concerned with her famous letter.

This 'untitled mamafesta' has had many names (Joyce gives us three full pages of these, from *The Augusta Angustissimost for Old Seabeastius' Salvation* to *First and Last Only True Account all about the Honorary Mirsu Earwicker, L.S.D., and the Snake (Nuggets!) by a Woman of the World who only can Tell Naked Truths about a Dear Man and all his Conspirators how they all Tried to Fall him Putting it all around Lucalizod about Privates Earwicker and a Pair of Sloppy Sluts plainly Showing all the Unmentionability falsely Accusing about the Raincoats*). There is a learned scholar at work here who, before he plunges into the depths of a lecture about the letter, tells us (and this is also Joyce telling us): 'Now, patience; and remember patience is the great thing, and above all things else we must avoid anything like being or becoming out of patience.' We need patience, wading through abstract theory before we learn anything about the provenance of the letter. At length we are told how a clever little hen called Belinda scratched up 'a goodish-sized sheet of letterpaper originating by transhipt from Boston (Mass.)' from a mud-mound flavoured with bits of orange-peel. The letter mentions wedding cakes and the 'grand funferall of poor Father Michael' (Michael Finnegan?) and sends love to the twins. It is tea-stained and unsigned. (Think of the Boston Tea Party, the release from ancient bondage and the start of a new epoch in history. Marriage, family life have replaced the old theocratic but unfruitful paternalism. And the Orange shall decay, says the Shan Van Vocht.) As for interpreting this old page of family gossip, is it not evident that ALP sees no great fault in HCE: 'Dancings (schwrites) was his only ttoo feebles. With apple harlottes'?

The letter (there is a strong element of parody of pedantry in this chapter) is accorded the reverence given to the *Book of Kells* (that ancient Irish psalter, magnificently illuminated, that was buried to protect it from the invading Danes). Indeed, it is stated roundly that the letter plainly inspired 'the tenebrous *Tunc* page' of the *Book of Kells*–the page which has written, in a mass of magnificent illumination, the words '*Tunc crucifixerunt XPI cum eo duos latrones*'–'Then they crucified Christ and with him two thieves', the 'XPI' (first three letters of the Greek word *Christos*) being an interpolation. This stained old hen-grubbed scrawl is marvelled at; marginal portraits are descried in it; niceties of punctuation are gravely discussed. But beneath the dream-satire there is seriousness of a dreaming sort, since the principle of family–finding expression in a half-literate bit of chat–underlies all civilisation. The archetypes of the crucified triumvirate (the Son who is also the Father in the middle, the thieves of his substance on either side) are to be found in HCE and the twins.

We have the letter, then, but can we be sure that it is really the letter that ALP wrote? Of course not: dreams do not disclose their hidden truths so easily. But this missive from Boston may be taken as a palimpcestuous précis of *Finnegans Wake* itself, and what follows in the next chapter is a pretty full presentation of its main characters (all of whom are allegedly mentioned in the letter) through the medium of a mad quiz. This is apparently conducted by the horrible four–'old Jeromesolem, old Huffsnuff, old Andy Cox, old Olecasandrum'–and it begins with a fatuous-seeming salutation: 'Who do you no tonigh, lazy and gentleman?' The lazy one is probably Shem, and the gentleman undoubtedly Shaun, prize quiz-kid, who 'rated one hundrick and thin per storehundred on this nightly quisquiquock of the twelve apostrophes, set by Jockit Mic Ereweak'. Who is 'Jockit'–Shaun (John, Jack, Jock) or Shem (Jacob)? The confusion is, as always, deliberate.

The 'twelve apostrophes' begin with a gigantic question (thirteen pages long) that seeks the identity of a 'maximost bridgesmaker' who stutters 'fore he falls and goes mad entirely when he's waked; is Timb to the pearly morn and Tomb to the mourning night', and so on. The answer is 'Finn MacCool!'–one of the manifestations of Finnegan-HCE. The next question, 'Does your mutter know your mike?', is apparently addressed to Shaun, since he appears later as Mike or Mick or the Archangel Michael, would-be destroyer of the devilish Nick or Shem. 'Ann alive, the lisp of her' is part of the answer. So far, then, we have the father and mother. Then comes a dream version of the motto on the arms of the city of Dublin: 'Thine obesity, O civilian, hits the felicitude of our orb!'[1] This stands above the little orb, or world, of a fat and happy home. But this home is only a part of all Ireland, and the next question asks about Ireland's four main cities (of special interest to the four old men, who represent the four provinces whose capitals these cities are). The answers are suitably disguised: Delfas; Dorhqk; Nublid; Dalway. I need not translate. Questions 5 and 6 refer to Earwicker's bartender, 'Pore ole Joe!', and cleaning-woman ('Summon In The Housesweep Dinah'–a deformation of a song in *Ulysses*–'There's someone in the house with Dinah'). The old woman herself is heard, grumbling: '. . . who bruk the dandleass and who seen the blackcullen jam for Tomorrha's pickneck I hope it'll pour.'

The Twelve are now mentioned. They stand for the whole of human society and they have lowly but bizarre trades–'the doorboy, the cleaner, the sojer, the crook, the squeezer, the lounger, the curman, the tourabout, the mussroomsniffer, the bleakablue tramp, the funpowtherplother, the christymansboxer'. We are told their names and places of origin and even given a specimen of their characteristic way of speaking:

. . . are the porters of the passions in virtue of retroratiocination, and, contributing their conflingent controversies of differentiation, unify their voxes in a vote of vaticination, who crunch the crusts of comfort due to

[1] The motto of the city of Dublin is *Obedientia civium urbis felicitas.*

depredation, drain the mead for misery to incur intoxication, condone every evil by practical justification and condam any good to its own gratification . . .

But, when asked who they really are, the answerer says: 'The Morphios!' The twelve citizens are sleepers, deliberating on life in pretentious polysyllables but letting life pass them by – as, in fact, it has passed by the four old men, the quizzers.

Next come the 'maggies', the girls in the park who melt into one girl, a daughter, a temptress ('yeth cometh elope year, coach and four, Sweet Peck-at-my-Heart picks one man more'). After that, Number 9, comes a description of the big dream itself and of this very book that enshrines it – 'a collideorscape' (lovely and exact word). Question 10 is important, since – 'What bitter's love but yurning, what' sour lovemutch but a bref burning till shee that drawes doth smoake retourne?' – it ushers in an answer from the primal temptress, Issy or Iseult, herself, all in Swiftian 'little language', coy girly-wirly talk, ghastly but fascinating:

. . . Now open, pet, your lips, pepette, like I used my sweet parted lipsabuss with Dan Holohan of facetious memory taught me after the flannel dance, with the proof of love, up Smock Alley the first night he smelled pouder and I coloured beneath my fan, *pipetta mia*, when you learned me the linguo to melt.

She is all woman, but not in the ALP sense (mature mother, transmitter of life and her dead lord's good name): ogling, inflaming passion but withholding its satisfaction, she loves her mirror best and provides another explanation for her appearance as a duo in the sinful park. 'With my whiteness I thee woo,' she says, 'and bind my silk breasths I thee bound! Always, Amory, amor andmore. Till always, thou lovest!' She is, of course, quite irresistible.

The penultimate question calls for a twenty-page answer. It is addressed to Shaun, whose name is changed to Jones for the occasion and who takes on rather petulant professorial qualities, and it concerns fraternal charity. The rhythm of the question derives from Thomas Moore's poem about the Exile of Erin, and it beats most pathetically when set out as verse:

> If you met on the binge a poor acheseyeld from Ailing,
>> when the tune of his tremble shook shimmy on shin,
> while his countrary raged in the weak of his wailing,
>> like a rugilant pugilant Lyon O'Lynn;
> if he maundered in misliness, plaining his plight or
>> played fox and lice, pricking and dropping hips teeth,

or wringing his handcuffs for peace, the poor blighter,
   praying Dieuf and Domb Nostrums foh thomethinks to eath;
if he weapt while he leapt and guffalled quith a quhimper,
   made cold blood a blue mundy and no bones without flech,
taking kiss, kake or kick with a suck, sigh or simper,
   a diffle to larn and a dibble to lech;
if the fain shinner pegged you to shave his immartial,
   wee skillmustered shoul with his ooh, hoodoodoo!
broking wind that to wiles, woemaid sin he was partial,
   we don't think, Jones, we'd care to this evening, would you?

The drunken, ailing, eye-aching exile is, of course, Joyce himself, poor artist seeking succour and soul's salvation from a better endowed brother (or Buck Mulligan, with whom Shaun is sometimes identified in his real-life form of Oliver St John Gogarty). Shaun will give no help, but, after his 'No, blank ye!', he finds it necessary to indulge in lengthy explanations of his attitude. He wants 'to conclusively confute this begging question' (he is embarrassed, though: he says 'hasitate') by referring to the 'dimecash problem' and expatiating on '*talis qualis*'.

But Shaun-Jones finds the only way to keep his audience awake is to give them a couple of fables, both of which work out the brother-opposition theme. Bruno Nolan is told to take his tongue out of the inkpot, and then the professor translates from the Javanese the story of the Mookse and the Gripes, beginning formally: 'Gentes and laitymen, fullstoppers and semicolonials, hybreds and lubberds!' The tale combines Aesop's Fox and Grapes and Lewis Carroll's Mock Turtle and Griffon, but it soon becomes clear that the Mookse is English Pope Adrian ('Bragspear') and the Gripes the Irish people and the old Irish Church of the *Book of Kells* (more Byzantine than Roman). The bull *Laudabiliter* is worked into the Mookse's threats – 'That is quite about what I came on *my* missions with *my* intentions *laudabiliter* to settle with you, barbarousse' – and we remember that it was with the blessing of that bull that Henry II annexed Ireland, thus bringing Ireland into the Roman fold as well as under the English crown. With British bragging and 'poposity' the Mookse wades into the 'poor little sowsieved subsquashed Gripes', and the battling sons of the one Mother Church (Anna Livia is subtly invoked in '*Amnis Limina Permanent*') fail to notice that a little girl is looking down on them from the 'bannistars'. This is Nuvoletta, the little cloud, who is both Issy-Iseult and ALP in her source-capacity. The stupid quarrel blinds the Mookse and the Gripes to the permanent fact of their one river-mother (who

213

flows along quietly all this while); the fighting brothers ('Bullfolly answered volleyball') miss the proffered beauty of 'the daughter of the queen of the Emperour of Irelande'. Two women–Valkyries or banshees–gather up severally the Mookse and the Gripes on the river-bank, and nothing is left but an elm-tree and a stone. The big theme of the Shem-Shaun antipathy has been expounded. 'Nolan Browne, you may now leave the classroom.'

But Professor Jones has another, more privy, story to tell. This concerns Caseous and Burrus (Cassius and Brutus, but also Cheese and Butter). These come from the same mothering milk, and in Burrus we see Shaun ('a genuine prime, the real choice, full of natural greace') and in Caseous ('a hole or two, the highstinks aforefelt and anygo prigging worms') Shem's less sunny properties. We are asked to 'pursue Burrus and Caseous for a rung or two up their isocelating biangle', and in this figure we see ALP (Joyce's symbol for her is, in fact, an isosceles triangle). The whole tragedy of Shem and Shaun–whatever form or fancy dress they put on–lies in their twinhood. The successor of HCE should be the 'genuine prime', the first-born, and there is no first-born. If Shaun is daddy's favourite, Shem must be mummy's, but a natural bequest to the father's favourite son is not only the right of rule but the monopoly of the mother. The sexual struggles between Shem and Shaun ironically get in the way of sexual conquest. In this present fable both Burrus and Caseous love Margareen ('*I cream for thee, Sweet Margareen*'), but she, eternal woman, wants neither:

A cleopatrician in her own right she at once complicates the position while Burrus and Caseous are contending for her misstery by implicating herself with an elusive Antonius, a wop who would appear to hug a personal interest in refined chees of all chades at the same time as he wags an antomine art of being rude like the boor.

Whenever the brothers quarrel and fight, they seem to call into being a third personage (the third soldier?) like this Antonius who, 'a wop', possibly Antonio with his ice-cream cart, is also the dreamer's own tentative image of himself. Margareen, or whatever her name is, is the desired incestuous bride of the father and brothers alike.

The conclusion of Shaun-Jones's long lecture is unequivocal. If the 'proud pursebroken ranger' came to him 'to beg for a bite in our bark *Noisdanger*', he would–'were we tucked in the one bed and bit by the one flea'–have no hesitation in footing him out. The last question of all asks '*Sacer esto?*', in which the Latin *sacer* means both 'blest' and 'accursed'–here, undoubtedly, the latter only: 'Will

you be accursed?' The answer comes from Shem: '*Semus sumus!*' –
'Shem we are!' And now – 'Shem is as short for Shemus as Jem is
joky for Jacob' – we are ready for a very entertaining and yet shocking chapter, in which mother's-boy Shem is revealed all too candidly
as James Joyce ('Shame's voice') – the exiled artist, reviled by the
sanctimonious, finding his salvation in being a sewer (back to 'The
Holy Office'), perverse, 'a sham and a low sham', but still the scribe
who penned his mother's letter, a hated but feared 'greekenhearted
yude' like Bloom himself.

This chapter is a Rabelaisian triumph, though – in the true Joyce
manner – it uses laughter for a bitter end. Shem's 'lowness' is so
thoroughly celebrated that it takes on a kind of grandeur. It comes
out first in his rejection of good plain food (that which fed the Irish
literary Renaissance):

So low was he that he preferred Gibsen's teatime salmon tinned, as in-
expensive as pleasing, to the plumpest roeheavy lax or the friskiest parr or
smolt troutlet that ever was gaffed between Leixlip and Island Bridge and
many was the time he repeated in his botulism that no junglegrown pine-
apple ever smacked like the whoppers you shook out of Ananias' cans,
Findlater and Gladstone's, Corner House, Englend. None of your inch-
thick blueblooded Balaclava fried-at-belief-stakes or juicejelly legs of the
Grex's molten mutton or greasilygristly grunters' goupons or slice upon
slab of luscious goosebosom with lump after load of plumpudding stuffing
all aswim in a swamp of bogoakgravy . . .

The rejected Irish salmon is that salmon of wisdom cooked by Finn
MacCool; he will not belong to the native 'Grex' or flock. His art is
nourished on poison ('his botulism'). If you want the good and
wholesome you must go to his brother Shaun: 'Johns is a different
butcher's . . . Feel his lambs! Ex! Feel how sheap! Exex! His liver
too is great value, a spatiality! Exexex! COMMUNICATED.'
Shaun is revealed as the space-man, lord of solid objects, as well as
the holy one who excommunicates the low artist. Shem's task is to
capture the rhythm of time, draw inspiration from the creative
mother-river.

A seedy Satan, rolled in the dirt, stinking, blasphemous, he has
committed the terrible crime of writing *Ulysses*, which not even he
can understand: 'amid the inspissated grime of his glaucous den
making believe to read his usylessly unreadable Blue Book of Eccles,
édition de ténèbres'. He is a pervert like the Jew of Eccles Street,
putting out a filthy 'abortisement' – 'Jymes wishes to hear from
wearers of abandoned female costumes . . . to start city life together.
His jymes is out of job, would sit and write.' His house – 'O'Shea or

215

O'Shame'–is called the Haunted Inkbottle, 'a stinksome inkenstink', and there he makes ink out of the nasty excretions of his own body (too terrible for English, this is put in good clean Latin) and uses that body as paper (he is the spider of Swift's *Battle of the Books*). The vilification is all too quotable. Here is the libel to end all libels. There is nothing like it in all literature. And yet this 'sniffer of carrion, premature gravedigger, seeker of the nest of evil in the bosom of a good word' is beloved of his mother ALP. Why? It is because he represents Mercy, while his brother only stands for justice. In his self-righteousness, JUSTIUS knows only how to sneer, threaten: 'I'll brune this bird or Brown Bess's bung's gone bandy. I'm the boy to bruise and braise.' MERCIUS, speaking 'of hisself', is full of 'agenbite of inwit' for 'my fault, his fault, a kingship through a fault'. Aware of the sins in himself, he is in no position to condemn others. Having reached the rock-bottom of wretchedness, he has a compensatory gift bestowed on him, the artist's gift: 'He lifts the lifewand and the dumb speak.' His mother is the creative current that flows through the solid Shaun-run city. She is coming now:

. . . little oldfashioned mummy, little wonderful mummy, ducking under bridges, bellhopping the weirs, dodging by a bit of bog, rapidshooting round the bends, by Tallaght's green hills and the pools of the phooka and a place they call it Blessington and slipping sly by Sallynoggin, as happy as the day is wet, babbling, bubbling, chattering to herself, deloothering the fields on their elbows leaning with the sloothering side of her, giddy-gaddy, grannyma, gossipaceous Anna Livia.

And so to the closing chapter of this first section of the book. The two banshees that took away the Mookse and the Gripes have been changed into washerwomen, scrubbing away on the banks of the Liffey and, in prose splashing with river-names, they celebrate in rich dream-Dublinese the water-mother who bears us forward gently to our next epoch of Viconian history. The story they rehearse is that of Anna's marriage to HCE (Huges Caput Earlyfouler–a fusion of French Hugh Capet and German Henry the Fowler, both foreigners). They have little time for him–'Or whatever it was they threed to make out he thried to two in the Fiendish park. He's an awful old reppe . . . And how long was he under loch and neagh?'– but Anna Livia herself comes in for some censure: 'Do you know she was calling bakvandets sals from all around, nyumba noo, chamba choo, to go in till him, her erring cheef, and tickle the pontiff aisy-oisy?'

Anna Livia is, after all, a river—yielding, dipped into by many, unpossessive herself, herself much possessed. She has had much experience since she was 'just a young thin pale soft shy slim slip of a thing'; it has taken her a long time to get to Dublin and HCE:

It was ages behind that when nullahs were nowhere, in county Wickenlow, garden of Erin, before she ever dreamt she'd lave Kilbride and go foaming under Horsepass bridge, with the great southerwestern windstorming her traces and the midland's grainwaster asarch for her track, to wend her ways byandby, robecca or worse, to spin and to grind, to swab and to thrash, for all her golden lifey in the barleyfields and pennylotts of Humphrey's fordofhurdlestown and lie with a landleaper, wellingtonorseher.

('Fordofhurdlestown'=Bailé átha Cliath=Dublin.) But our main concern is with her widowed aspect, her scotching of the scandal that was to put HCE under loch and neagh and leave the rule of the world to his sons, the halves of himself. 'She swore on croststyx nyne wyndabouts she's be level with all the snags of them yet.' She got a 'zakbag, a shammy mailsack . . . off one of her swapsons, Shaun the Post', she dressed herself queenlily, 'Annushka Lutetiavitch Pufflovah', and then 'with her mealiebag slang over her shulder, Anna Livia, oysterface, forth of her bassein came'. In the bag were fragments of the living substance of her dead lord—'a Christmas box apiece for aisch and iveryone of her childer'. Her childer are one hundred and eleven in number (111 is the symbol of plenitude), and their names and the presents she gave them fill two and a half pages. They are, of course, dream-fantastical—'a *Missa pro Messa* for Taff de Taff; Jill, the spoon of a girl, for Jack, the broth of a boy' and so on—but our final impression of overwhelming richness could not have been achieved by any other method than that of the Rabelaisian catalogue. The washerwomen wonder what happened to the children, but they are on opposite banks of Anna Livia herself and the river is widening: it is hard to hear. 'Can't hear with the waters of', they say. 'Can't hear with bawk of bats, all thim liffeying waters of.' Of all 'Livia's daughtersons' only the names of Shem and Shaun remain. Hoarsely the voices call for a tale of 'stem or stone'. We remember that this is what the Mookse and the Gripes became—an elm and a stone by the river. We end the chapter with those two images—the tree for change and life and creation; the stone for permanence, the deadness of the law. We are ready—'beside the rivering waters of, hitherandthithering waters of. Night!'—for the next epoch in the cycle, the world of the sons. But Anna Livia has brought us to this phase, redeeming the rumoured shame of her dead husband with the plurability of the gift of his gathered substance, to be used and misused by the 'twins of his bosom'.

When we have doubts about the value of *Finnegans Wake*–and doubts sometimes come upon us when we face its difficulties, the mad calculation of its experiments with language and time, the huge unclimbable mound of multiple myth–we have only to think of this wonderful final chapter of Book One for the doubts to be resolved. It remains one of the most astonishing pieces of audacity in the whole of world literature, and the audacity comes off. The language is cosmic, yet it is the homely speech of ordinary people. We seem to see a woman who is also a river and a man who is also a city. Time dissolves; we have a glimpse of eternity. And the eternal vision is made out of muddy water, old saws, half-remembered music-hall songs, gossip, and the stain on a pair of underpants. The heart bows down.

5: Brotherly Hate

WE ARE PRIMARILY IN A BED ABOVE A BAR IN CHAPELIZOD, Dublin, on a Saturday night, with a dry branch tapping or tipping at the window, and we must never let ourselves forget it. In the final section of *Finnegans Wake* we are not allowed to forget it. The fact that we have to look at the near-end of the book to find out where the dreamer is dreaming does not imply that the whole thing is badly made or that Joyce is withholding something from us. *Finnegans Wake* is cyclical like a riverrun, and we can enter the river at any point we wish. I have already done this in order to help beginners who, brought up like all of us on ordinary books where you start at page 1 and push on straight to the end, may think it cheating to treat *Finnegans Wake* in a different way. It is not cheating, and we ought to be aware of the inward movement of the pattern. In the first section we were in Dublin, by the Hill of Howth and the Liffey, in the Phoenix Park–for the most part out of doors. In the second section we come to the Earwicker home to learn something about the play and education of the children as well as to witness the downfall of the father in his own bar. We are away from the big timeless landscape which is proper for myth; we are here and now, in an age dominated by the demagogue.

We need not worry overmuch about the fact that Earwicker was shoved under Lough Neagh in the first section and here is to be seen alive again, alive but decaying. This is dream-stuff, and easy resurrection (going home from one's father's funeral to find him presiding over the cold ham and whiskified tea) is a dull commonplace of dreams. Besides, the twins–at play and at homework–need a family background in which the father is no longer a castle-crowned rock and the mother a river.

The play of the first chapter of Book Two is a real play, presented 'every evening at lighting up o'clock sharp and until further notice in Feenichts Playhouse. (Bar and conveniences always open, Diddlem

Club douncestears.)' It is called *The Mime of Mick, Nick and the Maggies* and, when you come to think of it, is really a play within a play. Earwicker's twin sons (whose waking names are Jerry and Kevin, but, as we shall see, only if HCE's waking name is Mr Porter) play Shem and Shaun in the dream; in the dream-play Mr Seumas McQuillad plays Glugg and Mr Sean O'Mailey plays Chuff. Those surnames are, of course, nicknames or trade-names playing at being patronymics – Shem is the lad of the quill or pen; Shaun delivers the post or mail: one writes the word and the other merely delivers it. The other actors are no strangers to us. Izod is played by Miss Butys Pott, the self-loving Issy, 'a bewitching blonde who dimples delightfully and is approached in loveliness only by her grateful sister reflection in the mirror'. She is supported by The Floras, 'a month's bunch of pretty maidens' from St Bride's (St Bridget's) Finishing Establishment. The month of February is Joyce's birth-month, and it may be this fact that made him limit his 'month's bunch' to twenty-eight, with the elusive Issy as leap-year girl. The part of Ann (Miss Corrie Corriendo – riverrunner) is, as it were, played by herself, as the part of Hump (Mr Makeall Gone – all-creator who dies) is played by Hump Earwicker. The St Bride's girls are more or less balanced by the alumni of St Patricius' Academy for Grownup Gentlemen – the twelve customers of the pub. Kate is there ('kook-and-dishdrudge'), and the bar-help's name is revealed as Saunderson – 'scherinsheiner and spoilcurate'.

What is the play about? It is a version of a game of Joyce's own childhood, in which angels fight devils. Glugg (Shem) is Old Nick, battered young Satan, 'the bold bad bleak boy of the storybooks', and Chuff (Shaun) is Mick or the Archangel Michael, 'the fine frank fairhaired fellow of the fairytales':

Chuffy was a nangel then and his soard fleshed light like likening. Fools top! Singty, sangty, meekly loose, defendy nous from prowlabouts. Make a shine on the curst. Emen.

Michael, as the prayer said at the end of Mass reminds us, is the defender of the Church in the day of battle. This ties up with Shaun as the Mookse, head of the Church and imposer of Roman rule on Book-of-Kelly (has anybody here seen?) Ireland. Glugg-Shem is not a very fearsome devil, but, after all, he is only a child:

... the duvlin sulph was in Glugger, that lost-to-lurning. Punct. He was sbuffing and sputing, tussing like anisine, whipping his eyesoult and gnatsching his teats over the brividies from existers and the outher liubbocks of life.

He is, we learn, loved of none of the month-girls, and Izod has jilted him, being now fatally fascinated by Chuff. But Glugg wants love, and not even ALP will give him anything more than pity: 'This poor Glugg! It was so said of him about of his old fontmouther. Truly deplurabel!' The girls tease him; he chases them but can catch none. 'Not Rose, Sevilla nor Citronelle; not Esmeralde, Pervinca nor Indra; not Viola even nor all of them four themes over.' The month-girls have become rainbow-girls (four days=one colour).

They perform a sort of phonetic mime of a colour and ask Glugg to guess what the colour is ('Up tighty in the front'–*heli*; 'down again on the loose'–*o*; 'drim and drumming on her back'–*tr*; 'and a pop from her whistle'–*ope*). Glugg asks the four elements (the four old men) for an answer, but they cannot help him. To increase his embarrassment, he seems to want to make water, and the rainbow girls, 'holding their noises', insinuate that he is making 'peace in his preaches and play with esteem'. These giggling girls dance round Chuff, 'for they are an angel's garland', but their 'rompride round in rout' spells R-A-I-N-B-O-W. This act of spelling (an act ful- filled in time) pushes them into the future, and we see them as they will be–mature ordinary women with age coming upon them. They dance widdershins–W-O-B-N-I-A-R–and they are once again 'all the flowers of the ancelles' garden'.

Glugg is enraged. He curses, blasphemes, swears that he will have his own back on all of them. He will turn himself into a sort of James Joyce, complete with 'carberry banishment' (exile), 'mum's for maxim' (silence), and 'handy antics' (cunning). He will 'go in for scribenery with the satiety of arthurs' and even write *Ulysses*. Some of the episodes of *Ulysses* are now mentioned, in appropriate dream- form: 'Ukalepe. Loathers' leave. Nemo in Patria. The Luncher Out. Skilly and Carubdish. A Wondering Wreck. From the Mermaids' Tavern. Bullyfamous. Naughtsycalves. Mother of Misery. Wal- purgas Nackt.' But after his rage and threats to show up even his own hovel-home he calms down: 'He threwed his fit up to his aers, rolled his poligone eyes, snivelled from his snose and blew the guff out of his hornypipe.' As a seeming reward for his return to good, though diabolic, humour, he is given a letter from we-know-who: 'Stop up, mavrone, and sit in my lap, Pepette.' There is a new riddle for him: 'Find the frenge for frocks and translace it into shocks of such as touch with show and show.' He cannot answer it, and so he is told: 'Get!'

And he did a get, their anayance, and slink his hook away, aleguere come alaguerre, like a chimista inchamisas, whom the harricana hurries and hots foots, zingo, zango, segur.

He lies in filth while the flower-maidens dance around their angelic Chuff, chanting praises out of parodied prayers. But Glugg returns, 'shrivering, with his spittyful eyes and his whoozebecome woice', and says he will never sin again. But the sins he now confesses are not his own but his father's and also those of 'his fiery goosemother, laotsey taotsey, woman who did'.

The moon rises, it grows dark, we are 'circumveiloped by obscuritads'. The animals prepare for sleep. 'Witchman, watch of your night?' Joyce's night-prose again triumphs: 'Darkpark's acoo with sucking loves.' But on Vico Road, where 'vamp, vamp, vamp, the girls are merchand', the fight between Glugg and Chuff is ready to begin. And, indeed, Glugg makes a frightful dash at his adversary. A proffered prize for the conqueror, Issy-Iseult appears: 'Wink's the winning word.' And, of course, she is for Chuff, as are all the girls. The whole twenty-nine of them rise against Glugg, taunting, teasing. He ceases then to be comic; he becomes identified with the assassin Macbeth:

> For a burning would is come to dance inane. Glamours hath moidered's lieb and herefore Coldours must leap no more. Lack breath must leap no more.

Living evil, he must stay on his own wicked side of the street:

> If you cross this rood as you roamed the rand I'm blessed but you'd feel him a blasting rod. Behind me, frees from evil smells! Perdition stinks before us.

This does not mean the Chuff-Glugg struggle is over. Glugg has been established as the enemy but, because of the Brunonian law of merging opposites, there is a moment when we cannot be quite sure which twin is which: '. . . trumpers are mixed up in duels and here's B. Rohan meets N. Ohlan for the prize of a thou.' The girls 'are in such transfusion just to know twigst timidly twomeys, for gracious sake, who is artthoudux from whose heterotropic'. But Glugg is defeated. 'Creedless, croonless hangs his haughty. There end no moe red devil in the white of his eye.'

And yet the warring of these opposites has to remind us of the great personage in whom thesis and antithesis are not presented in battle but in harmony, composed to a synthesis—the all-father, 'an isaac jacquemin mauromormo milesian'. He is 'Hocus Crocus,

Esquilocus' but also 'Finnfinn the Faineant'. He sleeps now, he
cannot be resurrected. He will reawaken, but not just yet. As for
sleeping, it is time for the children to go home to bed. 'The play
thou schouwburgst, Game, here endeth. The curtain drops by deep
request.' But the children are still noisy and quarrelsome. Only when
their father HCE slams the door in thunder and they are reminded
of the voice of God will they turn to their night-prayers:

O Loud, hear the wee beseech of thees of each of these thy unlitten
ones! Grant sleep in hour's time, O Loud!
That they take no chill. That they do ming no merder. That they shall
not gomeet madhowiatrees.
Loud, heap miseries upon us yet entwine our arts with laughters, low!

One knows of no better prayer.

The next chapter is devoted to work, not play. The children must
prepare for the taking over of their father's world. They must study
the great book of life 'from tomtittot to teetootomtotalitarian' –
the origins of God and man, the arts and sciences. Joyce presents us
with a dream-version of the all-including primer. There are mad
footnotes which seem to be the work of irreverent Shem and which
hardly ever seem to bear even the remotest relationship to the corresponding parts of the text. In the right-hand margin Shaun has
very serious, very pretentious, very learned guides to the subject-
matter, always in upper-case letters. In the left-hand margin Shem
has rude, irrelevant, rebellious or nonsensical comments in italic
letters. About halfway through, the twins, remembering Brown and
Nolan, change sides. A good example of their respective attitudes
to learning can be seen on the very first page. Shaun has 'UNDE ET
UBI' and 'SIC' and 'IMAGINABLE ITINERARY THROUGH
THE PARTICULAR UNIVERSAL.' Shem has '*With his broad
and hairy face, to Ireland a disgrace*' (presumably he means God),
'*Menly about peebles*' and '*Dont retch meat fat salt lard sinks down
(and out)*.' The footnotes on the first page are as follows:

[1] Rawmeash, quoshe with her girlic teangue. If old Herod with the
Cormwell's eczema was to go for me like he does Snuffler whatever about
his blue canaries I'd do nine months for his beaver beard.
[2] Mater Mary Mercerycordial of the Dripping Nipples, milk's a queer
arrangement.
[3] Real life behind the floodlights as shown by the best exponents of a
royal divorce.

Of course, our first this-is-nonsense reaction to both footnotes and
Shem-marginal-comments tends to be modified after many readings.

These three footnotes, for instance, make a kind of pattern of fatherhood and motherhood, revealed first in its divine aspects and then brought down to HCE and ALP (*A Royal Divorce* is Earwicker's favourite dramatic entertainment). As for Shaun's marginal pointers, these always, alas, make too much sense: they are the very voice of the student who plans great things for himself in the world. The right-hand ant toils away, the left-hand grasshopper chirps like a mad thing.

The text with its three-sided frame is very difficult to follow, but this is chiefly because it hides under its surface of dream Dublin chatter the strict doctrines of the ancient Cabbala. This makes much of the mystical significance of numbers. Thus, the Creator– 'Ainsoph' in the Cabbala–is represented by the number 1. His heavenly consort is 0 (Joyce calls her 'Zeroine'). As he moves towards her, the numbers 2 to 9 are produced, and, when they achieve union, the great 10 comes about. The first thing the twins have to learn is the immanence of this divine creative force in the innumerable forms of the universe. Behind all the kinds of knowledge, from history to music, lies the ultimate knowledge of the One. Joyce's achievement in setting forth all this lies, as it does throughout *Finnegans Wake*, in making the abstract not merely concrete but local, not merely local but comic. *Unde?*–whence have we come? *Ubi?*–where are we? Our 'imaginable itinerary through the particular universal' is the path we take in order to find out:

Quick lunch by our left, wheel, to where. Long Livius Lane, mid Mezzofanti Mall, diagnosing Lavatery Square, up Tycho Brache Crescent, shouldering Berkeley Alley, querfixing Gainsborough Carfax, under Guido d'Arezzo's Gadeway, by New Livius Lane till where we whiled while we whithered. Old Vico Roundpoint.

These great names represent the seven main branches of knowledge, beginning with Livy the historian and ending with him, old Vico there too to remind us of the cyclical nature of our progress: history does not, as Mr Deasy thought, lead to God's manifestation; God is behind everything, unseen, unknowable:

Ainsoph, this upright one, with that noughty besighed him zeroine. To see in his horrorscup he is mehrkurios than saltz of sulphur. Terror of the noonstruck by day, cryptogam of each nightly bridable. But, to speak broken heaventalk, is he? Who is he? Whose is he? Why is he? Howmuch is he? Which is he? When is he? Where is he? How is he?

Shem's marginal comments on God are very much those of Stephen Dedalus: '*Swiney Tod, ye Daimon Barbar! Dig him in the rubsh! Ungodly old Ardrey, Cronwall beeswaxing the convulsion box.'*

But it is not the God of the Irish Catholics, the butcher who kills us like pigs (*Swiney Tod=Schweinstod*=pigsdeath), who is under discussion. We are concerned with the cabbalistic One and Zero, the creation of the world of multiplicity which we can see, as well as anywhere, in HCE's pub and household (those famous initials are never long out of the text–'*Haud certo ergo*', for instance; ALP is triply celebrated in '*Apis amat aram. Luna legit librum. Pulla petit pascua*'). The Earwicker home is a tiny figure of the cosmos. Once, however, we examine this figure, we leave questions of theology and become preoccupied with the building of human societies. We enter HCE's house, climb 'from the murk of the mythelated' to civilisation, represented by 'Harington's invention', the WC, and visit 'the clarience of the child light in the studiorium upsturts'. The twins in their nursery will enact the 'urges and widerurges' of primitive man. They will fight over a girl, even, while she 'with her tootpetty-pout of jemenfichue will sit and knit on solfa sofa'. (The footnote says: 'Let me blush to think of all those halfwayhoist pullovers.') In the nursery, as in the greater world, the two great driving forces of cupidity and concupiscence will be at work–'early notions of acquired rights' and the 'pursuit of panhysteric woman'. At the same time, the process of transmitting knowledge from one age to the next proceeds: old granny teaches little Issy about man the winner and woman the loser, asking her to 'Note the Respectable Irish Distressed Ladies and the Merry Mustard Frothblowers of Hum-phreystown Associations.'

The right-hand margin now presents the nine principles of that bigger human history adumbrated in the nursery: 'CONCOMI-TANCE OF COURAGE, COUNSEL AND CONSTANCY. ORDINATION OF OMEN, ONUS AND OBIT. DISTRIBU-TION OF DANGER, DUTY AND DESTINY. POLAR PRIN-CIPLES.' It seems to add up to C.O.D.–cash on delivery, a typically Shaunian summation: we expect the goods of life and we will pay with the stoic virtues when we get them. When we come to Number 10–marriage of King One and Queen Zero–we see that all life is based on the polar principle of sex. Can we really learn much from past history, then? (The notes BC and AD are played in the left-hand margin.) 'Please stop if you're a B.C. minding missy, please do. But should you prefer A.D. stepplease.' The completed Viconian eras–the theocratic and aristocratic–have nothing to teach the coming democratic age. Heroes like Humpty are done for ('By old

Grumbledum's walls'); the rainbow of the future spreads ('Heil, heptarched span of peace!'–the footnote says: 'I'm blest if I can see') and now we are to have 'Impovernment of the booble by the bauble for the bubble'. Or look at it another way: the special things we were taught to look for in the past are not in the past at all; they are here, in the present: 'Number Thirty two West Eleventh streak looks on to that (may all in the tocoming of the sempereternal speel spry with it!) datetree doloriferous' of past time: 1132 is here and now.

Here, though, there seems to be a great philosophical paradox. Present and past may be brought together because of recurring archetypes, but we cannot doubt that the *individual* forms of one age are never an exact reproduction of corresponding forms in another age. We accept the notion of new species–'one world burrowing on another . . . Standfest, our topiocal sagon hero, or any other macotther, signs is on the bellyguds bastille back'–and the fact that the older world lies underneath the new world: 'THE MONGREL UNDER THE DUNGMOUND. SIGNIFICANCE OF THE INFRALIMINAL INTELLIGENCE.' It is in the darkness of the unconscious that the old hero Finnegan subsists:

Aught darks flou a duskness. Bats that? There peepeestrilling. At Brannan's on the moor. At Tam Fanagan's weak yat his still's going strang. And still here is noctules and can tell things acommon on by that fluffy feeling.

'OFFRANDES' says the marginal note, and the text 'Dogs' vespers'. It may be that, as we propitiate the God of the heavens, so we must make offerings to our deeper, more primitive, natures. 'Keep the dog far hence', says T. S. Eliot–those animal forces inside us we fear so much. Perhaps we should bow down occasionally to that dog.

And now 'INCIPIT INTERMISSIO'. We rest from our studies a little, and the temptress Issy, who has already been thrusting her way into the footnotes ('Pipette. I can almost feed their sweetness at my lisplips'), fills three-quarters of a page with a footnote letter which seduces us to a mood of temporary languor. We have not yet learned much about sex. Issy turns herself into a love-goddess:

Wasn't it just divining that dog of a dag in Skokholme as I sat astrid uppon their Drewitt's altar, as cooledas as culcumbre, slapping my straights till the sloping ruins, postillion, postallion, a swinge a swank, with you offering me clouts of illscents and them horners stagstruck on the leasward!

Cities fall, broken in war, but still the flowers remain, fresh and smiling as in the days of old battles (Joyce tells us this not in his own dream-words but in the undistorted French of Edgar Quinet). Flowers of love beckon, but the boys 'totient quotients', 'Bruto and Cassio', are more concerned with the manlier matter of their eternal opposition. They get down then to doing their sums, inscribing first 'At maturing daily gloryaims' (the Jesuit *Ad Majorem Dei Gloriam*) at the head of their paper. Every theme of the book obscurely appears as a mathematical problem, and we become aware of how large a part number has so far played in it. The boys' names are now given as Dolph (Shem) and Kev (Shaun)–'singlebarrelled names for doubleparalleled twixtytwins'–and it is Kev who comes to his brother for help. The problem they are going to work out is evidently important–'Concoct an equoangular trillitter'–for Joyce, in Latin, invites the spirits of the dead to come and watch: *'Venite, preteriti.'* Apparently, though, young Dolph-Shem has some obscene purpose in mind, for–both the sets of marginal comments disappearing–we have a lengthy piece of confused moralising, alluding much to the Tristram-Iseult legend and, addressing the two lovers by their Irish names–Diarmait and Grainne distorted to 'diarmuee and granyou', saying: 'if that is what lamoor . . . seems circling toward out yondest heaven help his hindmost'. When the marginal comments are resumed, we see that Shaun has his grave pointers in italic, at the left, and Shem's irreverence, in the dignity of capitals, is on the right.

The letters ALP are now seen as the points of the isosceles triangle (the fertile *delta*) which is Anna Livia's own sign. In a diagram made up of two interlocking circles and two isosceles triangles with a common base (ALP and *alpha lambda pi*), Dolph-Shem finds his thesis, an obscurely obscene exposition of his own sexual curiosity, while Kev-Shaun makes learned but ingenuous comments in the margin:

Outer serpumstances being ekewilled, we carefully, if she pleats, lift by her seam hem and jabote at the spidsiest of her trickkikant (like thousands done before since fillies calpered. Ocone! Ocone!) the maidsapron of our A.L.P., fearfully! till its nether nadir is vortically where (allow me aright to two cute winkles) its naval's napex will have to beandbe. You must proach near mear for at is dark. Lob. And light your mech. Jeldy!

The whole process of learning, of scientific investigation and the hugging of secret knowledge, is revealed as mere curiosity about what lies up our mothers' skirts. Kev-Shaun is slow in realising his brother's drift, but when he does he turns on him, and the fraternal battle is resumed – Michael versus Old Nick. The footnote says 'Picking on Nickagain, Pikey Mikey?' The archangel calls Satan 'the divver's own smart gossoon, aequal to yoursell and wanigel to anglyother, so you are, hoax! You know, you'll be dampned, so you will, one of these invernal days . . .'

The real point is, I think, that Shem, with all his tendency to make game of learning, has more understanding of the mystical significance of signs and letters (he is, after all, an artist) than has his twin, despite the earnestness of his application. Both boys, being the father split into two, are incomplete in themselves, and there are times when their recognition of this makes them turn in anger on each other. It is now a matter of 'Christ's Church varses Bellial!' But the narrator (being himself an artist and hence on the side of Dolph-Shem-Glugg-Nick) celebrates Irish literature as a sort of divine body – organs listed in the margin, names garbled in the text: 'Steal, Barke, Starn, Swhipt, Wiles, Pshaw, Doubblinbbayyates.' This does not prevent Shaun from delivering a blow to Shem's mortal body – 'Wince wan's won! Rip!' (footnote: 'A byebye bingbang boys! See you Nutcracker Sunday!').

But, surprisingly when we consider that Shem is the devil, not so surprisingly when we remember that he is also Stephen Dedalus, there is no retaliation. In his brain he must conquer. He says: 'Thanks eversore much, Pointcarried! . . . I'm seeing rayingbogeys rings round me . . . By Saxon Chromaticus, you done that lovely for me!' He calls on his little-cloud sister for confirmation of the skill and strength of Shaun's blow. Before they go out into the great world, Shem is revealed as the monopolist of spiritual power, his brother as the extroverted politician-fighter. 'And that salubrated sickenagiaour of yaours have teaspilled all my hazeydency', says Shem to Shaun. '. . . I'm only out for celebridging over the guilt of the gap in your hiscitendency. You are a hundred thousand times welcome, old wortsampler, hellbeit you're just about as culpable as my woolfell merger would be.' We remember the double significance of 'hesitency/hesitancy'. The guilt of HCE, Parnell and Piggot is in both the sons, revealed equally in Shaun's jealous blow, Shem's failure to strike back. The Shem-margin is full of HCE stuttering.

Peace, then – the thrice-repeated Sanskrit word for it which concludes Eliot's *The Waste Land*: 'Shantih' distorted to 'slanty scanty shanty'. The end of learning and the beginning of the time for action. Shaun's margin sums up, in great names from Cato to

Darius, the scope of their studies; the text, with a Rabelaisian catalogue, indicates the subjects of their essays. *'Castor, Pollux'* in the margin relates to 'Compare the Fistic Styles of Jimmy Wilde and Jack Sharkey' in the text; *'Julius Caesar'* leads us to 'A Succeesful Career in the Civil Service' (footnote: 'R.C., disengaged, good character, would help, no salary'). Shem's margin says: 'MAW-MAW, LUK, YOUR BEEFTAY'S FIZZIN OVER!' and we know that it is supper-time. The mystic numbers of the Cabbala – summary of all knowledge – are set out from 'Aun Do Tri' to final 'Geg'. At the number five or 'Cush' – halfway down the ladder of numbers – the split of creation into its two opposing brother-elements takes place. The footnote says: 'Kish is for anticheirst, and the free of my hand to him!' and a thumbed nose is shown in the margin. 'Anticheirst' combines 'Antichrist' and 'anti-cheiros' – 'counter-hand', 'back of my hand': both Shem and Shaun oppose the Christ-element, as manifested in each other. The other drawing – one of crossed bones – sums up everything: the kiss of love, the crucifixion, love-through-death, death-through-love, the whole of murderous history, the arrangement into a pattern of the dead and dry – knowledge itself. 'Their feed begins', says the text. They eat the substance of their father. Then they go off to the New World, sending a 'NIGHTLETTER':

With our best youlldied greedings to Pep and Memmy and the old folkers below and beyant, wishing them all very merry Incarnations in this land of the livvey and plenty of preposperousness through their coming new yonks

The day of the brothers has arrived; the day of their father – as we shall see in the remaining two chapters of this section of the book – is finished.

6: Mactation of the Host

FROM SINBAD THE SAILOR TO TINBAD THE TAILOR WAS A STEP
of Leopold Bloom's descent into sleep. Earwicker's descent to
misery and a sense of uselessness involves the same word-play, but
the words of his dream are its very substance, not just its garment.
HCE is at the most complex and tight-knit phase of his dream, a
dream that we ourselves, along with Joyce, are dreaming. The matter
of the dream is so dense and confused that HCE seems to require a
mise en scène of great familiarity to hold the dream down (as a simple
canto fermo or even an unmoving pedal-point serves as a strong bass
for highly involved counterpoint). HCE is dreaming that, before
going off to dream in bed, he is presiding over his tavern, and its
noisy guest-patrons – the four, the twelve, and more – are reducing
their host from hero to butt, as well as hero to villain, turning the
provider of heart's sustenance into the very butcher's carcase which
must be growlingly devoured, gaffing the sailor and turning him into
a tailor and then into the garment itself which – the outward show of
pride and dignity – will be rent to shreds and atoms. This must be
done so that the world of the brothers can come into existence and
Shaun, full-fed of his father, can exchange 'greedings' with the
constituents of a mean democracy that was once a hero's kingdom.
It is the eating of the host – God made man made bread – by which
the life of small creatures is sustained. Thus, as with every sad thing
in this book, we are reminded of the nobility of sacrifice as well as
the joy of resurrection. Pound HCE to atoms and those atoms prove
to be adams: the great circle of creation will roll again.

   This part of *Finnegans Wake* is the very devil to summarise: it
is like saying what Bach's *Art of Fugue* is about, bar by bar. But we
must (and this should be said often) never expect anything approaching waking sense. The confused density of the narrative is caused
partly by the shame of its hero and partly by his rending, the division
of his substance. The sense of what is happening in the dream and

what is imagined as happening in the dream is clouded by the noise of drunkenness and vituperation, by many tongues brought back from abroad by roving seamen, and the whole mixture is further thickened by the bark of television and radio. We start off with a tale about a 'Norweeger's capstan', a sort of wild Flying Dutchman figure. He is HCE as he was, old Nordic rover-invader, and he represents HCE's past sins re-enacted in the present. The present HCE is reduced to a mere 'ship's husband', a server of sailors, the dupe of a rascally mariner, and the wrongs done to him are matter for a new kind of humiliation. The captain (let us use waking language) has the ship's husband arrange for the making of a suit of clothes, and, when the clothes are ready, the captain will not pay for them. A young man called Kersse (kersey) underlines the tailoring motif. He offers to go after the captain when the latter, jeering, puts back to sea. He is a kind of emanation of Earwicker in his 'Persse O'Reilly' form (remember Hosty's scurrilous ballad), 'k' being the Erse equivalent of the Brythonic (Welsh or Breton) 'p' (e.g. Welsh *pa*—what=Erse *ca*). Thus Kersse, who works for a tailoring firm, is the side of HCE that will undo him, unpick him, in both his forms –ageing husband (ship's or otherwise) and absconding rogue-seaman. After this tale there are shared memories of a great fall, and the customers' talk turns to the ship's husband's daughter. She fell for the captain: 'there were no peanats in her famalgia so no wumble she tumbled for his famas roalls davors' ('royal divorce'–Earwicker's favourite play). Double shame again for HCE.

The next appearance of the rascal-rover is greeted by the ship's husband very nordically: 'he made the sign of the hammer', Thor's sign:

God's drought, he sayd, after a few daze, thinking of all those bliakings, how leif pauses! Here you are back on your hawkins, from Blasil the Brast to our povotogesus portocall, the furt on the turn of the hurdies, slave to trade, vassal of spices and a dragon-on-the-market, and be turbot, lurch a stripe, as were you soused methought out of the mackerel. Eldsfells! sayd he. A kumpavin on iceslant! Here's open handlegs for one old faulker from the hame folk here in you's booth!

There is no rancour, since HCE and the captain are one and the same man. Moreover, these seaman's visits are pure ritual, like those earlier visits of Grace O'Malley: they are fairy-tale stuff. This time the captain orders food and drink but, as before, goes off without paying. The prose is thick with tailoring terms (for the food and the suit are the same thing), and we even hear the voices of three tailors who seem to represent the three Fates. When the captain comes into the tavern for the third time, he is followed by Kersse, who greets all cheerily: 'Peiwei toptip, nankeen pontdelounges. Gives fair day. Cheroot. Cheevio!' He has apparently been to the races, since he is asked, 'And, haikon or hurlin, who did you do at doyle today, my horsey dorksey gentryman.' Pidgin English mingles with the tongues of the Norsemen, and, through a fug of noise and drink, we hear a voice of vituperation raised against 'the bugganeering wanderducken . . . the coarsehair highsaydighsayman . . . the bloedaxe bloodooth baltxebec, that is crupping into our raw lenguage navel through the lumbsmall of his hawsehole'. The villain is evidently HCE, foreigner, invader, cheat, lecher.

And now, after a weather forecast on the radio, we hear a tale of the catching and taming of the rover. 'Birdflights', the radio assures us, 'confirm abbroaching nubtials.' The mariner is to be made to marry the ship's husband's daughter, a confusion of Issy and ALP. 'Come Bastabasco and hippychip eggs' (HCE) 'she will make a suomease pair and singlette, jodhpur smalls and tailorless, a copener's cribful, leaf, bud and berry, the divlin's own little mimmykin puss (hip, hip, horatia!) for my old comrhade saltymar here . . .' The 'suomease pair' is obviously the twins and the 'singlette' the daughter. An Irish marriage will calm the wanderer down, stop his tricks. Soon he is 'Cawcaught. Coocaged'. There are great celebrations; somebody even sings a negro spiritual: 'He goat a berth. And she cot a manege. And wohl's gorse mundom ganna wedst.' The marriage is consummated ('if hec dont love alpy then lad you annoy me') and, since there is an element of incestuous guilt in it all, we hear the hundred-letter thunderclap, the fall-word in the form 'Pappappapparrassannuaragheallachnatullaghmonganmacmacmacw-hackfalltherdebblenonthedubblandaddydoodled'. The taming of the tempestuous rover is summed up in 'his loudship was converted to a landshop'.

But we cannot get away from that primal guilty act in the park, and, as we have committed ourselves to a marine context, the park quite naturally becomes the sea. We have gone back even further than the Garden of Eden and see man himself arising from a watery element. The theme of guilt is not developed, only mentioned, for we now have an 'enterruption'. That this is to have a strong Slav flavour is prefigured in 'Check or slowback. Dvershen.' Kate the cleaning-woman is introduced with Czechoslovak prepositions (which, like those of Russian, are single letters – *v, s* and so on). The children are asleep, she says, and the mistress of the house is in bed. If Earwicker is 'whishtful to licture her caudal' he can join her. The mention of the bedroom brings in the sound of the branch tapping at the window–'Dip'. Kate is in her guise as keeper of the Wellington Museum in Phoenix Park and this, far from sending HCE to join his lady in repose, opens up the old world of imperialistic war again. A picture on the wall of the bar shows the Charge of the Light Brigade, with hunting overtones (horses, HCE as John Peel, the sound of the horn or bugle) and Earwicker is dream-drawn to telling a story about 'Arthur Duke'. Inevitably, this is full of HCE's own guilt–'it was of him, my wife and I thinks, to feel to every of the younging fruits, tenderosed like an atlantic's breastswells or . . . a bright tauth bight shimmeryshaking for the welt of his low. And where the peckadillies at his wristsends meetings be loving so lightly dovessoild the candidacy, me wipin eye sinks, of his softboiled bosom should be apparient even to our illicterate of nullatinenties.' Here we are again–the two creamy roses in the park, the lobsters or redcoats, the stuttering guilt:

Imagine twee cweamy wosen. Suppwose you get a beautiful thought and cull them sylvias sub silence. Then inmaggin a stotterer. Suppoutre him to been one biggermaster Omnibil. Then lustily . . . immengine up to three longly lurking lobstarts . . . How do, dainty daulimbs? So peached to pick on you in this way, prue and simple, pritt and spry! Heyday too, Malster Faunagon, and hopes your hahititahiti licks the mankey nuts!

The pushing of the guilt back to the beginning, to the giant Finnegan reposing in the unconscious, is not to be permitted. The customers call for a television show presented by Butt and Taff (Shem and Shaun disguised as cross-talk comedians) and they are anxious that they should re-enact the old story of Buckley and the Russian general ('How Burghley shuck the rackushant Germanon'). There is, in fact, an apocryphal tale in existence about an Irish soldier, Buckley, who, fighting for the British in the Crimean War, was in a position to shoot a Russian general when this latter had let down his trousers to defecate. But humanity and a feeling for human dignity prevailed; Buckley did not fire. So the story (it was, to make due acknowledgements, John Joyce's story) went. Now it is changed to fit the dream and engineer Earwicker's ultimate humiliation.

The Butt and Taff episode is presented in dramatic form, complete with stage directions. This makes the battle-sounding, guilt-echoing gallimaufrey seem more lucid than it really is. The three redcoat witnesses of Earwicker's nameless crime (which seems now to involve defecation and innumerable sexual perversions) form a link between the park and the battlefield. Butt is one of the soldiers; he easily changes into Buckley, making the two stories into one. The cross-talk act is interrupted for the report of a race-meeting, but even this is thick with the HCE horror-tale:

Emancipator, the Creman hunter (Major Hermyn C. Entwhistle) with dramatic effect reproducing the form of famous sires on the scene of the formers triumphs, is showing the eagle's way to Mr Whaytehayte's three buy geldings Homo Made Ink, Bailey Beacon and Ratatuohy while Furstin II and The Other Girl (Mrs 'Boss' Waters, Leavybrink) too early spring dabbles, are showing a clean pairofhids to Immensipater.

It is, of course, horses that link the themes of battle, hunt, and racing. When we resume the Buckley story, the wizards Browne and Nolan will (we must always expect this) confuse Butt and Taff to Tuff and Batt, but the general drift remains clear. HCE, prime brute, warmonger, imperialist, is identified with the Russian general, and, in this version of the Buckley story, he is shot, even though his pants are down. 'I gave one dobblenotch', says Butt-Buckley, 'and I ups with my crozzier. Mirrdo! With my how on armer and hits leg an arrow cockshock rockrogn. Sparro!'

To match the chaos of the soldier's blow in *Ulysses*, we must now have the annihilation of the atom, but Joyce puts the hope of resurrection even in that: 'the abnihilisation of the etym'. From nothing–*ab nihilo*–the etymon, root of truth, of all language, will re-emerge. And now, the tale ended, Butt and Taff melt into one person, make a moral and prophetic conclusion (this shooting of the Russian general by Buckley will happen again, recurring in a cycle, so long as the 'samuraised twimbs' are a principle of life–Shem versus Shaun, the split personality of HCE raging in inner war. 'So till butagain budly shoots thon rising germinal let bodley chow the fatt of his anger and badley bide the toil of his tubb').

But Earwicker makes the mistake of sympathising with the Russian general, while the customers approve what Butt-Buckley did. HCE says that that story is the story of all great men who fall; indeed, it is everybody's story: 'And that is at most redoubtedly an overthrew of each and ilkermann of us, I persuade myself, before Gow, gentlemen, so true as this are my kopfinpot astrode on these is my boardsoldereds.' A hero is ruined because nature leads him to the exposure of his baser part. HCE, that very hero, is seen for an instant in his noblest aspect, sea-warrior coming to land, 'flying the Perseoroyal'. And now comes the crushing of the hero, the mactation of the host. This is so big an undertaking that we have to prepare for it somewhat remotely, converting it into a ritual. The radio announces, after calling for order in the voices of the three soldiers ('Attention! Stand at!! Ease!!!'), the twofold song of the nightingales (the two girls), and the very leaves of the trees sing of the destruction of 'the marrer of mirth and the jangtherapper of all jocolarinas'. The customers rehearse his sins ('Has they bane re-neemed? Soothinly low'). But the brave old Adam stands up for himself, admitting his guilt but drawing his accusers into it: 'Guilty but fellows culpows!' He has been misunderstood or 'missaunder-staid', he says. His crime was a little one. His Swiftian little loves, 'my dears, the estelles', merge into one, then become two again, and all he did was this: 'my palmspread was gav to a parsleysprig, the curliest weedeen old ocean coils around'. The witnesses have not played cricket: 'Wickedgapers, I appeal against the light!' He is out with it now, in a full confession: 'the lilliths oft I feldt, and, when booboob brutals and cautiouses only aims at the oggog hogs in the humand', then let him, like Caesar, be assassinated: 'thit thides or marse makes a good dayle to be shattat. Fall stuff.' Fall staff, fall soldier's pole, he has finished. 'Here endeth chinchinatibus.'

The four old men have their say now. They are the four gospel-lers, the four Irish provinces, the four Viconian phases. They are Russia (Gregorovitch), Greece (Leonocopolos), Italy (Tarpinacci) and Ireland (Duggelduggel). Their words carry weight. They state what men may not do, and what men may not do consists of what HCE is already supposed to have done, including shooting Russian generals (hardly fair) and being a 'pedestaroly'. Then they are tucked away inside an 'Omar Khayyam' stanza: 'And thus within the tavern's secret booth The wisehight ones who sip the tested sooth Bestir them as the Just has bid to jab The punch of quaram on the mug of truth.' Six of the twelve (Mr G. B. W. Ashburner, Mr Faixgood, Mr I. I. Chattaway, Mr Q. P. Dieudonney, Mr T. T. Erchdeakin and Mr W. K. Ferris-Fender) add a word or so: 'They had heard or had heard said or had heard said written.' But who is anyone to accuse or judge? 'You were in the same boat of your-selves too, Getobodoff or Treamplasurin.'

From afar we hear the sound of a ballad. Hosty is at it again ('Ostia, lift it! Lift at it, Ostia!'):

> Dour douchy was a sieguldson.
> He cooed that loud nor he was young.

> He cud bad caw nor he was gray
> Like wather parted from the say.

It is time to turn out the customers and lock the door. 'The humming, it's coming. Insway onsway.' In good Norse English, HCE cries, 'Tids, genmen, plays.' Outside the streets are filling, the mobs marching, bells are clashing out. The pub is cleared. The song comes nearer:

> His bludgeon's bruk, his drum is tore.
> For spuds we'll keep the hat he wore
> And roll in clover on his clay
> By wather parted from the say.

There is going to be a 'lyncheon partying'. Still, the doors are locked and only the 'for eolders' refuse to be turned out. But HCE cannot lock his ears to the voices without that proclaim his guilt to the world. His sins know no end. Some are fantastic but one or two very privy: 'Begetting a wife which begame his niece by pouring her youngthings into skintighs'; 'You cannot make a limousine lady out of a hillman minx'; 'For a frecklesome freshcheeky sweetworded lupsqueezer.' We hear dangerous noises: BENK and BINK and BUNK and BANK and BONK – falling noises, hitting noises. HCE's doom is nigh.

But all this is a story within a story within a dream. There will be no violence. All we have heard is part of the narrative recounted by the customers. Earwicker ends his evening not dead but depressed. He goes round the beery bar lapping up all the leavings – 'whatever surplus rotgut, sorra much, was left by the lazy lousers of maltknights and beerchurls' – and, in a pub that is also a ship, collapses. He is dead out. 'Farvel, farerne. Goodbark, goodbye!' He sails into the next chapter.

The next chapter is the last chapter of Book II of *Finnegans Wake*, a sad little *envoi*. In his drunken dream, HCE says farewell to youth, but, in the imagined flesh of a son of his body, welcomes its coming. The four old men turn themselves to seagulls, 'overhoved, shrillgleescreaming', wheeling above the ship that is the bridal-bed of Tristram and Iseult (*Iseult-la-belle*, Isobel, Earwicker's own daughter). They mock old King Mark:

> *–Three quarks for Muster Mark!*
> *Sure he hasnt got much of a bark*
> *And sure any he has it's all beside the mark . . .*
> *Hohohoho, moulty Mark!*
> *You're the rummest old rooster ever flopped out of a Noah's ark*

And you think you're cock of the wark.
Fowls, up! Tristy's the spry young spark
That'll tread her and wed her and bed her and red her
Without ever winking the tail of a feather
And that's how that chap's going to make his money and mark!

Mark, whose destined bride Iseult is, lies there on the floor, a snoring sack, done, past the handling of the glory of young flesh. His son, Shaun, has taken over from him (not, of course, that the dream imputes incestuous desire to Shaun; Issy there plays any young girl who is all sex).

To see the young lovers brings back the lovely cuddling past to the watching four. Johnny MacDougal remembers first, and among the things he remembers, strangely, is 'poor Merkin Cornyngwham, the official out of the castle on pension, when he was completely drowned off Erin Isles'. This, of course, is Martin Cunningham of *Ulysses*, and we are surprised to see him turned into a type of the drowned man in *The Waste Land*. Marcus Lyons recalls the year 1132, the beginning of history, the Flemish armada wrecked 'off the coast of Cominghome and Saint Patrick, the anabaptist, and Saint Kevin, the lacustrian . . . and Lapoleon, the equestrian, on his whuite hourse of Hunover'. Lucas Tarpey is vaguer about dates — was it 1132 or 1169 or 1768 'when Carpery of the Goold Fins was in the kingship of Poolland'? But those were the fine old Eden days when love started and nobody had fallen yet. Finally Matt Gregory comes before us, very symbol of dead times that were to be 'devoured by active parlourmen, laudabiliter' (that bull again, that gave Ireland to the English). In their impotence they look on the lovers, drooling, remembering:

> So that was the end. And it can't be helped. Ah,
> God be good to us! Poor Andrew Martin Cunningham!
> Take breath! Ay! Ay!

We see the act of consummation — 'Amoricas Champius, with one aragan throust, druve the massive of virilvigtoury flshpst the both lines of forwards (Eburnea's down, boys!) rightjingbangshot into the goal of her gullet' — and the myth is washed clean of its romantic incrustations. What is Iseult? She is only

a strapping modern old ancient Irish prisscess, so and so hands high, such and such paddock weight, in her madapolam smock, nothing under her hat but red hair and solid ivory . . . and a firstclass pair of bedroom eyes, of most unhomy blue, (how weak we are, one and all!) the charm of favour's fond consent!

237

The love of the fabulous operatic pair is celebrated–'Hear, O hear, Iseult la belle! Tristan, sad hero, hear!'–in a delightful free-verse song which fuses the bardic and the backyard:

It was of a wet good Friday too she was ironing and, as I'm now to understand, she was always mad gone on me.
Grand goosegreasing we had entirely with an allnight eiderdown bed picnic to follow.
By the cross of Cong, says she, rising up Saturday in the twilight from under me, Mick, Nick the Maggot or whatever your name is, you're the mose likable lad that's come my ways yet from the barony of Bohermore.

And so the seagulls finally screeching away–'Mattheehew, Markeehew, Lukeehew, Johnheehwheehew!'–watch the boat sail into the future ('The way is free. Their lot is cast'). Poor Martin Cunningham, who was something in Dublin Castle, is drowned with the good days gone. On the floor-deck the ruined hero snores. But it is in his dream that the rule of Shaun will be made manifest.

7: Shaun to Jaun to Yawn

IN CLIMBING, AS WE DO NOW IN BOOK III OF *Finnegans Wake*, to the bedroom of HCE to dream about the future of his sons, we are not leaving the dream-world in order to re-enter it. There are moments when the thickness clears, when we approach the verge of waking, when we even sleepily get out of bed with Earwicker and his wife, but never once do we really find ourselves in the sunlit land where we can pinch ourselves to confirm that dreaming is over. The author's dream enfolds the sleep, half-sleep and morning yawning of his hero; the sheets of the dream are well tucked in. The author has dreamed that HCE has dreamed that he has awakened from his drunken stupor to go up to bed to start a new dream. This new dream is about the future, the rule of the ruling son, but all is controlled by the father. This is still the book of Earwicker.

In the first chapter of the three devoted chiefly to Shaun and his demagogy, we start with the sound of night-bells chiming an hour of some sort, a universal hour of mixed languages. Strange shapes from the historical past appear in the dreamed bedroom, and then a voice calls: 'Shaun! Shaun! Post the post!' And Shaun himself appears, 'dressed like an earl in just the correct wear', R.M.D. (Royal Mail, Dublin) embroidered on his 'starspangled zephyr with . . . crinklydoodle front' (he stands for the New World). He is the true politician, the popular voice, deliverer of the word but not its originator. Who is seeing all this, who is telling the story? Not one of the 'concordant wiseheads', the four old men, but their donkey. We have heard vaguely of this donkey before and marked its significance – the four feet a humbler figure of Ireland's four provinces but, in its palmy associations, perhaps the great donkey-rider Christ himself. Now the donkey takes the stage, vicar of bray.

Shaun has been eating in a 'porterhouse' called Saint Lawzenge of Toole's (back to the British conquest of Ireland) and his huge meals – 'threepartite pranzipal . . . *plus* a collation' – are fully itemised.

All the meals in *Finnegans Wake* are curiously appetising, and this long merging series of menus is no exception, from the 'half of a pint of becon with newled googs and a segment of riceplummy padding' to the 'pair of chops and thrown in from the silver grid . . . and gaulusch gravy and pumpernickel to wolp up and a gorger's bulby onion' and more, much more, with 'the best of wine *avec*'. He is, of course, eating his father, ingesting his substance like a sacrament before taking over his office. Full, he is ready to address the people ('the voce of Shaun, vote of the Irish'), though yawning from the sleepy feeding: 'Alo, alass, aladdin, amobus!'

He speaks humbly, admitting his unworthiness to bear 'these postoomany missive on his majesty's service'. It should have been his brother, 'for he's the head and I'm an everdevoting fiend of his', but Shaun himself is 'the heart of it'. His audience interposes mild questions, calling him 'dear Shaun' and asking 'who out of symphony gave you the permit' to carry the letter or manifesto of rule. Shaun is always vague in his answers, but he has a number of plausible slogans which point his practical wisdom:

Never back a woman you defend, never get quit of a friend on whom you depend, never make face to a foe till he's rife and never get stuck to another man's pfife. Amen; ptah! His hungry will be done! On the continent as in Eironesia. But believe me in my simplicity I am awfully good, I believe, so I am, at the root of me, praised be right cheek Discipline! . . . Down with the Saozon ruze! . . . Like the regular redshank I am. Impregnable as the mule himself.

'How mielodorous is thy bel chant, O songbird', say his listeners, and they even – after a passage about his money (where did he get it? What did he do with it?) and his love affairs (plenty of Swiftian or HCE guilt here) – ask him to sing them a song. He says he would rather 'spinooze' them a fable. But before he can start on the tale of the Ondt and the Gracehoper he coughs ('husstenhasstencaffincoffintussemtossemdamandamnacosaghcusaghhobixhatouxpeswchbechoscashlcarcarcaract' – the word for 'cough' in many languages appears here) and we recognise the thundred-letter clap which recalls the fall. Some of his own sexual guilt has been passed from dreaming HCE to his favourite son, hinted at previously in references to Swift's father-lover love for his two Esthers (or 'two venusstas', as Shaun's audience calls them). Sexual guilt, which the artist can purge, has been the lot of so many leaders.

The fable that follows is delightful. The Gracehoper is always 'jigging ajog, hoppy on akkant of his joyicity', and always asking

Floh and Luse and Bienie and Vespatilla (flea and louse and bee and wasp) to 'commence insects with him' (ah!). He is the irresponsible artist, writing works like *Ho, Time Timeagen, Wake!*, while the Ondt, 'not being a sommerfool', is more concerned with building a money-empire: 'As broad as Beppy's realm shall flourish my reign shall flourish!' The Gracehoper, after jingling 'through a jungle of love and debts' and 'horing after ladybirdies', meets the Ondt 'prostrandvorous upon his dhrone, in his Papylonian babooshkees, smolking a spatial brunt of Hosana cigals', 'as appi as a oneysucker or a baskerboy on the Libido'. Moreover, it is the Ondt who is now playing about with Floh and Luse and Bienie and Vespatilla, enjoying 'the melody that mints the money. *Ad majorem l.s.d.*' The Gracehoper forgives the Ondt his laughter at his own artist's poverty and sickness and dejection:

> *Teach Floh and Luse polkas, show Bienie where's sweet*
> *And be sure Vespatilla fines fat ones to heat.*
> *As I once played the piper I must now pay the count*
> *So saida to Moyhammlet and marhaba to your Mount!*
> *... Your feats end enormous, your volumes immense,*
> *(May the Graces I hoped for sing your Ondtship song sense!),*
> *Your genus is worldwide, your spacest sublime!*
> *But, Holy Saltmartin, why can't you beat time?*

He is able to forgive, for he is not really able to envy. The Ondt is welcome to his wealth, for the Gracehoper's temperament rejects the sort of life that is needful for the attaining of it. What is the Ondt doing but filling up space with possessions? He cannot, like the artist, conquer time, the only thing worth doing.

It is significant that Shaun sees the point of the Shem way of life (after all, he made up the fable). He is aware of what is missing in his own temperament, the nature of the split which makes each brother only half the man his father was. Now, being handed the 'letter, carried of Shaun, son of Hek, written of Shem, brother of Shaun, uttered for Alp, mother of Shem, for Hek, father of Shaun' and asked if he can read it, he denounces it as filth and flummery, a libel on his father ('How they wore two madges on the makewater. And why there were treefellers in the shrubrubs'—the sin in the park). But, gently asks the audience, has not Shaun himself 'used up slanguage tun times as words as the penmarks used out in sinscript with such hesitancy by your cerebrated brother'? Shaun at once picks up that word 'hesitancy' and turns it to 'HeCitEncy'— a reference to HCE's guilty stutter. 'Your words grates on my ares',

he says. And then he tears into absent Shem, angrily affirming that
it was not Shem who wrote the letter about the 'liliens of the veldt,
Nancy Nickies and Folletta Lajambe': he merely took down what
his mother kept squealing, the 'cribibber', trying to make a Swift of
himself—

. . . aspiring like the decan's, fast aslooped in the intrance to his polthrone-
chair with his sixth finger between his catseye and the index, making his
pillgrimace of Childe Horrid, engrossing to his ganderpan what the idio-
glossary he invented under hicks hyssop! Hock! Ickick gav him that
toock, imitator! And it was entirely theck latter to blame.

Shem is terrible, unforgivable—'weird, I tell you, and middayevil
down to his vegetable soul . . . That's why he was forbidden tomate
and was warmed off the ricecourse of marrimoney, under the
Helpless Corpses Enactment.' But what is the true reason for
Shaun's hate of his brother, the audience wants to know. Shaun
replies: 'For his root language, if you ask me whys.' And then, surprisingly, we hear a thunder-word made up out of ancient mytho-
logical names—'Ullhodturden weirmudgaardgringnirurdrmolnirfen-
rirlukkilokkibaugimandodrrerinsurtkrinmgernrackinarockar! Thor's
for yo!' We remember that Vico taught that language was an attempt
to make meaning out of God's thunder. Shem has the gift of language: he can explain what the thunder said. But the political leader
thrives on vague speech, the antithesis of truth and clarity. The
artist is the demagogue's true enemy; the truth made many a great
man fall. The audience recognises the thunder-word: 'The hundred-
lettered name again, last word of perfect language. But you could
come near it, we do suppose, strong Shaun O', we foresupposed.
How?' Shaun blusters: he is a better word-man than his brother,
and one day he will show it, but the whole thing is not worth the
trouble really, and the sort of thing that Shem writes is disgusting:
'I will commission to the flames any incendiarist whosoever or
ahriman howsoclever who would endeavour to set annyma roner
moother of mine on fire.' He is, all of a sudden, slobbering with
mother-love: Shem's letter has shamed her.

And now Shaun melts out of the dream: 'he spoorlessly disap-
paled and vanesshed, like a popo down a papa, from circular circu-
latio. Ah, mean!' He is gone and his people miss him, heaping
blessings on his memory:

And may the mosse of prosperousness gather you rolling home! May
foggy dews bediamondise your hooprings! May the fireplug of filiality
reinsure your bunghole! May the barleywind behind glow luck to your
bathershins!

Till he returns, 'may the tussocks grow quickly under your tramp-thickets and the daisies trip lightly over your battercops'. But there is something strange about this disappearing Shaun. Has he not ceased to be a man and turned into a barrel? He has certainly eaten enough.

But when we next meet him, in the chapter following, Shaun is 'amply altered for the brighter' and has even changed his name to Jaun, which has liverish overtones of a great lover. He is on his travels, delivering the word to the people, but he has stopped for a breather 'at the weir by Lazar's Walk'. Seated upon the 'brink-spondy' are the twenty-nine girls from St Bride's or St Bridget's or 'Benent Saint Berched's national nightschool', and Jaun gives them greeting, turning at the same time into a priest whose hands are speedily kissed by the maidens, 'kittering all about, rushing and making a tremendous girlsfuss over him pellmalc, their *jeune premier* and his rosyposy smile, mussing his frizzy hair and the golliwog curls of him'. Among the girls he recognises (leap-year is still with us) his own sister, called Izzy here, and it is evident that his attitude to her is ambiguous, but honest Jaun is 'brotheroesides her benedict godfather' and love to him is not quite what it was to his sinning father, stutterer in the park.

He addresses her fondly and then launches into a sermon to all the girls: 'Words taken in triumph, my sweet assistance, from the sufferant pen of our jocosus inkerman militant of the reed behind the ear.' He has reviled Shem's writing but it is all he has in the way of Holy Writ. The sermon itself is shocking, full of the sly wisdom of the world masquerading as the distillation of sanctity: 'Never lose your heart away till you win his diamond back . . . Lust, thou shalt not commix idolatry. Hip confiners help compunction. Never park your brief stays in the men's convenience . . . Collide with man, collude with money . . . Where vou truss be circumspicious and look before you leak, dears . . . Where it is nobler in the main to supper than the boys and errors of outrager's virtue. Give back those stolen kisses; restaure those allcotten glooves . . . Leg-before-Wicked lags-behind-Wall where here Mr Whicker whacked a great fall . . . Scenta Clauthes stiffstuffs your hose and heartsies full of temptiness . . . Slip your oval out of touch and let the paravis be your goal. Up leather, Prunella, convert your try! . . . Dress the pussy for her nighty and follow her piggytails up their way to Winkyland . . . Love through the usual channels, cisternbrothelly . . . Deal with Nature the great greengrocer and pay regularly the

monthlies.' And so on and so on and so on till the final warning:
'If ever I catch you at it, mind, it's you that will cocottch it! I'll
tackle you to feel if you have a few devils in you. Holy gun, I'll give
it to you, hot, high and heavy before you can say sedro.' All that the
son has become, it seems, is a more articulate and far more hypo-
critical dirty-old-man copy of the father. It is the tragedy of insuffi-
ciency – half an egg, not half of a double yolk.

Under cover of a continuation of the sermon, Jaun addresses his
sister only, telling her what men, and for that matter what books, to
avoid, ambiguously recommending the '*Weekly Standerd*, our verile
organ that is ethelred by all pressdom', and works like '*Through Hell
with the Papes* (mostly boys) by the divine comic Denti Alligator
(exsponging your index) and find a quip in a quire arisus aream from
bastardtitle to fatherjohnson.' Shaun will, with a certain greed,
guard her virtue for her. If anybody makes scoundrelly advances to
Izzy 'we'll dumb well soon show him what the Shaun way is like
how we'll go a long way towards breaking his outsider's face for
him'. He has to go away now, spreading the word, but he will be
back to 'cover the two pure chicks of your comely plumpchake with
zuccherikissings, hong, kong, and so gong'.

But, when he returns to his general sermonising, a certain confidence has gone out of Shaun already:

Do you know what, liddle giddles? One of these days I am advised by the
smiling voteseeker who's now snoring elued to positively strike off hiking
for good and all as I bldy well bldy ought until such temse as some mood
is made under privy-sealed orders to get me an increase of automoboil
and footwear for these poor discalced and a bourse from bon Somewind
for a cure at Badanuweir (though where it's going to come from this
time –) as I sartunly think now, honest to John, for an income plexus that
that's about the sanguine boundary limit. Amean.

A lot of them want him to retire on pension, but where is the money
to come from? He would be ready enough to turn back from glory
if he could only find the girl of his heart, a teashop nippy, 'my lady
of Lyons', to look after him. But his dream of tea-caddy homeliness,
protected by the umbrella-saint James Hanway from the big world,
is shot through with Swift-guilt – 'vanity of Vanessy . . . peepet!
peepet!' (Swift's little language: ppt). His grandiose dreams take on
a new form. If he had money he would invest it in 'vestments of
subdominal poteen at prime cost'; he is, he says, the gogetter that'd
make it pay like cash registers as sure as there's a pot on a pole'.
Rich, he would plant Izzy 'on the electric ottoman in the lap of

lechery, simpringly stitchless with admiracion, among the most uxoriously furnished compartments'.

This odious young man is all wind, a loud mouth concealing inner doubt. This Viconian phase will not do at all. Before he goes off on a mission he represents as Christlike, he paints a tawdry after-life, 'when the Royal Revolver of these real globoes lets regally fire of his *mio colpo* for the chrisman's pandemon to give over and the Harlequinade to begin properly SPQueaRking Mark Time's Finist Joke. Putting Allspace in a Notshall.' Soon, to no surprise, he becomes Christ himself, guzzling a vulgar last supper whose mastication is all too clearly to be seen, steak and peas and bacon becoming 'kates and eaps and naboc' and (x=consonant; o=vowel) cabbage and boiled protestants (potatoes)[1] pounded and gnashed to a gluey meat-extract-like bolus: 'xoxxoxo and xooxox xxoxoxxoxxx'. He is ready for off: 'Me hunger's weighed.' He asks Izzy to write to him, and she responds in the fascinatingly horrible little language we have come to know so well: 'my sapphire chaplets of ringarosary I will say for you to the Allmichael and solve qui pu while the dove-doves pick my mouthbuds . . . with nurse Madge, my linkingclass, she's a fright, poor old dutch, in her sleeptalking when I paint the measles on her and mudstuskers to make her a man'. (She must always have her mirror to turn herself into the two temptresses in the park.) The episode thickens with Swift-Stella allusions. Jaun raises his chalice and says: 'Esterelles, be not on your weeping what though Shaunathaun is in his fail!' The holy cup is also a 'bridle's cup' filled with champagne bubbling with concupiscent connotations. 'So gullaby, me poor Isley!'

Issy-Izzy-Iseult is the Church he leaves behind, to be comforted by 'Dave the Dancekerl' who 'will arrive incessantly in the fraction of a crust'. The Paraclete and the Eucharist appear in one image. Issy's name is changed to Julia Bride (Christ's bride, the Church) and Dave, the Holy Ghost, is introduced to her. But, if we are to prune away excess characters with Occam's razor, this Paraclete must be Shem, and, indeed, we hear: 'He's the mightiest penum-brella I ever flourished on behond the shadow of a post!' It is right that Shem, artist, vessel of inspiration, should play the descending dove. But Jaun-Christ has to struggle with impulses of an old en-mity–'We're as thick and thin now as two tubular jawballs. I hate him about his patent henesy, plasfh it, yet am I amorist. I love him.

---

[1] In the year of the Irish potato famine Protestant evangelists made converts through the bribe of potato soup. Hence potatoes have ever since been called 'protestants'.

I love his old portugal's nose'–and we are not surprised to find later that Jaun starts a grumbling programme of disparagement. It begins with a discussion about church music and Shem's vocal gift: '. . . he could be near a colonel with a voice like that'. Shem becomes Stephen Dedalus-Joyce and Jaun becomes Buck Mulligan-Gogarty: 'The misery billyboots I used to lend him before we split' (we are back in the Martello Tower). The latter identification is a pregnant one when we remember Mulligan's mockery of the Mass, his ballad about Joking Jesus. As for the real Joyce behind these dream-masks, he is there in the 'beurlads scoel' (his first job in exile was as a teacher in the Berlitz School), placing 'the ocean between his and ours', trying to be 'as homely gauche as swift'. The sacred spirit (Holy Ghost) is reduced to ('homely gauche') a mocking, rather inept satirical sneerer. But–'my positively last at any stage!'–Jaun has done talking: ' 'tis time to be up and ambling'.

He is becoming, though big, vague and pitiable. He is 'Jaun the Boast', but the twenty-nine girls of St Bride's are prepared to accord him a hero's farewell. More, they will hymn this grotesque barrel of wind like the god Osiris, like a fertile tree or a spring in the desert:

> Oasis, cedarous esaltarshoming Leafboughnoon!
> Oisis, coolpressus onmountof Sighing!
> . . . Pipetto, Pipetta has misery unnoticed!

Issy-Izzy-Iseult is there, Swiftian little language and all, now turned into Isis, wife-sister of the god. Off, mourned, he goes down the river, 'with a posse of tossing hankerwaves to his windward like seraph's summonses on the air . . . along the highroad of the nation, Traitor's Track', poor stuff compared with his father. But does he not seem to take on, in the distance, the mirage qualities of a true god, fertiliser not mere dirt? His name becomes Haun.

The silent cock shall crow at last. The west shall shake the east awake. Walk while ye have the night for morn, lightbreakfastbringer, morroweth whereon every past shall full fost sleep. Amain.

Sleep, though, is Shaun's meed from now on. In the next chapter, his own last, he has become Yawn, a great swollen hulk, a torpid giant lying on a hill, a wretched parody of Finnegan. To him there come the eternal four–'Shanator Gregory . . . Shanator Lyons . . . his Recordership, Dr Shunadure Tarpey . . . old Shunny Mac-Shunny, MacDougal the hiker, in the rere of them on the run' (Johnny MacDougal, last gospeller, also represents Ulster, behind the other Irish provinces in finding freedom from British rule), and with them is their donkey, the 'skygrey globetrotter'. They question Yawn, being assured that he is not dead but sleeping, and a kind of ventriloquial voice booms out at them in answer from the prostrate giant-form. What the four wish to know is Yawn's 'historical grouns': after all, he has been set up as their ruler. The voice of Yawn refers them back to the 'prehistoric barrow . . . the orangery' –in other words, the heap of dirt and orange-peel where the hen scratched up the letter. The questioners say that they have heard from their donkey that in Yawn there is no way to the better life, despite his big boastful kingly vocabulary: 'no moorhens cry or mooner's plankgang . . . to lead us to hopenhaven'. Yawn's reply is evasive and in French: '*Moy jay trouvay la clee dang les champs.*' He found, like St Patrick, the key in the fields, the shamrock that is a figure of the Holy Trinity. But his attempt to identify himself with the saint is confused by the tones of guilty love (Swift was Dean of St Patrick's, Dublin): 'Trinathan partnick dieudonnay. Have you seen her? Typette, my tactile O!' Given by God ('dieudonnay') he is nevertheless 'partnick' (part the devil, part his brother): he lacks the solidity, the confident unity (despite the guilt) of HCE.

Succeeding questions strive to reach the old solidity that lies somewhere beneath this soft, lumpish, decaying giant. What does Yawn know about the 'oxeyed man' who sailed from 'Daneland'? The initials we have missed for so many pages reappear, with most heroic associations: 'Ecce Hagios Chrisman!' (behold the saintly Christman); 'Hunkalus Childared Easterheld' (Easter hero); 'Hill-cloud encompass us.' Yawn will not at first admit that HCE was his true father, since he wants no share in his guilt, but soon he utters a Nordic rune made out of the great initials:

> –*Hail him heathen, heal him holystone!*
> *Courser, Recourser, Changechild . . . . ?*
> *Eld as endall, earth . . . . ?*

And then Yawn accepts that Original Sin that springs from his father: 'By him it was done bapka, by me it was gone into . . .' And he states HCE's name as it appeared in Hosty's ballad: 'Me das has or oreils. Piercey, piercey, piercey, piercey!' But there is something else there, too: 'Midas has (gold) ears–ass's ears': was not this another secret that soon, through the whispering of the reeds, spread abroad about another great man? HCE can transmute common things to gold, the all-father, but he is also part-animal (ass's ears). Yet the heroic wheel comes full circle when we remember that, in *Finnegans Wake*, Christ is identified with the ass he rode on.

247

After the father, the twins. The four suspect that Shaun, though he represented himself as the originator of the Word, as well as its deliverer, is hiding the truth, the fact that it was Shem who found the letter when the hen scratched it up: 'The gist is the gist of Shaum but the hand is the hand of Sameas' (echo of Isaac's words). Yawn is asked if he thinks Shem is a 'counterfeit Kevin' (it was St Kevin who was believed to be the wisest of Ireland's saints): 'have you reasonable hesitancy in your mind about him?' Shaun-Yawn's confusion affects his language, turning it to gibberish, a macaronic mixture of tongues, making it end as pidgin: 'Me no angly mo, me speakee Yellman's lingas' and so on. 'Hell's Confucium and the Elements!' cry the four. '. . . Thot's never the postal cleric, checking chinchin chat with nipponnippers!' And, pressed as to whether he is really St Patrick, Yawn will give no direct answer, only the riddling '*Quadrigue my yoke. Triple my tryst. Tandem my sire*', which hides the date of Patrick's coming to Ireland: 432 ('*Quad . . . triple . . . tandem*'). Eventually it appears that there is no real question of establishing identity for Yawn at all, nor is there for his brother. Shem and Shaun are 'alionola equal and opposite brunoipso, *id est*, eternally provoking alio opposite equally as provoked as Bruno at being eternally opposed by Nola. Poor omniboose, singalow single-arum . . .' Bruno the Nolan has been once more invoked to show how opposites are reconciled under God. But the trouble here is that there is no God: this is a phase of history without belief. The brothers do not merge into their great positive father; they merely cancel each other out. All they can do in their pathetic attempt to affirm identity is to borrow from their father, and all they can borrow is the sin he committed in the park. Is the only real being, then, HCE? No, we must not forget the sexual polarity, a positive thing, unlike the brother polarity, which is negative. We come now to ALP once more.

But ALP is not primarily concerned with talking about herself. Her voice comes from the depths, rehearsing yet again the tale of the scandal. HCE was wronged. He was blackmailed:

The said Sully, a barracker associated with tinkers, the blackhand, Shovellyvans, wreuter of annoyimgmost letters and skirriless ballets in Parsee Franch who is Magrath's thug and smells cheaply of Power's spirits, like a deepsea dibbler, and he is not fit enough to throw guts down to a bear.

Magrath (the cad with the pipe?) is the enemy. But while ALP as 'Your wife. Amn. Anm. Amm. Ann' is HCE's defender, she remains an aspect of the women he is said to have wronged, and we must not be surprised to hear tones of complaint from her. She is many voices, the river of woman in many tributaries, but she ends up as the loyal ALP we know: nobody 'on allad the hold scurface of the jorth would come next or nigh him, Mr Eelwhipper, seed and nursery man'.

We want further information about HCE. We hear the very title of that book about *Work in Progress* which was written by Joyce's twelve: 'Your exagmination round his factification for incamination of a warping process. Declaim!' We know that the eternal twelve are here, but what is this 'warping process'? It is an image of two opposed things – a building-up (weaving) and a breaking-down (twisting out of shape) – and we are not surprised to see the empire of HCE honoured in a 'Dunker's durbar' and then, 'after his life overlasting . . . reduced to nothing'. And what is *Work in Progress*? It is another name for *Finnegans Wake*. Here then he lies, the great man on his bier. 'But', cry the voices, 'there's leps of flam in Funnycoon's Wick. The keyn has passed. Lung lift the keying . . . God save you king! Muster of the Hidden Life!' It is only a vision, though. We have not yet reached the undying heart of HCE.

To contact the master, hidden somewhere in the earth beneath the vast slack body of Yawn, requires much preparation. First we have to hear strange voices out of the past, voices of war and love – 'Slog slagt and sluaghter! Rape the daughter! Choke the pope! . . . Pipette dear! Us! Us! Me! Me! . . . O! Mother of my tears! Believe for me! Fold thy son!' – and mixed up with these ancestral voices is the metallic 'Zin' or 'Zinzin' which may be the tap of a dry branch ('Tip') with life put back into it. The enquirers, excited, cry: 'Now we're gettin it. Tune in and pick up the forain counties! Hello!' but almost at once there is nothing but SILENCE. Still, the interred presence of HCE seems to be sending out shoots of life and violence, and we feel justified in setting the stage for his appearance at last: 'Act drop. Stand by! Blinders! Curtain up. Juice, please! Foots!' But we still get nothing but voices. At length, though, one voice describes two objects we have already seen, earlier, in Anna Livia Plurabelle's own chapter:

– The flagstone. By tombs, deep and heavy. To the unaveiling memory of. Peacer the grave.

– . . . There used to be a tree stuck up? An overlisting eshtree?

– There used, sure enough. Beside the Annar. At the ford of Slivenamond. Oakley Ashe's elm.

The stone and the elm were, we remember, the manifestations of Shaun, with his dead law, and Shem, with his living inspiration. But the sons have melted into the father, and the tree of life—round which a whole universe burgeons and plays—is the symbol of the union of HCE and ALP. We look in the dense text for Yggdrasill, the world-tree of the Northmen, and sure enough it is there, suitably disguised: 'cock robins muchmore hatching most out of his missado eggdrazzles for him'. The 'steyne of law' is 'tod' (German for 'death'), while the tree combines 'the form masculine. The gender feminine'. We are getting closer to the great father and family-man.

But the huge fish takes some catching:

> —*There's an old psalmsobbing lax salmoner fogeyboren Herrin Plunde-*
> *howse*
> *Who went floundering with his boatloads of spermin spunk about.*
> *Leaping freck after every long tom and wet lissy between Howth and*
> *Humbermouth.*
> *Our Human Conger Eel!*

Reminiscences of the sin in the park, arguments as to whether it was really a sin and, if a sin, whether it might not have been evil-producing-good (O Foenix Culprit!) lead at length to Issy-Izzy-Iseult as the primal temptress in duplicate. She talks to her mirror-image and she tells us plainly what the dreamer has been doing with his dream:

It's meemly us two, meme idoll. Of course it was downright verry wickred of him, reely meeting me disguised . . . How me adores eatsother simply (Mon ishebeau! Ma reinebelle!), in his storm collar, as I leaned yestreen from his muskished labs, even my little pom got excited, when I turned his head on his same manly bust and kissed him more.

The four old men—who have appeared in this scene at their most intelligent and dignified—can do little more. The task of enquiry must be handed over to younger men—'We bright young chaps of the brandnew braintrust'—whose methods are brisker. After a brief questioning of Kate, who seems to say that HCE was frisky enough for sin ('Fuddling fun for Fullacan's sake!'), the boys of the brain-trust bid the buried sinner-hero appear: 'Fa Fe Fi Fo Fum! Ho, croak, evildoer! Arise, sir ghostus!' And at last we listen to the genuine voice of HCE:

—Amtsadam, sir, to you! Eternest cittas, heil! Here we are again! I am bubub brought up under a camel act of dynasties long out of print, the first of Shitric Shilkanbeard (or is it Owllaugh MacAuscullpth the Thord?), but, in pontofacts massimust, I am known throughout the world . . . as a cleanliving man and, as a matter of fict, by my halfwife, I think how our public at large appreciates it most highly from me that I am as cleanliving as could be and that my game was a fair average since I perpetually kept my ouija ouija wicket up.

Here is the old stutter and the old desperate facetiousness in self-defence, though we become aware gradually (we are warned in 'ouija ouija') that HCE is speaking through a 'control' and that this is a séance. The drift of his statement is the fundamental harmlessness of all his acts. He, in his position as innkeeper and solid citizen, could never afford 'to be guilty of crim crig con of malfeasance trespass against parson with the person of a youthful gigirl frifrif friend'. Anna is his 'bestpreserved wholewife'; he loves her dearly. There is not one 'teaspoonspill of evidence at bottomlie to my babad'; the libel that has spread all over the city, all over the world, must be laid at the door of the 'caca cad' with the pipe in the park. 'Hole affair is rotten muckswinish porcupig's draff. Enouch!'

Reception is bad. HCE becomes confused with another character, perhaps the 'control', whose name is 'Whitehed'. But this name changes to 'Whitehowth', and 'poor Haveth Childers Everywhere' is dream-identified with Finnegan himself, the head of Howth. HCE is the hill, the castle, the city. Nobility starts through the comic bubbling. His history is not a history of shame but of achievement:

... here where my tenenure of office and my toils of domestication first began, with weight of woman my skat and skuld but Flukie of the Ravens as my sure piloter, famine with Englisch sweat and oppedemics, the twotoothed dragon worms with allsort serpents, has compolitely seceded from this landleague of many nations and open and notorious naughty livers are found not on our rolls. This seat of our city it is of all sides pleasant, comfortable and wholesome. If you would traverse hills, they are not far off. If champain land, it lieth of all parts. If you would be delited with fresh water, the famous river, called of Ptolemy the Libnia Labia, runneth fast by. If you will take the view of the sea, it is at hand. Give heed!

Give heed, in fact, to this tale of a fair city, a tale qualified with wrongs and failures, but still a heartening chronicle. Here is the great boon of a life, drunk with variety, built 'on me, your sleeping giant'. The hill-giant wed the woman-river; he 'knew her fleshly when all my bawdy did I her whorship, min bryllupswibe: Heaven, he hall-thundered; Heydays, he flung blissforhers'. The very forces of the sky flashed and drummed their union. HCE fed, loved, dressed, glorified his spouse, planted Chesterfield elms and Kentish hops, a Queen's garden; 'I brewed for my alpine plurabelle, wigwarming

wench . . . my granvilled brandold Dublin lindub, the free, the
froh, the frothy freshener.' He laid down roads, rich with traffic, all
for her pleasure. (We hear no stutter now.) The voice of the giant,
wine-god, city-maker, calls from beneath and beyond the crushed
lump of the body of his failed successor, false redeemer. Trumpet
his fame, four gospellers: 'Mattahah! Marahah! Luahah! Joahana-
hanahana!'

8: Bed and Ricorso

Spring dawn, the master bedroom of the Bristol tavern, a stirring out of sleep: 'What was thaas? Fog was whaas? Too mult sleepth. Let sleepth . . . But really now whenabouts? Expatiate then how much times we live in. Yes?' Yes, indeed, for the decayed times are not just the décor of the dream of Earwicker; they are here and now, the gods and city-builders underground, love a travesty, faith dead. Our own dream of life, which sees the pair asleep or half-awake, twitching at the light, awaits the *ricorso*, the return to nobility and creativeness.

The twins, Kevin and Jerry, 'nicechild' and 'badbrat', sleep, watched over by 'kinderwardens', the Mamalujo bedposts and the ass that is Christ. Isobel, Saintette Isabelle, lies prettily, 'wild-wood's eyes and primarose hair . . . in mauves of moss and daphne-dews . . . child of tree, like some losthappy leaf, like blowing flower stilled.' As for the parents—

in their bed of trial, on the bolster of hardship, by the glimmer of memory, under coverlets of cowardice, Albatrus Nyanzer with Victa Nyanza, his mace of might mortified, her beautifell hung up on a nail, he, Mr of our fathers, she, our moddereen ru arue rue, they, ay, by the hodypoker and blazier, they are, as sure as dinny drops into the dyke . . . A cry off.

The king and queen (or queen and consort, Victoria and Albert, two great African lakes of sleep) are deposed to mere father and mother when they hear this cry. 'Where are we at all? and whenabouts in the name of space?' They are in a house. They are in a bedroom which is a stage-set (is not ordinary life just one of our acts, a play we are condemned to?). We see now the provenance of some of the characters of the bigger play of sleep–'Adam's mantel . . . over mantelpiece picture of Michael, lance, slaying Satan, dragon with smoke . . .' We see a man with a nightcap and a woman with curlpins.

To our surprise we discover that it is not sleep which has been disturbed by the 'cry off' but the act of intercourse. We see this from the viewpoints of their own four bedposts—like Christ's life, reported by four cold gospellers, their uncreative act is blazoned to the world. At the end of the bedroom inventory comes 'man's gummy article, pink'.

The first gospeller describes the two with cold exactness—the man's 'beastly expression, fishy eyes', exhibiting rage. He is 'ruddy blond, Armenian bole, black patch, beer wig, gross build, episcopalian, any age'. She has a 'haggish expression, peaky nose, trekant mouth'; she is 'undersized, free kirk, no age'. These are not the HCE and ALP we have known. Soon they are designated as Mr and Mrs Porter. At last we learn their real names. 'Earwicker' is comic, romantic, better for a dream than for real life; 'Porter' is right for a stout-seller, one who carries burdens. But we will still call them by the names we have known longest.

Upstairs are the Porter babes—the Corsican brothers in one room; little pussy, whose 'pessname' is Buttercup, in the other. The parents enter the twins' room, where 'our bright bull babe Frank Kevin' is happily asleep. 'Jerry Jehu', though, has had a nightmare, and it is his cry that disturbed the queasy dawn act of love. Shem the Penman to come, he has not yet made ink flow, but 'he has pipettishly bespilled himself from his foundingpen as illspent from inkinghorn'. An incontinent child.

The 'second position of discordance' describes Earwicker, who 'partially eclipses the femecovert', from the back. His hairy bottom becomes Phoenix Park ('how the nature in all frisko is enlivened by gentlemen's seats'), and we become dimly aware that perhaps all the history that has been enacted there throughout *Finnegans Wake* has come about because a man dropped his trousers or lifted his nightshirt. Is history all ordure—'hystorical leavesdroppings'? Was the fall, with dropping leaves, initiated not with the tree of knowledge but with the removal of figleaf aprons? We must leave such questions because the wife is now soothing her crying child in a kind of Russian (Anna is of Russian stock. We have met hints before). Joyce soothes us as well, who have cried sometimes at the nightmare of his book: 'Tis jest jibberweek's joke', pure 'Jabberwocky'. The crying child may be more than Joyce's readers, though: 'Sonly all in your imagination, dim. Poor little brittle magic nation, dim of mind!' Is Jerry Ireland? It is no comfort to know that history's nightmare will clear with the coming of Kevin-Shaun: 'While elvery stream winds seling on for to keep this barrel of bounty rolling and the nightmail afarfrom morning nears.'

The court, says the evangelist, is to go 'into half morning'. An act remains to be completed. 'Then the court to come in to full morning. Herein see ye fail not!' In a kind of Esperanto we learn that both children can see their father's erection: '*Vidu, porkego! Ili vi rigardas. Returnu, porkego. Maldelikato!*' It is not decent. The sight of the 'stark pointing pole' starts Joyce off on a fantasy of flags, bells, fireworks: ' 'Tis holyyear's day! Juin jully we may!' The sexual ecstasy that promises can best be figured in such festival terms. It is time to seek it, back in the master bedroom:

–He is quieter now.
–Legalentitled. Accesstopartnuzz. Notwildebeetsch. Byrightofaptz. Twainbeonerflsh. Haveandholdpp.
–S! Let us go. Make a noise. Slee . . .
–Qui . . . The gir . . .

There is an echo of marriage-vows, as though intercourse is a duty or form or entitlement, nothing more. The real love-urge is gone. And the young are making ready to show how strong and lusty they are, how eager to take over from their elders; they 'will be soon heart-pocking on their betters' doornoggers'. But back to bed.

And now Joyce attacks us yet again with the unexpected. Instead of entering the bedroom we plunge into a cold and legalistic vision of the horror of a world in which the sexual act is divorced from the desire of fertility, in which every perversion is calmly accepted and susceptible of discussion in utilitarian terms. What has religion to say about the death of sexual morality? The two main Christian churches of the kingdom–the Catholic and the Anglican–have become as cold as their defecting members, mere firms called, respectively, Tangos, Limited and Pango ('a rival concern'). Reading the following, in all its frigid clarity, one longs to be folded back into dream-language again:

Honuphrius is a concupiscent exservicemajor who makes dishonest propositions to all. He is considered to have committed, invoking *droit d'oreiller*, simple infidelities with Felicia, a virgin, and to be practising for unnatural coits with Eugenius and Jeremias, two or three philadelphians. Honuphrius, Felicia, Eugenius and Jeremias are consanguineous to the lowest degree. Anita the wife of Honuphrius, has been told by her tire-woman, Fortissa, that Honuphrius has blasphemously confessed under voluntary chastisement that he has instructed his slave, Mauritius, to urge Magravius, a commercial, emulous of Honuphrius, to solicit the chastity of Anita. Anita is informed by some illegitimate children of

Fortissa with Mauritius ... that Gillia, the schismatical wife of Magravius, is visited clandestinely by Barnabas, the advocate of Honuphrius, an immoral person who has been corrupted by Jeremias.

See, then, how the lawful lust of HCE (Honuphrius) and the twitch of longing for his daughter, as well as his natural love for his sons, have opened up a hell of total sexual corruption. The above is only the mouth of hell. It proceeds with details so twisted and knotted, so intricate a net of debauchery, that one tries to catch at anything clean and innocent, and, seeing the names of the four old men, transmuted to Gregorius, Leo, Vitellius and Macdugalius, one's heart momentarily lifts. But they are in it too. Sulla, 'an orthodox savage (and leader of a band of twelve mercenaries, the Sullivani)', is going to procure Felicia for them. Even the thirty-nine articles of the Church of England are debased to the 'thirtynine several manners' in which Honuphrius pretends to possess his 'conjunct ... whenever he has rendered himself impotent to consummate by subdolence'.

The legal question is: has Honuphrius hegemony and shall Anita submit? The legal answer is: 'so long as there is a joint deposit account in the two names a mutual obligation is posited'. The financial position of the couple is reviewed, and we are led into a sort of ecclesiastical history in strictly commercial terms, full of bad cheques. We recall Samuel Butler's Musical Banks in *Erewhon*:

Since then the cheque, a good washable pink, embossed D you D No 11 hundred and thirty 2, good for the figure and face, had been circulating in the country for over thirtynine years among holders of Pango stock ... though not one demonetised farthing had ever spun or fluctuated across the counter in the semblance of hard coin or liquid cash.

A musical bank, indeed, without any music. The number DUD 1132 implies that there is neither real fall nor real resurrection; the cheque itself is a condom. The Church of England is bogus, an illogical absurdity (remember what Stephen says at the end of *A Portrait* about Protestantism), infertile, its thirty-nine articles matched by a history that, in the long annals of Catholic Christianity, seems no longer than thirty-nine years. It stands, in this dream-mythology, for a sterile civilisation which cries out for a *ricorso*, the wheel to turn and the thunder to startle us into belief again.

This interlude is horrific or vastly comic, just as we prefer (Mr Edmund Wilson finds it very funny). But we are glad to get back to the Earwicker bedroom, though we must first abide a prayer for them, delivered, in the absence of God, to 'Big Maester Finnykin', who is 'Prospector projector and boomooster giant builder of all causeways woesoever'. A review of the imperfections of 'Humpfrey, champion emir' is bumblingly tolerant. He is, after all, our begetter, so 'let us . . . presently preposterose a snatchvote of thanksalot to the huskiest coaxing experimenter that ever gave his best hand into chancerisk'. And now let us all watch him and Anna in the 'third position of concord! Excellent view from front. Sidome. Female imperfectly masking male.' They copulate:

The field is down, the race is their own. The galleonman jovial on his bulky brown nightmare. Bigrob dignagging his lylyputtana. One to one bore one! The datter, io, io, sleeps in peace, in peace. And the twillingsons, ganymede, garrymore, turn in trot and trot. But old pairamere goes it a gallop, a gallop. Bossford and phospherine. One to one on!

Not only do we in the room watch, along with the Mamalujo bedposts, but the whole world watches too, in shadows cast on the blind. 'The man in the street can see the coming event. Photoflashing it far too wide. It will be known through all Urania soon.' It is to be thought of, wrily, as a great creative act, but we know that HCE is wearing a condom; it is nothing more than a parody of divine copulation, best described in tepid cricketing terms ('how's that? Noball, he carries his bat!') while the first cock–true emblem of fertility, though also of betrayal–crows 'Cocorico!'

The act ends:

Withdraw your member! Closure. This chamber stands abjourned. Such precedent is largely a cause to lack of collective continencies among Donnelly's orchard as lifelong the shadyside to Fairbrother's field. Humbo, lock your kekkle up! Anny, blow your wickle out! Tuck away the tablesheet! You never wet the tea! And you may go rightoway back to your Aunty Dilluvia, Humphrey, after that!

'You never wet the tea!' There seems not even to have been an ejaculation. Sex between these two is coming to an end. 'Others are as tired of themselves as you are. Let each one learn to bore himself.' Ironical thanks are returned to all participants in this little play, including the mattress and the condom, 'while the dapplegray dawn drags nearing nigh for to wake all droners that drowse in Dublin'. And here is the end of Humphrey: '. . . ultimatehim, fell the crowning barleystraw, when an explosium of his distilleries deafadumped all his dry goods to his most favoured sinflute and dropped him, what remains of a heptark, leareyed and letterish, weeping worrybound on his bankrump . . . That's his last tryon to march through the grand tryomphal arch. His reignbolt's shot. Never again!'

And so to the fourth and last position, 'tableau final'. Dawn shines

257

over 'our all honoured christmastyde easteredman', and, the couple lying dozing, the third phase of the Viconian cycle comes to an end. We are ready for the *Ricorso*–Book IV, a single short chapter–a period of refreshment, renewal, readjustment, that the wheel may turn and life resume its dream.

We begin our final phase with a language older than the English of the Anglo-Irish or the Latin of the Church. Eliot's *The Waste Land*, with its call for renewal through purgation, interpreted the voice of the thunder in Sanskrit and ended with a threefold *Shantih*, word of peace. Joyce begins now with 'Sandhyas! Sandhyas! Sandhyas!'–a prayer-word, but nothing to do with the Catholic '*Sanctus*' it suggests. The *sandhyas* is the Hindu prayer that is said when time seems most pregnant with change–at dawn, at sunset, at noon, at midnight; the term itself means 'twilight, zone of change, the moment between one period and another'. The first pages of the *Ricorso* are crammed with punning Sanskrit. The little folk of that Dublin that is the world cry: 'Svadesia salve! We Durbalanars, theeadjure.' They are calling not on the God of the Catholics but on the Hindu *Svadesia* who is the self-moved mover; *Durbala* means 'weak'.

'Calling all downs', we hear, and 'O rally, O rally, O rally!' It is Perse O'Reilly, Earwicker, who is being told to wake to the new day, but also the spirits who will re-make time are being summoned from above to be sent down to earth. 'Gud modning, have yous viewsed Piers' aube?'–have you washed off the dirt of the past, have you seen Earwicker's dawn? 'A hand from the cloud emerges, holding a chart expanded'–the clean new parchment of time asks to be written on. The branch of the tree of life taps at the window: 'Tep! . . . Top.' But Earwicker sleeps on, despite the crow of the cock: 'Conk a dook he'll doo. Svap' (*svap* is the Sanskrit for 'sleep'). 'So let him slap, the sap! Till they take down the shatter from his shap.' All about him is past history, the creation of opposites: 'Death banes and the quick quoke. But life wends and the dombs spake!' Space is summed up in the 'Hill of Hafid' and in the 'geoglyphy' of the river. We hear a 'friarbird' 'faraclacking' the tale of the coming of sleeping HCE, but his time is now no more than a tale. His sound night's sleep 'is just about to rolywholyover . . . Every talk has his stay . . . and all-a-dreams perhapsing under lucksloop at last are through. Why? It is a sort of a swigswag, systomy, dystomy . . .' The rhythm of life is the heart's rhythm, the 'swigswag' of a pendulum. The old tide goes out, the new tide comes in.

'The torporature is returning to mornal'—morning dissolves the torpor of the sleeper—and we see now why the prose is so drenched in Hinduism and Sanskrit: we are looking eastwards—'Lotus spray'. Like Omar Khayyam, we prefer a drink ('There's a tavern in the tarn') to a congealed paragraph of dawn philosophy, and it is in the very potion that we hear the knock of life: 'Tip. Take Tamotimo's topical. Tip. Browne yet Noland. Tip.' The drink, the dawn combine in an image of the pool of fertility, from which the new will emerge: '. . . the dart of desire has gored the heart of secret waters . . . Bring about it to be brought about and it will be, loke, our lake lemanted . . . the citye of Is is issuant (atlanst!), urban and orbal, through seep froms umber under wasseres of Erie'—a drowned city but a re-emergent one—Ys, Atlantis, sacked and triumphant (*'urbi et orbi'*) Rome.

Out of the waters now rises the new maker, son of Earwicker, but not the shameful son of the dream past. The time of decay will come, as it has for Earwicker himself, but now we see the dawn of Christian Ireland personified in the youthful saint Kevin. He is hymned joyously in a 'clangalied' by the twenty-nine maidens of St Bride's, themselves all promoted to sainthood (or rather to churches with saint's names), punctually at the end our leap-year girl ('trema! unloud!! pepet!!!)' as S. Loellisotoelles. The old playfulness has become 'prayfulness'. Though the ass may prophesy the appearance one day of a certain 'Shoon the Puzt', greedy eater of his father's substance, a 'smeoil like a grace of backoning over his egglips . . . as royt as the mail and as fat as a fuddle', we must rejoice at this dawn-moment of 'Kevin, of increate God the servant, of the Lord Creator a filial fearer . . . in the search for love of knowledge through the comprehension of the unity in altruism through stupefaction.' But, generally, and saints on one side, we must accept this new world of youth and hope. It is time 'for old Champelysied to seek the shades of his retirement and for young Chappielassies to tear a round and tease their partners loveoftfun at Finnegan's Wake . . . And it's high tigh tigh. Titley hi ti ti'—a time to dance.

But, whether we will or not, we cannot conceive of the true dawn of youth and hope as being secular. We move towards a theocratic re-birth, and this is best figured in the coming to Ireland of that man with whom Shaun-Yawn tried, in a distant dream of decay, to identify himself. The time has come to draw together many of our historical threads in a kind of fugal stretto: 'The while we, we are waiting, we are waiting for. Hymn.' And here are two we have met before—Mutt and Jute, Butt and Taff, perennial cross-talk comedians now called Muta and Juva (their names stand for change and youth and help). They are looking at the lord of the land, the 'Dorminus master' who has already some sleep in him as the new order threatens. Already he is a 'diminussed aster', a diminished star, for who should be arriving now but 'the Chrystanthemlander with his porters of bonzos, pompommy plonkyplonk, the ghariwallahs, moveyovering the cabrattlefield of slaine'—the ruler of an empire, but of what sort we cannot yet see. Still, it is one with hope in it. Surprisingly Muta and Juva leave their dog-Latin, pidgin and primitive cries to speak good clear waking language:

Muta : So that when we shall have acquired unification we shall pass on to diversity and when we shall have passed on to diversity we shall have acquired the instinct of combat and when we shall have acquired the instinct of combat we shall pass back to the spirit of appeasement?
Juva : By the light of the bright reason which daysends to us from the high.

The one who has come is St Patrick, and the law he will supersede is represented by a character called variously Bulkily, Bookley and Balkelly, described as the 'archdruid of islish chinchinjoss'. He is the Buckley who shot the Russian general, he is also Berkeley the idealistic philosopher (things exist only as ideas, creations of the mind). Evidently he represents a doctrine of dreams, of appearances, while 'Same Patholic' stands for the 'petrificationibus' of the Church, its solidity, its hard sense and tangibility (is not the Church 'Tangos, Limited'?). The old and the new confront each other, while 'Uberking Leary' (High King Lughaire, pronounced 'Leary'—the monarch who reigned in Ireland when Patrick came) looks on. Like HCE, like Finnegan, he has no essential stake in this epoch, so he has laid bets (Muta and Juva tell us this) on both: 'Haven money on stablecert?... Tempt to wom Outsider!'

'Bilkilly-Belkelly' spouts sesquipedalian idealism which makes as much sense as blackfellow's gibberish. Patrick confutes him by proclaiming the doctrine of the Trinity, helped by a 'handcaughtscheaf of synthetic shammyrag'. The crowd cheers: 'Good safe firelamp!' All pray: 'Per ye comdoom doominoom noonstroom. Yeasome priestomes. Fullyhum toowhoom.' The archdruid, hearing the 'skyfold high' re-echo those words ('*Per eundem Dominum Nostrum Jesum Christum Filium Tuum*'), accepts defeat. The Christian dawn has arrived.

We must remember, though, that we are not dealing with Mr Deasy's history, a road leading to the ultimate manifestation of the

godhead, but with the Viconian cycle. We have seen the coming of
Patrick presented as a new thing, fresh as a shamrock, but nothing
is new: that story belongs to A.D. 432. Things merely recur, old
promises looking like new: only the forms change: 'Yet is no body
present here which was not there before. Only is order othered.
Nought is nulled. *Fuitfiat!*' That portmanteau-Latin sums it all
up: 'It was; let it happen!' Forget not the cycle: 'Our wholemole
millwheeling vicociclometer.' Here the wheel (HCE ALP PLA
ECH) is seen turning: 'Have we cherished expectations? Are we for
liberty of persuasiveness? . . . A plainplanned liffeyism assemble-
ments Eblania's conglomerate horde.' The present is past and the
past is present, and all is hot, fresh-cooked, 'as sure as herself pits
hen to paper and there's scribings scrawled on eggs'.

Hen? Paper? We never really got to know what was in that letter
the hen scratched up from the dirt-heap gilded with orange-peel.
Here it is, then, with the final secret of life embedded in it. But if
we expect some great revelation, angels choiring as the ultimate
mystery unfolds, we shall be disappointed. The letter addresses the
city and the whole earth–'Dear Dirtdump'–and says that 'we have
frankly enjoyed more than anything these secret workings of natures
(thanks ever for it, we humbly pray) and, well, was really so de-
nighted of this lights time'. People have raked up muck to soil the
name of a great man, but 'yon clouds will soon disappear looking
forwards at a fine day'. Still, let all revilers be warned: 'Wriggling
reptiles, take notice! Whereas we exgust all such sprinkling snigs.'
Ultimately, though, 'once you are balladproof you are unperceable
to haily, icy and missile-throes'. For the rest, 'we are all at home in
old Fintona, thank Danis . . . whool wheel be true unto lovesend so
long as we has a pockle full of brass'. The opposites persist, but they
change places with ease: 'Tomothy and Lorcan, the bucket Toolers,
both are Timsons now they've changed their characticuls during
their blackout.' We shall have a funeral; we shall have a wake. In
other words, there is no secret behind life: life is what it is and we
push on with it. You can find this same letter in your own 'leather-
box' if you look for it. And you can, with the rest of us, thank 'Adam,
our former first Finnlatter . . . for his beautiful crossmess parzel'.
That is what life is–a combination of crossword puzzle and Christmas parcel. The letter ends with a reference to 'the herewaker of our
hamefame . . . who will get himself up and erect, confident and
heroic when but, young as of old, for my daily comfreshenall, a wee
one woos'. It is signed: 'Alma Luvia, Pollabella.'

'A wee one woos.' HCE looks for a renewal of youth in the love of a young one, a daughter, but he will not find this in his own person, only in the life of the son who will take his place. He will cling to his deluded fancy, though, lying beside his ageing wife. His wife, however, is the eternal river; she has seen too much not to see clearly how man's life, with its city-building, its lechery and wars, is dream upon dream. Aware of growing old, she knows that only by entering the great renewing sea of personal death can she be re-born. We come now to her great final monologue, the cry of the river as it flows, the filth of man's city on its back, to the sea.

Soft morning, city! Lsp! I am leafy speaking. Lpf! Folty and folty all the nights have falled on to long my hair. Not a sound, falling. Lispn. No wind no word. Only a leaf, just a leaf and then leaves. The woods are fond always. As were we their babes in. And robins in crews so. It is for me goolden wending. Unless? Away! Rise up, man of the hooths, you have slept so long!

She is, of course, not just the 'Leafy' (or Liffey). She is the leaves of the tree of life, now falling; she is any wife telling any husband (even though it is in the words of J. M. Synge) to get out of bed and start a new day. But, as the monologue develops, the river colours everything: 'The trout will be so fine at brookfisht.' The rhythm broadens, the wifely complaining takes on a certain majesty:

A hundred cares, a tithe of troubles and is there one who understands me? One in a thousand of years of the nights? All me life I have been lived among them but now they are becoming lothed to me. And I am lothing their little warm tricks. And lothing their mean cosy turns. And all the greedy gushes out through their small souls. And all the lazy leaks down over their brash bodies. How small it's all!

As she approaches her great father, the sea, how alien from nobility, how petty seems her husband the hill and the city:

I thought you were all glittering with the noblest of carriage. You're only a bumpkin. I thought you the great in all things, in guilt and in glory. You're but a puny. Home! My people were not their sort out beyond there so far as I can. For all the bold and bad and bleary they are blamed, the seahags. No! Nor for all our wild dances in all their wild din. I can see meself among them, allaniuvia pulchrabelled.

She foresees her becoming a cloud ('allaniuvia') rising in freshness from the sea, borne in to the source where she will rise in youth, a girl from the hills. But now she must lose herself in the vast bitter waters:

I am passing out. O bitter ending! I'll slip away before they're up. They'll never see. Nor know. Nor miss me. And it's old and old it's sad and old it's sad and weary I go back to you, my cold father, my cold mad father, my cold mad feary father, till the near sight of the mere size of him, the moyles and moyles of it, moananoaning, makes me seasilt saltsick and I rush, my only, into your arms. . . . My leaves have drifted from me. All. But one clings still. I'll bear it on me. To remind me of. Lff! So soft this morning, ours. Yes. Carry me along, taddy, like you done through the toy fair! If I seen him bearing down on me under whitsspread wings like he'd come from Arkangels, I sink I'd die down over his feet, humbly dumbly, only to washup.

She has reached her father, who will tempestuously carry her through the clamour of the waves to his bosom. But she has one word more for her husband, the hill, the city, the 'humbly dumbly' egg of life, soon to fall again. And again, and again, for ever:

A gull. Gulls. Far calls. Coming, far! End here. Us then. Finn, again! Take. Bussoftlhee, mememormee! Till thousendsthee. Lps. The keys to. Given! A way a lone a last a loved a long the

Start again. This is the end, but also the beginning. And so we turn back to the opening of *Finnegans Wake* to complete the sentence:

riverrun, past Eve and Adam's, from swerve of shore to bend of bay, brings us by a commodius vicus of recirculation back to Howth Castle and Environs.

And we are led on once more to suffer the sentence of life or, which is the same thing, joyfully unwrap its 'crossmess parzel'. And, when Anna Livia promises the keys, she seems to fulfil that promise ('Given!'), for a new lucidity seems to shine through the turning zoetrope: we feel that the 'hundred cares' of the artist, his 'tithe of troubles', have not been in vain: we are beginning to understand.

9: In the End is the Word

Finnegans Wake IS A WORK OF LITERATURE AND HENCE, THEORETI-
cally at least, a subject for literary criticism. The trouble is that,
though we may legislate for the literature of waking life, it is im-
possible to lay down rules for books of dreams. In the foregoing
chapters I have attempted to do little more than say what, as far as
I can see, is going on in Earwicker's dream, and my view of what is
going on is greatly conditioned by my desire to struggle out of the
dream and pretend that we have all really been awake all the time.
The language of simple exposition cannot cope with Joyce's ten-or-
twelve-part counterpoint, and I have been forced to ignore much
that is important – the metaphysics, for instance, that is personified
in the characters; the vast array of historical personages that are
dragged out of Mr Deasy's time and made to ride the Viconian
cycle. To attempt a critical appraisal would, at this stage of my own
understanding of the book, be an impertinence. I have enough to
do, and so has everybody else, in trying to comprehend Joyce's
seventeen-year palimpsest.

What I must try to do here, though, is to attempt to confute
Joyce's critics, meaning those who, failing totally to appreciate what
Finnegans Wake is trying to do, attack it where, by ordinary literary
standards, it seems most vulnerable. I had better start by saying
that there seems to be a great deal of dream-literature in existence –
the dream was a popular literary convention in the Middle Ages, for
instance; two of the world's best-loved books, *Pilgrim's Progress* and
the *Alice* diptych, recount dreams – but that there is usually very
little of the true dream about it. Bunyan's book is a waking allegory,
as is *The Pearl* or *The Vision of Piers Plowman*. Genuine dream-stuff
is, before *Finnegans Wake*, to be found perhaps only in *Alice*,
Clarence's big speech in *Richard III*, Kafka (though he presents less
dream than sick hallucination), Dostoevsky, and the Bible. Joyce is
the only author who has tried, in a work of literature as opposed to

a work of science, to demonstrate what a dream is really like without making any concessions at all to those who will accept a dream as a literary convention, an intermission between waking states, or a bit of fanciful garnishing, but not as the whole essence of a work of epic proportions. Thus, when the classical critics turn on *Finnegans Wake* the beams of their bull's-eye lanterns, they see something unique, unsubmissive to their waking rules, and hence to be condemned for what it does not pretend to be rather than appraised in terms of what is is. They denounce night because the sun is not shining; they upbraid the eternal because their watches cannot time it; they produce their foot-rules and protest that there is no space to measure.

The first thing that conventional criticism cries out against in Joyce is his alleged unintelligibility. Critics have always been howling about unintelligibility, though, if a difficult book has existed long enough (like the Book of Revelation or *Gargantua and Pantagruel* or *Tristram Shandy* or Blake's *Milton*), they will not complain too loudly of what they say they cannot fully understand. The moss that attacks classical statues is a wonderful mitigator of unintelligibility. The late, revered T. S. Eliot was once in the van of unintelligibility, but age and the Order of Merit enlightened a lot of his readers. No important and difficult work of art is permanently unintelligible, since great writers create both the sensibility of the future and the language of the future, but there is a sense in which the author of *Finnegans Wake* must always murmur '*Mea culpa, mea maxima culpa*' to the priests of clarity, since it is in the very nature of his subject-matter to be elusive and difficult. For one who will say '*O felix culpa*' there are ninety-nine who will give no absolution. But, before we go any further, let us be entirely clear in our minds as to what we mean when we say that a piece of writing is unintelligible.

A writer may fail to be understood when he is either incompetent or demented. No one will deny Joyce's competence and, as far as I know, only Mr Evelyn Waugh has asserted that Joyce went mad, and then, said Mr Waugh, it was because certain influential Americans asked him to go mad. A writer may be unintelligible when he is seeking a verbal equivalent for a state of mind not yet fully understood or a complex psychological experience that will not yield to ordinary language. He will be unintelligible when he is essaying extreme naturalism, trying, for example, to capture the quality of real-life language which is blurred through distance, drink, sleep, or madness. He will be unintelligible when he is deliberately separating language from its referents (the objects or concepts of real life to which language refers) in order to create a quasi-musical pattern. Finally, he may be unintelligible when he is so loading words with referents (usually a number of secondary associations that cluster round the denotation, or dictionary definition) that the reader becomes bewildered and does not see what the primary referent is. Joyce, if he is unintelligible at all, is unintelligible in all these non-pathological ways, and they seem, on analysis, to be all artistically legitimate – in other words, they all seem to aim at a mode of communication rather than a wanton muffling or quelling of sense. Is the traditional critic, then, quite sure what he means when he accuses Joyce of unintelligibility?

Our educational tradition, both in Britain and America, has conditioned us to look on words as mere counters which, given a particular context, mean one thing and one thing only. This tradition, needless to say, is geared to the legalistic and commercial rather than to the aesthetic. When a word is ambiguous we are uneasy, and we are right to be uneasy when that word is set in a contract or official directive. But the exploitation of the ambiguity of a word is, as Professor Empson has been pointing out for a long time, one of the joys of the literary art. Gerard Manley Hopkins says: 'Brute beauty and valour and act . . . here buckle', and that word 'buckle' conveys two opposed notions – the sense of fastening a belt for action; the sense of becoming distorted and broken, as when we talk of the buckling of a bicycle-wheel. Conflict is of the essence of Hopkins's poems – glory and guilt, confidence and doubt – and, in this other great Catholic writer, we have the same (though far more self-conscious) urge to convey opposed principles of life simultaneously, in one and the same word or expression. When life is freed from the restrictions of time and space, as it is in dreams, the mind makes less effort to sort out contradictions, or gentler ambiguities, and a word may ring freely, sounding all its harmonics. This free ringing, in a zone of psychological experience which has all the doors open, may well set jangling all the phonetic and etymological associations which the mind is capable of accommodating – foreign languages not taught in public schools, songs little known in the great world of singing, scraps of conversation almost forgotten, dead slogans, posters long torn from their walls. Joyce was psychologically right in refusing to limit the associations of dream-words to what some abstract image of a reader or critic could most easily take in. In throwing vocables of great, though arbitrary, complexity at us he was being true to his principle of artistic communication. Paradoxically, when an essential word or phrase in a book about a dream is least intelligible, then it may be most intelligible.

Waking literature (that is, literature that bows to time and space) is the exploitation of a single language. Dream-literature, breaking down all boundaries, may be more concerned with the phenomenon of language in general. Living in the West, I have little occasion to use Malay, a tongue I know at least as well as I know French. In dreams, I am no longer in the West; with the collapse of space, compass-points have no meaning. Hence English and Malay frequently dance together, merging, becoming not two languages conjoined but an emblem of language in general. A better linguist than I may well make his dream-picture of language by mixing six or seven tongues. We can only learn about dreams by introspection. I do not see how Joyce could have made his great piece of dream-literature without looking into his own polyglot mind.

It is the wealth of this mind that is most persistently attacked. Joyce's great crime, apparently, is to know too much. Blows against *Finnegans Wake* are often oblique thrusts at *Ulysses*, another monster of erudition. Erudition was once Eliot's crime: since Wordsworth had done well enough without benefit of Sanskrit, it was unforgivable to make the thunder of *The Waste Land* say 'Datta Dayadhvam Damyata'. But, as our world grows smaller, we become less satisfied with what an insular tradition can teach us. We are English-speaking first, but we ignore at our peril what is enshrined in the phonemes and rhythms of Europe and the great (mostly untranslatable) religious monuments of the East. Now, Eliot may be forgiven since his learning is apparently harnessed to an end of high seriousness; Joyce, on the other hand, seems to throw his library about to promote froth (which is all a dream is) and facetiousness (what the Irish call wit). It would appear that, obscure or lucid, he cannot win. We are still unwilling to concede profundity to the deeper places of the mind; we cannot quite forgive Christ for (as Joyce himself put it) founding His Church on a pun. We have a lot to learn.

If difficulty seems to reside in Joyce's language rather than in the reader's own brain, the reader may have a legitimate grouse when he says that Joyce might at least explain a little and not seem to revel in the mystification. But was explanation in the form of notes or author's signposts really possible with *Finnegans Wake*? A barrage of glosses, whether concentrated at the end, as with *The Waste*

Land, or slily worked into the text would have made the whole book look even more fearsome than it looks already; moreover, it would have impaired the artful spontaneity, rendered the dream less dream-like. And, like all good poets, Joyce aspires to be God rather than mere man; God sets His creations all about us, but He leaves the glory of interpretation to fallible minds. The ultimate meaning of *Finnegans Wake* rests with ourselves; the communication of artists is not the communication of government departments.

But Joyce, who died only two years after the publication of *Finnegans Wake*, had time to leave one clue. His book, he said, would come clear to the reader if the reader listened to its music. Indeed, Joyce demonstrated how potent this music is when he made a recording of part of the end of Book I, the *Anna Livia Plurabelle* section. But, alas, *Finnegans Wake* does not disclose a great deal of its music to a reader unschooled in interpretation of the artist's notation; the script is not phonetic, so that we are often unsure how to pronounce a word, and much of the richness and complexity is only revealed to the eye. We cannot chant a geometrical figure, an E on its back, or a hundred-letter thunder-word (paradoxically, it is only the eye that can recognise the thunder). Many of the puns have a strong visual element, 'hesitancy' and 'hesitency' sound the same, and the whole point of the Shem-Shaun lesson is that we should imagine ourselves looking at a book with marginal glosses and foot-notes. But the appeal is ultimately to the auditory imagination, which is what Joyce probably meant, and the book is music perhaps in the sense that the orchestral score one reads in bed is music. A bad score-reader tackling, say, Wagner's *Ring* (which *Finnegans Wake* in some ways resembles) may not be able to hear much with his inner ear, but he may be able to recognise the recurrence of the *Leitmotive* by their configurations on the stave. So when we see an allomorph of the 'ppt' which Swift used when he wrote to Stella, we can be pretty sure that Iseult la Belle is somewhere around. When the great initials HCE[1] appear, often imperceptible when the enshrining phrase is read aloud, we know that, however much we may seem to have modulated, we are really not very far from home. Sometimes, on the other hand, sheer sound triumphs. The bird that traditionally calls 'More pork' cries instead 'Moor Park', and we are with Swift, caged in the home of Sir William Temple. Hidden verse-rhythms only come out of the prose when hearing is switched on. In other words, we need two things for the full appreciation of the

---

[1] HCE is a genuine musical phrase, incidentally; in Germany, H is B natural.

texture of *Finnegans Wake*–the printed book and the voice of Joyce on long-playing records. Some day a gramophone company–redeeming lost opportunities in Joyce's lifetime–may receive an enlightened subvention from some cultural body, but it is easier to find money than to find an actor who is willing to ruin his career by yielding his total personality to a dead author. And does anybody living possess a voice as miraculous?

In *Finnegans Wake* the characters themselves have voices, but they have little else. They call clearly and recognisably and give their true selves away, but these true selves, knowing neither time nor space, are never allowed to materialise in flesh, nor even in ectoplasm. We cannot see them and we cannot see (no matter how well we may know Dublin) the setting in which they act. The merging of one character into another, the simultaneous identification of the actual with the historical with the mythical cannot, in fact, be achieved without fleshlessness. Mary Manning's very clever dramatisation of *Finnegans Wake*, which she calls *The Voice of Shem*,[1] is shocking and diminishing because it fixes the personages in time and place and appearance, reducing them to actors on a lighted stage; it establishes (and this may be its main virtue) the danger of trying to turn *Finnegans Wake* into an experience for the visual imagination as opposed to the reading eye. But those critics who hate verbal ambiguities tend to love sharp visual images, and Joyce (not only in this book) has been repeatedly attacked for the low visibility of his writing. Yet literature at its most literary (for instance, when it is poetry) is not well able to make a strong appeal to the eye: visualisation is the death of true image-making. When we think of Hamlet we think of an actor playing the part; when we read Hamlet's speeches we are more strongly aware of responses of smell, taste, feeling, movement than of sight. There is little to look at in *Paradise Lost*, Blake's *Jerusalem*, Keats's *Ode to a Nightingale*, or Eliot's *Four Quartets*. Poetry may take fragments of visual experience but only for the purpose of combining them, of creating a complex that it is perilous to try to see clearly. 'Where the bus stops there shop I', says HCE from the dead, and vague visions of shopping and bussing are swallowed up in the little joy of the parody. *Finnegans Wake* does not deprive us of sight (though it nearly deprived Joyce of it); it frees us from the burden of having to project coherent images on the imaginative retina; it performs *in excelsis* the job that literature was born to perform.

[1] Faber and Faber, 1958.

Only in one respect is *Finnegans Wake* more solidly spatial than real dreams. I once dreamed of a plate which had seven slices of bread and butter on it; I took away three and six remained. This sort of thing never happens in Earwicker's dream. Joyce often spoke of his book as mathematical, and one thing in it that the vast chaotic dreaming mind never impairs is number. Half of 1132 is always 566, and out of that basic figure of fall and recovery some of the significant numbers of the book are made: 1 for HCE, 1 for ALP, 3 for the children, 2 for the sons. $1+1=2$; $3\times2=6$; 6×2 gives us the eternal twelve. $1+1+2$ gives us the four old men. The sum of the four figures of 1132 is 7, number of the rainbow girls. 4×7 gives the 28 days of February, the number of the St Bride's girls, divisible by 4 to bring back the rainbow. Every four years comes the leap-year girl. The two girls in the park and the three watching soldiers, HCE and his enemy—all are in the *ricorso*-and-fall number; the three and the two are always there to remind us that falling bodies, whether of Finnegan, Parnell, HCE or Humpty Dumpty, go down at 32 feet per second per second.

It is this devotion to number which makes *Finnegans Wake* the long book it is. Joyce had enough of algebra, with its generalising letters, in *Ulysses*; in *Finnegans Wake* he glorifies humble arithmetic, dwelling with a kind of awe on the rich multiplicity conveyed by the number of ALP's children, for instance, so that each of the 111 is fully named and the 111 gifts (fruit of the father) specified. Even the mention of *Ulysses* is enough to make Joyce want to dream-enumerate the chapters. Number is the reality behind the illusion of name and appearance. Critics have spoken of the book's diffuseness, but that seeming sprawl is really numerical exactness. The counting fingers are at their work, however deep the sleep, and those thunderwords always have exactly a hundred letters, no more, no less. This is not childishness; the profundity of the meaning of number, set out seriously beneath the joke of the lesson-chapter, permeates the whole book.

If critics will accept the logic of *Finnegans Wake*, hidden beneath what seem to be mad words and intolerable length, they will still shy at the lack of what they call action. This, they say, is presented to us as a novel, and in a novel things are supposed to happen. Very little muscle is exerted in either *Finnegans Wake* or *Ulysses*, but we have to avoid lamenting the fact that Joyce was never strong on action of the Sir Walter Scott kind, that, though he was drawn to epic, he early rejected the bloody substance of epic. We have seen in his work how even the least gesture of violence will provoke earthquakes or Armageddon, even shiver the universe to atoms–events too apocalyptical to be more than static, comic rites, final mockeries of action as the best-sellers know action. He did not reject such action as a vulgarity, only as a property that might damage language by inflating it. The representation of passion or violence had best be limited to thought or speech, since the thrust of fist or phallus, being a physical cliché, seems to call for a verbal cliché in the recounting. The clichés of Dublin pub-talk or an advertising canvasser's interior monologue are mere naturalism; the frame of symbol and poetry is a new creation out of words and the rhythms of words, static rather than kinetic. The novel should aspire to Shakespeare's language, not Shakespeare's stage-directions.

But, of course, Joyce was a family-man, and the small events of the family day had far more meaning than the big passionate public events of the books on the sitting-room shelves. In both *Ulysses* and *Finnegans Wake* he attempts to cut history down to size, measure it against his son's cold or his daughter's toothache, his wife's plea for more housekeeping money and the broken dental plate he cannot afford to have repaired. He committed himself to glorifying the common man and his family, anointing them with a richer language than the romantics, whose eyes were full of the universe, ever gave themselves time myopically to amass. Examine that stain on the table-cloth, the crescent of dirt in your thumb-nail, the delicacy of that frail cone of ash on your cheap cigar, the pattern on the stringy carpet, and see what words will most exactly and lovingly render them. The words that glorify the commonplace will tame the bluster of history. The moon is in a cup of cocoa and the Viconian cycle turns with the sleeper on the bed with the jangling springs. At the same time, take words as well as give them, so that eternal myths are expressed in exactly caught baby-talk, the slobbering of the crone in the jug-and-bottle, or a poor silly song on the radio. This is Joyce's art.

It is, finally, an art of scrupulous rendering. I do not mean by this that Joyce's great achievement was solely to find the right word and the right rhythm for the thing that was already there, waiting in the DBC tea-shop where Parnell's brother 'translates a white bishop' or on the banks of Shakespeare's Thames where the pen is 'chivying her game of cygnets'. I mean rather that he set himself the task of creating exact and inevitable language for the conceivable as well as the actual, and that *Finnegans Wake* is an exercise in rendering the

271

almost inconceivable. From this point of view alone it cannot be ignored, though imaginative writers continue to ignore it, being perhaps frightened of admitting that they, like young Stephen Dedalus, 'have much, much to learn'. Joyce continues to set the highest standards of any author except Shakespeare, Miiton, Pope and Hopkins to those who aspire to writing well. His mountain looms at the end of the street where so many of us work with the blinds down, fearful of looking out. So long as we ignore his challenge we can go on being content with what the world calls good writing—mock-Augustanism, good manners and weak tea, the heightened journalistic, the no-nonsense penny-plain, the asthmatic spasms of the open-air invalid, the phallic jerks of the really impotent. But when we have read him and absorbed even an iota of his substance, neither literature nor life can ever be quite the same again. We shall be finding an embarrassing joy in the commonplace, seeing the most defiled city as a figure of heaven, and assuming, against all the odds, a hardly supportable optimism.